MURDER
AT
HOLY CROSS

MURDER AT HOLY CROSS

Peter Davidson

BERKLEY BOOKS, NEW YORK

THE BERKLEY PUBLISHING GROUP
Published by the Penguin Group
Penguin Group (USA) Inc.
375 Hudson Street, New York, New York 10014, USA
Penguin Group (Canada), 90 Eglinton Avenue East, Suite 700, Toronto, Ontario M4P 2Y3, Canada
(a division of Pearson Penguin Canada Inc.)
Penguin Books Ltd., 80 Strand, London WC2R 0RL, England
Penguin Group Ireland, 25 St. Stephen's Green, Dublin 2, Ireland (a division of Penguin Books Ltd.)
Penguin Group (Australia), 250 Camberwell Road, Camberwell, Victoria 3124, Australia
(a division of Pearson Australia Group Pty. Ltd.)
Penguin Books India Pvt. Ltd., 11 Community Centre, Panchsheel Park, New Delhi—110 017, India
Penguin Group (NZ), 67 Apollo Drive, Rosedale, North Shore 0632, New Zealand
(a division of Pearson New Zealand Ltd.)
Penguin Books (South Africa) (Pty.) Ltd., 24 Sturdee Avenue, Rosebank, Johannesburg 2196,
South Africa

Penguin Books Ltd., Registered Offices: 80 Strand, London WC2R 0RL, England

The publisher does not have any control over and does not assume any responsibility for author or
third-party websites or their content.

MURDER AT HOLY CROSS

A Berkley Book / published by arrangement with the author

PRINTING HISTORY
Berkley mass-market edition / November 2007

Copyright © 2007 by Peter Davidson
Cover design by Steven Ferlauto
Book design by Laura K. Corless

ISBN: 978-0-425-21792-4

BERKLEY®
Berkley Books are published by The Berkley Publishing Group,
a division of Penguin Group (USA) Inc.,
375 Hudson Street, New York, New York 10014.
BERKLEY® is a registered trademark of Penguin Group (USA) Inc.
The "B" design is a trademark belonging to Penguin Group (USA) Inc.

PRINTED IN THE UNITED STATES OF AMERICA

10 9 8 7 6 5 4 3 2 1

For Sister Michelle Lewis

May she find peace in the arms of God.

MURDER AT HOLY CROSS[*]

WHO'S WHO

The Victim
Michelle "Shelly" Lewis, aka Sister Michelle

The Priests
Father Abbot Gregory Wendt, aka Father Gregory,
aka Father Abbot, aka Father Wendt,

Father Damian Gibault, aka Father Damian,
aka James Gibault

The Monk Trainees
Mykhaylo "Misha" Kofel
Petro Terenta, aka Petro Terenta Wendt
Vasyl Kopych
Alexander "Sasha" Korsak
Illya Hrytsak
Ivan Kalynych
Yosyp Lembak

The Lawmen
Jorge Gonzalez	Tom Romagni
Art Nanni	Joe Malott
John King	Jose Cabado
Larry Belyeu	Steve Signori
Bill Gilliland	Toby Wolson
Doug McCoy	

[*]Refers only to the Monastery of the Exaltation of the Most Holy Cross and Holy Cross Academy, both of Miami, Florida, and no other entity named Holy Cross.

The Prosecutors

Gail Levine
Priscilla Prado
Penny Brill

The Public Defenders

Edith Georgi
Ray Taseff

Witness Lawyers

Mel Black
Richard Hersch
Clark Mervis
Joseph Blonsky

The Judge

Hon. Manuel Crespo

1

It was just before midnight and South Beach was jammed, typical of a balmy weekend evening. But on Saturday, March 24, 2001, the neon-lit Art Deco district on the southern tip of Miami Beach was even more crowded. Thirty thousand DJs, music bigwigs and club goers had descended on Miami for the annual Winter Music Conference, and it seemed that they were all intent on having a good time in the one-square mile, multicultural melting pot known as "SoBe."

While palm trees swayed with the breeze that blew in from the Atlantic Ocean, an endless line of shiny SUVs, sleek Mercedes convertibles, and stretch limos crawled bumper to bumper along Ocean Drive, where sidewalk bistros were filled with sexy young women in skimpy halter tops, muscular young men in T-shirts and Prada suits, and starry-eyed tourists from all over the world.

They were all there on this clear but moonless night to take in the scene or visit ultrahip nightspots like Crobar, Liquid, and Krave where, if they were lucky, they might rub elbows with pop divas like Madonna and Cher, Hollywood luminaries like Sylvester Stallone and Cameron Diaz, or supermodels like Nikki Taylor and Naomi Campbell.

On the other side of Biscayne Bay, thirty-nine-year-old Michelle Lewis, Sister Michelle, had already turned in for the night. She had been living in Miami for nineteen years but was immune to its steamy temptations. She did not wear halter tops and she had no interest in hobnobbing with celebrities. Instead, she wanted to get close to God, but before the sun would rise again over South Beach, Michelle Lewis's earthly life would come to a brutal and bloody end.

Michelle Ann Lewis was born in Akron, Ohio, on April 16, 1961, the older of Don and Beverly "Bev" Lewis's two children. Everyone called her Shelly.

Don earned his living as a chemical engineer with Goodyear, while Bev worked as a secretary at an auto parts company. By all accounts, the Lewis family was solidly middle-class. They lived in a comfortable three-bedroom ranch house with a fenced-in yard on Dennison Avenue, a tree-lined street in the Ellet neighborhood of Akron, a city that liked to call itself the "Rubber Capital of the World."

Despite the social upheavals of the 1960s and '70s, the Lewis family remained close and deeply religious—traditional Roman Catholics who regularly attended Mass on Sundays and did not eat fish on Fridays, not even after the Second Vatican Council deemed it okay in 1965. From the time she was a toddler, Shelly showed a strong will and an independent streak, and an abiding love for cats that manifested itself in her devotion to virtually every stray that wandered into the neighborhood.

Don was a strong believer in community service. He volunteered his spare time to the local Red Cross, where he taught CPR classes. He also devoured books on philosophy and science, and frequently engaged Shelly and her younger brother, Tim, in spirited discussions about their faith and what it meant to be a good Catholic.

While Don could be demanding and authoritative, Bev was always warm and loving. She baked holiday cookies for her children's friends and their families and kept the home and hearth clean and tidy.

By all accounts, Shelly's childhood was an ordinary one. She was brilliant, a straight-A student from the day she entered first grade at Ritzman Elementary School through her senior year of college. From an early age she loved reading and excelled at every subject, but she showed a special affinity for math, especially algebra and calculus. She was also a talented musician who played the flute in her middle-school and high-school orchestras and sang soprano in a clear, perfectly pitched voice with the school choirs.

She suffered from asthma and was severely nearsighted. From age ten she needed to wear eyeglasses all the time, but by age sixteen the eyewear was replaced by contact lenses. Shelly never smoked cigarettes, experimented with drugs, or chased boys, and she was not one to go joyriding once she got her driver's license. Instead, her trips in the family car were always undertaken with a purpose—to get a book at the library or bookstore, or to go to school or church. Every now and then she would drive to a nearby pizza joint for a slice or two of her favorite food.

By the time she was a junior in high school, Shelly had blossomed into an attractive, brown-eyed brunette. She was petite with delicate features, a ready smile, a wry sense of humor, and a flair for fashion and makeup.

There was never any doubt, however, that academics were her first priority. She preferred books to boys and, even though her friends and classmates were fans of '70s heavy metal bands like AC/DC and Judas Priest, she preferred opera and classical music.

Beverly Dreher was Shelly's best friend growing up. Starting as youngsters and throughout their teenage years, they would spend hours walking and talking, sharing their hopes and dreams for the future. By the time she was a senior in high school Shelly was talking about becoming a high school or college math teacher, and she hoped one day to marry.

Beverly remembers her best friend as a "deep thinker with a deeply-rooted belief system, someone who loved to learn and could easily grasp difficult math and science concepts and explain them to her fellow students." Students and faculty at Central-Hower High School, a magnet school for gifted students, were dazzled by her whiz-kid-like brainpower and musical talent.

In her senior year, Shelly's classmates voted her "Most Intellectual," while the school's faculty chose her class valedictorian when she graduated in 1979. She was also named to the prestigious National Honor Society, which recognizes outstanding high school students for their excellence in the areas of scholarship, leadership, service, and character.

Shelly's parents could not have been prouder. "Academics were hugely important in the Lewis family," Dreher said.

After graduating from high school Shelly enrolled at the University of Akron with two scholarships—one from the university and the other from Goodyear. She planned to major in math and, from high school on, always held a part-time job.

"My daughter was never a lazy person," her mom recalled. While in high school she worked the counter at McDonalds. During the summer following her graduation from high school, she worked in the office of Ohio Edison, the local utility company. As an eighteen-year-old college student she waited on tables at a local steakhouse, the Ponderosa, where she met and fell in love with coworker Gary Salmon. He was two years older and a student at a technical school where he was training to be a jet airplane mechanic.

Shelly and Gary tied the knot on June 12, 1981, less than two months after Shelly's twentieth birthday. They took their vows during a Nuptial Mass at Akron's St. Matthew's Catholic Church on Benton Avenue. Her white wedding gown was handmade—Shelly and her mother were excellent seamstresses. They had worked on it together for months. Don Lewis proudly walked his only daughter down the aisle to the altar. Beverly Dreher was one of her bridesmaids.

The newlyweds did not set up housekeeping in Akron. Instead, they immediately headed for sunny South Florida, where Gary landed a job working the night shift as a mechanic for Miami-based Eastern Airlines. Shelly was excited by the move, which took them from the bleakness of the Rust Belt to the warmth of the Sun Belt, believing with all her heart that it would be a good opportunity for her and for Gary.

The couple rented an apartment in Kendall, a sprawling suburb south of downtown Miami. Shelly enrolled at Florida International University where she majored in mathematics. Two years later she graduated with honors and went to work as an actuary, poring over statistics and calculating risks for the American Bankers Insurance Group, which sold life and other insurance products to consumers through their credit cards.

At first Shelly was happy with her job—and with good reason: She was very good at it, and it suited her personality. She was methodical and organized and enjoyed working in the structured atmosphere of a large corporation. It also helped that she was a quick learner and a fast worker. Her supervisors rewarded her with steady increases in responsibilities and salary, more than enough for her to begin acquiring the trappings of the good life.

She shopped at the Falls, an upscale mall anchored by Bloomingdale's and Macy's, as well as dozens of high-priced specialty boutiques where she bought designer suits and jewelry including platinum earrings, bracelets, and necklaces, and an eye-popping ring with large sapphires and sparkling diamonds. She collected silver knickknacks and expensive crystal and furnished the apartment with impeccable taste. The young couple took up boating and snorkeling and purchased a time-share in the Florida Keys, spending weekends there or on Captiva, a lush Eden-like barrier island on Florida's Gulf Coast.

It was a happy time; at least it started out that way, but it wasn't long before the bloom was off the rose. There was trouble in the marriage, and things had not turned out as Shelly had expected they would. She told friends that Gary was inattentive and that she was lonely. She confided that she felt trapped and stifled, and exasperated by her young husband's habit of spreading his tools all over the living room, as well as his inclination to spend his paycheck on the very latest electronic gadgets.

And she revealed that she was afraid of Gary who, at six-foot-two, towered over her. He had a terrible temper, she said.

Shelly had a temper, too, which meant that their arguments could be bitter. When they became especially heated things would get out of hand. Her husband, she confided, would hurl objects against the apartment's walls, and sometimes he would hurl them in her direction.

To deeply committed Catholics like Shelly, marriage is a sacred covenant between a man, a woman, and God. It can never be broken. Its purpose is creation, but Shelly decided that she did not want children. After four years of matrimony, she made up her mind to end the union. It was an excruciatingly painful decision, one that she agonized over for months before secretly consulting a Miami divorce lawyer. On Valentine's Day 1985, while her husband was at work, Shelly moved out.

When Gary returned home after working the night shift, he was astonished to discover that Shelly was gone, and that she had taken most of their furniture as well as his guns and ammunition. Later that day he was served with divorce papers. He was also served with a restraining order after Shelly told a judge that she feared for her physical safety. And she petitioned the Archdiocese of Miami for an annulment, which was granted.

Under Cannon Law, Catholic marriages are never dissolved. Instead, they're declared null, which means that in the eyes of the Church Shelly's marriage to Gary never happened; the union was invalid from the outset.

Shelly rented a town house and moved in, living alone for the first time in her life. On October 2, 1985, the divorce became final. While Shelly was proud that she was able to break loose and strike out on her own, she nevertheless was deeply troubled that the marriage had failed.

And she was frightened. Miami in the 1980s was a very scary place—the cocaine smuggling capital of the world. Billions of dollars in drug money poured into the city. They found their way into luxury car dealerships and dozens of new oceanfront hotels and condominium developments, and they also brought an explosion in violent crime, especially murders and home invasion robberies.

By the mid 1980s, Miami-Dade County had the highest crime rate in the nation. Its criminal justice system was overwhelmed, its courts disposing of cases with plea deals 98 percent of the time.

According to a study by the *Miami Herald* published August 28, 1994, criminals in the county had less of a risk of going to prison than criminals anywhere else in America, while its residents were at greater risk of becoming crime victims than residents anywhere else. Living in

Miami-Dade County, the *Herald* said, was even riskier than living in the most crime-ridden sections of Detroit or Washington, D.C.

Shelly felt especially vulnerable. She was frightened by the prospect that she could wake up one night to find an armed intruder in her bedroom.

"She did not feel safe," recalled Martha Dawson, a friend from her early days in Miami. To protect herself Shelly kept the doors and windows locked and her shades drawn day and night. She hoped that a steel pipe she had wedged into the track of the sliding glass patio door would keep the bad guys out.

Shelly threw herself into her work at American Bankers, and by 1990 she was earning sixty thousand dollars a year. She went to movies and the opera, plays and art museums. On Fridays she would attend happy hour after work, enjoying a frozen margarita or two with her colleagues at a nearby Bennigan's.

If Thanksgiving, Christmas, or Easter ever found her at home in Miami, she would host dinners for friends and neighbors who were spending the holidays alone. For a time there was a new man in her life, a coworker at American Bankers who had moved to South Florida from Canada. The romance was serious enough for her to travel with him to Toronto to meet his family, but the relationship ended when Shelly decided that she would never remarry.

But no matter how busy she was socially or at work, she could not shake the spiritual and emotional malaise that had enveloped her. Even though five years had passed since Shelly left her husband and filed for divorce, she confided to friends that she was deeply troubled, at times despondent, and still haunted by the failure of her marriage to Gary.

Her career as an actuary, though successful and financially rewarding, was unfulfilling. She had to force herself to get up each morning to go to work. As time went on, she found that she had less and less in common with her colleagues. She thought they were shallow and materialistic.

Deeply affected by the death of her father in 1988, Shelly desperately sought security and spiritual fulfillment. She focused more and more on religion, devouring books by and about the great thinkers of Catholicism, studying Gregorian chant, and praying the Rosary every day.

As she studied and meditated, Shelley became more and more disillusioned with her life in a dog-eat-dog secular world dominated by values that emphasized power, sex, and materialism. She came to believe that God had a plan for her, and it did not include marriage, motherhood, or a career as an actuary. As a young girl she had thought about joining a convent and living a monastic life, but as she blossomed into a young woman that idea faded. As a lonely divorcée, it would occur to her again.

She researched and visited convents whenever and wherever she could. After nearly two years of searching, she learned that Miami's Monastery of the Exaltation of the Most Holy Cross, on the campus of the Holy Cross Academy, was forming a convent.

She began attending Sunday services there, singing solos in her perfectly pitched soprano voice. The liturgy, she told friends, was so spiritually fulfilling it literally took her breath away. And she sought the counsel of Father Abbot Gregory Wendt, the monastery's spiritual leader and the chancellor-headmaster of the academy, which at the time was a grade school for grades four through eight.

In 1992, the monastery was nothing more than an ordinary one-story, three bedroom, single-family house in a modest residential neighborhood, while the academy held classes in portable classrooms and trailers on an adjacent parcel of land. Both were affiliated with the Byzantine Catholic Church.

•   •   •

Byzantine Catholics, originally known as Greek Catholics, trace their origins to the ancient city of Antioch in the days when the Roman Empire ruled most of Europe, North Africa, and the Middle East. In the year 312, the emperor Constantine I embraced Christianity, ending the persecution of Christians. Seventeen years later, Constantine moved the capital of the empire from Rome to the Greek city of Byzantium and renamed it Constantinople. In 1415, the city was conquered by the Ottoman Turks, who renamed it Istanbul.

The Byzantine Catholic Church flourished in the predominantly Greek-speaking eastern half of the Roman Empire. Its missionaries traveled freely throughout the Slavic regions of southeastern Europe, where they converted millions of people in countries known today as Bulgaria, Russia, Romania, and Ukraine, as well as the former Yugoslav republics of Macedonia, Serbia, and Montenegro.

They had great success in part because Mass was celebrated in the local languages rather than in Latin, the language of the Roman Catholic Church. Byzantine missionaries were able to establish hundreds of secluded religious communities, or monasteries, where monks and nuns lived, prayed, and worked in isolation.

Some monasteries became wealthy and powerful, and their leaders—called abbots—were among the most influential men in their regions.

Byzantine, or Eastern Rite, Catholics hold the same beliefs as Roman, or Latin Rite, Catholics. They accept the primacy of the pope in the Vatican, but they are not under direct papal authority. Instead, Byzantines have their own dioceses, called eparchies, which are under the authority of Eastern Rite bishops, and they follow different rituals and traditions.

For example, the entire liturgy, or Mass, is chanted, and incense is used from beginning to end. Byzantine churches are usually built in the shape of a Greek cross, and they are topped by as many as thirteen domes. The largest dome, usually over the middle of the nave of the church, symbolizes Christ hovering over the faithful. Smaller domes represent the evangelists Matthew, Mark, Luke, and John.

Inside every Byzantine church is the iconostasis, a large partition or screen decorated with medieval-looking icons that illustrate the life, death, and resurrection of Jesus. The doors of the iconostasis, called royal doors, symbolize the gates of heaven. The icons on the iconostasis appear in hier-archical order with Christ in the center leading the way up to God. Of all the icons, those of Mary, Mother of God—the *Theotokos*—are especially revered.

In their everyday dress, Byzantine clerics customarily wear long black robes, called cassocks, and pope-type hats, and priests in Europe are permitted to marry, but bishops and monastics are required to remain celibate.

Several months after she began attending Mass at Holy Cross, Shelly was certain that she had been called by God. She decided that she wanted to pursue a religious life at Holy Cross. As a Roman Catholic, she would not be converting. Instead she would simply change rites. Father Abbot Gregory Wendt agreed to accept her into the monastery and the twenty-nine-year-old divorcée promised to live a life of poverty, chastity, and obedience to God and to Father Gregory as the abbot of the monastery.

They were not the final vows of a nun, however. Those, the abbot told her, would come later. For now she would be a nun-in-training for at least a year before she'd be guaranteed a permanent home as a novitiate. She would wear a heavy black habit like those worn by nuns in eastern Europe centuries ago. It would cover her from head to foot, with only the front of her face exposed. She wore it with pride. It was a symbol of her faith and devotion, and it connected her to an earlier era in Catholic history.

She would not be allowed to receive phone calls at the monastery, nor could she make any without first getting permission from Father Gregory. And she was prohibited from wearing contact lenses or covering up the light brown mustache she had regularly bleached since middle school. To do so would be vain and worldly, Father Gregory told her.

Shelly acquiesced, believing that the austere rules of the monastery were but a small price to pay for the chance to escape the rat race and the uncertainties of the secular world. Besides, she'd be able to live a contemplative life, meditating, praying, and singing all day.

Contemplative prayer is the practice of a church tradition called mysticism. It dates back to the earliest years of the Catholic Church, when new believers went into the desert to escape the world in order to pray and meditate without distraction or interruption. That tradition is what drew Shelly to Holy Cross, so she gave everything she owned—jewelry, furniture, crystal, clothing, and her car—to friends and relatives. Although it broke her heart, Shelly even gave up Bat Woman and Robin, her beloved cats, and she donated her modest savings account to the Church.

On a sunny spring morning in 1992, Shelly Lewis, with not much more than a toothbrush, a bible, and the clothes on her back, moved into the Monastery of the Exaltation of the Most Holy Cross. Although it was just minutes from her town house, it was a world away from the life she had been living.

The monastery was the domain of Father Gregory, also known as the Right Reverend Doctor Gregory F. G. Wendt, or as he would explain, "My civilian name is Frank Gerard Wendt. I am also known in religion as Archimandrite

Gregory, Father Abbot—with one *T*—Gregory or Father Gregory."

It was a mantra that investigators would hear again and again as they probed the arcane world of Holy Cross seeking a killer and the truth behind allegations that priests there were sexually abusing boys living at the monastery.

2

"She got the two things she wanted most—security and the opportunity to serve God."

—Beverly Dreher

At six-foot-four, the Right Reverend Doctor Gregory F. G. Wendt is an impressive man, especially in his Eastern Rite clerical garments—black, ankle-length cassock and matching cylindrical hat and veil, called a *kamelavkion*.

He was born Frank Gerard Wendt on June 7, 1944, in the New York City borough of Manhattan. In 1947, the family relocated to Miami when his father went to work as a technician for Eastern Airlines.

During World War II, the military brought thousands of soldiers and sailors to the region for training. When the war ended many permanently settled in Miami with their families. At the same time tourism, construction, and the explosive growth of the aviation industry fueled a population boom. Pan American World Airways connected Miami with thirty-two countries in South and Central America while Eastern Airlines connected Miami to New York, Chicago, and points in between.

The Wendts settled in Coral Gables. Young Frank attended Catholic schools run by the diocese of Miami, which was elevated to an archdiocese in 1968 following the arrival of millions of new Catholic residents from northern states, Cuba, and other countries in South and Central America.

Wendt would say that he was called to the cloth while attending summer "vocation weeks" at St. Bernard Abbey, a Benedictine monastery in Cullman, Alabama, when he was fifteen years old. It was then that he realized "that the precepts of the Christian life were something very important, and at that point I decided to follow these and pursue the priesthood."

The following year Frank Wendt entered a Miami seminary, St. John Minor Vianny. After graduation he returned to St. Bernard Abbey where he studied philosophy and music, and where he was tonsured—a sacred rite that marks one's becoming a novice monk. It involves shaving the head and cloaking the novice in a monastic habit to symbolize the renunciation of worldly fashions.

Unlike priests who serve a parish, monks serve God. Unless they are priest-monks, they don't provide pastoral counseling. Their days are supposed to be highly structured with little time for leisure. Instead, they devote themselves to prayer and work that enhances their mission to do God's work on Earth.

It was while at St. Bernard that Wendt was first exposed to the Eastern Rite. "I fell in love with it," he would say. And it was while at St. Bernard, too, that he first realized his spiritual destiny: establishing an Eastern Rite monastery in South Florida. But first Wendt, a serious musician who played the organ and harpsichord, wanted to complete his secular education. He enrolled at Alabama College—later renamed the University of Montevallo—where he majored in music and minored in history. He graduated cum laude in 1966 with a bachelor of arts—"*Artium Baccalarius* in Latin," he liked to say.

After graduation, Wendt traveled to the Netherlands

where he lived in a monastery for four years and studied philosophy and theology. By 1970 he was back in Miami, where he was ordained a priest in his home church, St. Hugh's, in the Coconut Grove section of Miami. Frank Gerard Wendt became Reverend Wendt.

He would serve briefly at a parish in Oklahoma before returning to Miami in 1973 to work at St. Basil's Byzantine Catholic Church. Then he headed back to the Netherlands to complete his studies for a doctorate from the Catholic University of Nijmegan.

In 1978, while Shelly Lewis was a high school senior, Reverend Wendt sought permission to switch from the Latin Rite to the Eastern Rite so that his "spiritual life would be more enriched by the Byzantine tradition," he explained, adding that he "found the phraseology of the prayers more complete and more spiritually enriching."

His request was granted in a practice known as incardination, a formal process whereby a cleric is released from the jurisdiction of one bishop—in this case the Archbishop of Miami—and transferred to that of another.

With just the stroke of a pen, Father Gregory Wendt was no longer a Roman Catholic priest. He became a cleric under the auspices of the eparchy—or diocese—of Passaic, New Jersey, which then, as now, had jurisdiction over Byzantine Catholics in Florida.

The following year, the thirty-five-year-old clergyman founded the Monastery of the Three Holy Hierarchs on a rustic plot of land owned by the Passaic Eparchy near the Palm Beach County town of Lantana. According to the articles of incorporation, the monastery was established as a nonprofit entity "under the patronage of the Most Reverend Michael J. Dudick, D.D., Bishop, Eparchy of Passaic, N.J. The status shall be a Catholic order or community of the Byzantine Rite, Eparch of Passaic."

According to Wendt, the monastery's superior, the location was chosen because it was close to St. Vincent de Paul

Seminary in nearby Boynton Beach. Wendt hoped to attract young seminarians to the new monastic community.

The plan was to tend beehives, raise goats and chickens, and start a school of theology, but Wendt's ambitious plan didn't work out. He was the monastery's lone monk and after little more than a year the bishop ordered it shut down. Wendt, said to be suffering from severe colitis, returned to Miami.

"I left the monastery on a leave of absence for illness," Wendt said, but there were whispers and rumors that there was another more sinister reason for the shutdown. The rumors would follow the cleric all the way back to Miami.

Whatever the reason, without Wendt the monastery was doomed.

"After I left, the membership greatly diminished to nothing and, therefore, the eparchy allowed the corporation to expire," he remembered. "There was in fact no monastery left."

Despite the setback, the failure of the monastery was not a total loss for Wendt. It was where, during the summer of 1979, he met a young seminarian who was studying for the priesthood at St. Vincent de Paul Seminary in nearby Boynton Beach.

James Gibault was born on November 5, 1954, in Meriden, Connecticut, a small industrial city midway between Hartford and New Haven. He was the oldest of Albert and Geraldine Gibault's three children and their only son. After graduating from the University of Connecticut with a bachelor's degree in marketing, Gibault worked briefly as a bank teller and a personnel counselor. In 1978, he was living in Boynton Beach and working as a busboy when he applied for admission to St. Vincent de Paul.

On his application, Gibault was asked to write in a

"Yes" or "No" answer to a series of questions about his personal life:

- Has any member of your family been afflicted with mental disease?

- Are you in any way physically deformed or handicapped?

- Do you have any chronic disease?

- Are you now or have you been addicted to drugs or to marijuana or to alcohol?

- Have you ever been affiliated with a heretical or schismatic sect or a forbidden society?

- Have you ever married or attempted to contract marriage?

- Have you ever killed or mutilated a human being, even accidentally?

Next to each question, Gibault wrote "No."

He labored at the Lantana monastery for two steamy South Florida summers, performing mostly menial tasks such as cutting the grass, cleaning the facilities, and washing dishes. Then in December 1980, when he was just sixteen credits short of completing his seminary studies, Gibault's superiors at St. Vincent delivered a devastating blow—they asked him to leave.

He had a problem, and it was serious enough to raise doubts about his ability to serve the Church as a cleric. According to seminary documents, officials advised Gibault to take a leave of absence "due to his drinking habits and undesirable behavior associated with drink." And he was directed to seek psychological counseling and "more time for growth and development."

But Gibault's troubles didn't prevent Wendt from taking

the young seminarian under his wing. He became his spiritual advisor and mentor, while Gibault became Wendt's devoted subordinate. Together, the two men set out to realize Wendt's dream to establish an Eastern Rite monastery in South Florida.

For the next two years they taught school, Gibault at Cardinal Gibbons High School in Fort Lauderdale then at LaSalle High in Miami, while Wendt taught at the Francisco Baldor School, Gulliver Academy, and Columbus High School, all located in Miami.

They pooled their salaries and lived sparsely. In 1982 they launched the Byzantine Catholic Monastery, with Wendt and one other monk in residence—Gibault. It was located in a residential neighborhood in South Miami-Dade. The living room served as the chapel, but Wendt, then thirty-eight, said he planned to build a larger one in the garage. It would be a "stable vow monastery," which meant that its members would live together in a community, work, and serve God together as one spiritual family. Three years later the monastery's name was changed to the Monastery of the Exaltation of the Most Holy Cross.

"I do whatever I can to spread the Kingdom of God on earth," Wendt told an interviewer from the *Miami Herald* in 1982.

During this time Gibault, who had already followed his mentor into the Byzantine Catholic Church, was able to finish his theological training by following a course of independent study directed by Wendt. After passing oral and written exams at the seminary that had sent him packing in 1980, he was ordained a priest in 1992. He took the religious name Damian.

The two clerics launched Holy Cross Academy in 1985, in an area of Kendall, Florida, known as Horse Country, with nine lay teachers and about fifty students. At first they held classes for fourth- through eighth-grade boys and girls in makeshift classrooms rented from nearby churches and the Hacienda, an equestrian club and horse farm.

Sixteen months later, the clerics were able to set up portable classrooms and trailers on the first of several adjoining tracts they purchased over a period of several years. The funds came from their salaries, a Dutch benefactor who donated fifty thousand dollars, a bank loan, tuition, and fund-raisers. In 1994, the first permanent classroom building opened at Holy Cross at a cost of $1.5 million. It had the look of a medieval castle complete with turrets, towers, and ornate gold crosses.

"Our ideal is not so much to create a castle, but a monastery," Wendt told the *Miami Herald* at the time. "This is the only monastery school to our knowledge in South Florida, and we wanted an architecture with religious purposes."

Wendt said the location was chosen because the monks, all of whom were vegetarians, needed a location where they could tend goats and chickens. "We try to grow as much of our food as possible," Wendt told the *Miami Herald* in 1985.

The residents of Horse Country didn't exactly roll out the welcome mat for Holy Cross. The local homeowners, association opposed Wendt's plans, which included adding two additional adjoining structures that would form a sixty-six-thousand-square-foot U-shaped structure. The goal was to be able to accommodate more than five hundred students from pre-kindergarten through grade twelve.

In addition to classrooms, there would be state-of-the-art science and computer labs, a library, an auditorium, playing fields, and a chapel. Despite stiff community opposition, the county commission narrowly approved the plans by a vote of four to three, swayed in part by the school's popularity with Catholic parents desperate for the rigorous curriculum and structure that Holy Cross proposed. When completed, the Holy Cross complex would consist of seven structures—the school, a convent, a prefabricated structure serving as the school's business office, a chapel, a guest house that would be home to Christine Wendt, the abbot's mother, the monastery where Wendt resided, and the candidates' house, a converted barn that would be home to Gibault and the monks-in-training from Ukraine.

In many ways Holy Cross Academy was a throwback to an earlier era. Students from the youngest grades learned Latin and Greek; they studied the classics, art, music, chemistry, and biology, and they could count on at least two hours of homework daily. Classes were small, religious instruction was given to students at every grade level by teachers in clerical robes, and prayer was always part of the school day.

Discipline was strict, too. Every student was required to sign a behavior contract. They had to wear uniforms and were taught to stand whenever an adult entered a classroom. Boys couldn't wear earrings, and their hair could not touch their collars or hang in their eyes. Girls had to wear skirts that covered their knees. Older students, both boys and girls, wore school blazers and neckties and gray pants or skirts. Gum chewing and lateness were forbidden. Rule breaking could result in Saturday detentions, during which students would spend the day cleaning the school.

Some teachers found the atmosphere oppressive and left after a brief stay. Nevertheless, by 2001, Holy Cross Academy had become a multimillion-dollar operation with five hundred students paying as much as $5,900 a year in tuition. And overseeing it all was Father Abbot Gregory Wendt, who made it perfectly clear that he was head honcho, "the highest authority" at Holy Cross Academy.

"It is inappropriate and, in fact, useless to contact the

Bishops as there is no higher authority to whom to direct a suggestion, a concern, a complaint or appeal than the Chancellor-Headmaster who is the President and highest authority regarding the corporation," the Holy Cross faculty handbook warned.

There was nothing humble about Wendt. Many who had dealings with the bearded and bespectacled cleric—teachers, parents, and others—found him condescending, arrogant, and pompous. But while the holy man may have had the final word on everything at Holy Cross, when it came to the day-to-day running of the academy everyone agreed that Sister Michelle was the one who made things happen.

"She was the backbone of the school," a former student recalled. "She was on top of everything."

Sister Michelle Lewis was the school's financial administrator. She kept the books, collected tuition, and paid the bills. She was also in charge of registration and admissions, distributed report cards, organized the activities calendar and the yearbook, and taught calculus. When she had time, she'd clean the chapel and help prepare lunches for the academy's students.

She was also a familiar figure at all sports and extracurricular activities, and very often when a teacher was out sick, it was Sister Michelle who substituted. She even looked after stray dogs and cats that wandered onto the campus.

When asked if Sister Michelle was a Holy Cross employee, Wendt answered, "Monastics are not employed." Asked if she was compensated for her teaching or bookkeeping, Wendt said, "Yes, spiritually."

The holy man explained: "Everyone in monastic life does something that is work. In speaking to a monastic candidate we talk about their strengths, their weaknesses, their abilities, and obviously with her training she had the abilities which we could make use of, in which she wished to offer in the areas of mathematics. There was calculus and in the bookkeeping area, and that's what I was blessed with—her desire to do those as her work."

Michelle Lewis had signed on to spend her days in prayer, meditation, and song as a member of the Holy Cross monastery. As Sister Michelle she was constantly on call, the pager that she wore on her belt beeping relentlessly from morning until night every day of the week.

If she felt stressed or overwhelmed by her responsibilities and the demands made on her, Michelle never complained. Instead she became increasingly acid-tongued and short-tempered, the result in part of working twelve-hour days in South Florida's subtropical heat and humidity while covered from head to toe in the oppressively heavy medieval garments she was required to wear.

"She could be abrupt and businesslike," recalled her friend Heidi Browne, whose husband, Raymond, taught theology at Holy Cross and also served as the school's managing principal. Holy Cross's other nun, eighty-seven-year-old Sister Marie Lurz, agreed. "Sister Michelle was a very blunt person, very charitable person, but I didn't think she had any social skills."

Those who knew her before she joined Holy Cross were stunned and confused by the transformation. "She had become another person," observed her mom, Beverly Lewis. "But she loved the kids at the academy."

In the summer of 2000, Sister Michelle traveled home to Ohio to visit her mother. She brought with her the Holy Cross yearbook.

"Shelly was so proud," her mother recalled. "She pointed to all the kids and had something to say about each one of them. I could see the love in her eyes." It was the last time Bev Lewis would see her daughter alive.

"She was no longer the Shelly I knew," said her childhood friend Beverly Dreher. Over the years the two women had drifted apart and gone their separate ways: Shelly to Florida and Dreher to Columbus, Ohio, but they managed to stay in touch every now and then through phone calls, letters, and cards.

Dreher couldn't believe her eyes when she saw Michelle in her monastic habit. She remembers being taken aback by the oversized square eyeglasses her friend wore, "but it was the unbleached moustache that really shocked me."

To Dreher, Shelly's life at Holy Cross amounted to "indentured servitude." Shelly even confessed to her friend that she had been naïve about what her life would really be like at the academy, but she wasn't about to leave.

"She got the two things she wanted most: security and the opportunity to serve God," Dreher said.

Sister Michelle felt safe and secure. She had been living at Holy Cross for nearly ten years. She was part of a thriving monastic community that included the two priests and five young monks-to-be who had come from the remote and impoverished Transcarpathian Mountains of western Ukraine to live and study at Holy Cross. The work of the monastery was the academy, and Michelle was integral to its success. What's more, she was being spiritually guided by the Right Reverend Doctor Gregory F. G. Wendt, aka Father Abbot or Father Gregory, and his vicar, Father Damian Gibault.

In the late afternoon of Saturday, March 24, 2001, Sister Michelle hurried to the guest house on the Holy Cross campus, where the two clerics and the monk candidates had gathered for haircuts. A female barber from a nearby Supercuts was already there. Following her haircut, Sister Michelle asked the priests for permission to watch the World Figure Skating Championships, which were being televised later that night. With permission granted, Sister Michelle returned to the convent where she ate dinner with

Sister Marie Lurz, with whom she shared the three-bedroom, two-bath convent.

After dinner the two women sat in the living room where Marie, an English teacher at Holy Cross, sat on a sofa grading papers while Michelle, sitting on a love seat, worked on an embroidery of a Byzantine icon she had started some weeks earlier. Promptly at nine P.M., Sister Marie said good night and shuffled off to her bedroom at the north end of the house, while Sister Michelle remained in the living room watching intently as ice-skating great Michelle Kwan won her fourth figure skating championship. At ten o'clock she turned off the television set, turned out the lights, and walked to her bedroom at the south end.

Within hours Sister Michelle would be dead, her earthly life ended in an orgy of violence at the hands of an unlikely attacker who for years had kept his rage well hidden behind the twin façades of innocence and piety.

3

"I wasn't even sure if it was Sister's body because I was always used to seeing Sister, you know, in her dress, in her habit, and I said maybe it's not even Sister."

—Petro Terenta

March 25, 2001, started out as just another Sunday in sunny South Florida. On South Beach, the hipsters who had crowded the bistros and clubs the night before gave way to in-line skaters, joggers, and buff young men and women playing volleyball on the sandy expanse of beach that separates Ocean Drive from the Atlantic Ocean. Sunbathers were on the beach, too, and among them were shapely women, some young and some not so young, who preferred to soak up the sun topless.

Across Biscayne Bay, it had been a relatively quiet morning for the men and women on duty at the Miami-Dade County Police Department's emergency communications center. They hadn't fielded too many calls for help, and none that would come in that day would be as startling as the call that came in to an emergency operator at twelve minutes past eleven.

In a flat, matter-of-fact voice, the caller alerted authorities to the crime that would shock Miami and shake the Catholic Church.

911 OPERATOR: *Miami-Dade County Police and Fire. What is your emergency?*

CALLER: *Um, this is uh, Holy Cross Academy, 12425 SW 72nd Street.*

911 OPERATOR: *What's the emergency there?*

CALLER: *Ah, the emergency is that, ah, ah, one of the, uh, sisters didn't show up this morning for liturgy, and we sent someone over to look and they said that, ah, that there's, ah, like a nude body on the floor with blood.*

911 OPERATOR: *Where is that?*

CALLER: *This is in the convent.*

911 OPERATOR: *At one two four two five southwest seven-two street?*

CALLER: *Yes. That's the school address.*

911 OPERATOR: *That's where the body is at?*

CALLER: *Well, in the convent that belongs to the school.*

911 OPERATOR: *Okay, sir, is it at this same address?*

CALLER: *Yes. If you send someone to that address we'll show them which building.*

911 OPERATOR: *What's the phone number you are calling from?*

CALLER: *Pardon?*

911 OPERATOR: *What is the phone number you are calling from?*

CALLER: *Ah, uh, 305-598-0009.*

911 OPERATOR: *305-598-0009?*

CALLER: *No. 305-598-0009.*

911 OPERATOR: *That's what I said.*

CALLER: *I'm sorry. I didn't hear you. And I'm at extension fourteen.*

911 OPERATOR: *Extension fourteen?*

CALLER: *Yes.*

911 OPERATOR: *Okay, are you there now?*

CALLER: *I'm here, this is where, I'm not where the body is, no.*

911 OPERATOR: *Is it a male or a female body?*

CALLER: *A female. It was the nun's convent. Females.*

911 OPERATOR: *Okay. And no one ever saw her move or anything like that?*

CALLER: *No. Ah, we, no um, um. The person that we sent over was one of the brothers to see what was wrong and he found out and ran away right away. He was scared. Ran back here to tell me. We didn't know what happened, where she was.*

911 OPERATOR: *Okay. What's your last name?*

CALLER: *W-E-N-D-T.*

911 OPERATOR: *And it's Holy Cross?*

CALLER: *Right.*

911 OPERATOR: *And she's at the convent, right?*

CALLER: *Yes. They come to the main gates of the school.*

911 OPERATOR: *Okay. Police and Rescue are on their way.*

CALLER: *We'll have someone there to bring them to where the convent is.*

911 OPERATOR: *Okay.*

CALLER: *All right. Thank you.*

911 OPERATOR: *You're welcome.*

Wendt's emergency call lasted two minutes and thirty-eight seconds. Almost as soon as he hung up the phone, police and paramedics were at Holy Cross.

There are thirty-five incorporated cities, towns, and villages in Miami-Dade County. The larger ones, like the cities of Miami and Miami Beach, have their own police departments and crime scene investigation units. Many of the rest, as well as the 1.4 million residents who live in the unincorporated areas of the county, rely on the Miami-Dade Police Department (MDPD) for either all or most of the services related to law enforcement.

The first lawman on the scene was Jorge Gonzalez, one of the MDPD's three thousand sworn officers. Gonzalez, working out of the Kendall District Station, was on routine patrol in his green-and-white police cruiser when the radio crackled. The dispatcher ordered him to the sprawling seventeen-acre Holy Cross campus to investigate a report of a sick or injured woman found lying in a pool of blood.

In less than two minutes the lawman was there. As he steered his cruiser past the main gate and into the school's parking lot, Gonzalez noticed that two lime-green units from the Miami-Dade Fire Department—Rescue 9 with a team of paramedics and Engine 9—had pulled in ahead of him.

They had stopped on the east side of the school, in front of a three-story structure that looked as if it might have been built during the Middle Ages. Gonzalez watched as a priest in flowing robes and pope hat climbed aboard the Rescue unit, then followed as the Fire Rescue units made a beeline two hundred yards across an open field to the convent, a tan-colored single-story house on the northeast edge of the campus.

It had its own address—6950 Southwest 123rd Avenue. The house was set back about one hundred feet from the roadway on a nearly two-and-a-half acre plot. A seven-foot-high wooden fence hid the convent from the avenue, a two lane north-south roadway that runs past plant nurseries, stately homes, and horse farms.

The monastery's white Chevrolet pickup, Florida license plate UQE-80H, was parked outside. Gonzalez noticed no signs of forced entry or violence, nothing at all to indicate that anything was wrong.

As the paramedics of Rescue 9 removed their gear

from their vehicle, Gonzalez and Wendt hurried to the front door of the convent. While they walked, the cleric explained to Gonzalez that Sister Michelle had not appeared at the chapel for Sunday services. He gave Petro Terenta, one of the young monk candidates living at Holy Cross, a key to the front door of the convent and sent him there.

Within minutes, the monk-to-be returned. He was out of breath and frightened. He said Sister Michelle was lying on the floor and blood was everywhere. That's when Wendt dialed 911.

Later, investigators learned that it was Sister Marie Lurz who first sounded the alarm that something was amiss at Holy Cross. Heidi Browne recalls sitting in the chapel that morning with her husband and three young children.

"We were waiting for the liturgy to begin," the thirty-four-year-old principal's wife recalled. Wearing their robes, the five monk candidates were waiting, too, but the service could not start without bread for the liturgy, and it was Sister Michelle's job to bring it. Then, just before it was time for the service to begin, Sister Marie staggered into the chapel.

"I can't find Sister Michelle," the distraught elderly nun told the Brownes. It was customary for the two women to drive to the chapel in the monastery's white pickup truck with Sister Michelle behind the wheel, but this morning the frail nun had walked the two hundred yards from the convent.

"She told me, 'Sister Michelle did not come out for breakfast in the kitchen like she normally does,'" Browne recalled.

Sister Marie explained that she had knocked on Sister Michelle's bedroom door. When there was no answer she tried to open it, but it was locked. She even rattled the knob, but the door still did not open. Thinking that

Michelle might have gone on ahead without her, Sister Marie set out on the long walk to the chapel.

After listening to the elderly nun, Raymond Browne turned to Petro to ask if he had any idea where Sister Michelle might be.

"He asked me if I saw Sister today, and I said I didn't," Petro remembered. "Then he said 'She's missing. I think you should tell Father Abbot.'"

Petro immediately left and went to the candidates' house ninety feet away. Wendt and Gibault were on the phone, desperately trying to get in touch with Sister Michelle.

"As soon as I came in, before I could ask anything of them, they said, 'Where is Sister? Have you seen her? We need to start liturgy and she is missing.'"

The priests were concerned about not having bread for the service, so they sent Petro to the convent to get it. As soon as Wendt handed him the key, the young monk-to-be bolted out the door, running the two-hundred-yard distance.

At twenty-one years of age, Petro Terenta was the oldest of the monk candidates. He had come to the United States in 1996 at age sixteen along with another monk candidate, then-fourteen-year-old Mykhaylo "Misha" Kofel. Five more monk candidates would follow them, and three of them were still living at Holy Cross: Vasyl Kopych arrived in 1997, Alexander "Sasha" Korsak in 1999, and Yosyp Lembak in 2000. They had all come to Miami as adolescents on student visas. None had spoken more than a few words of English when they first arrived.

Petro was out of breath when he reached the front door of the convent.

"I knocked and waited for a response," Petro remembered. When there was none, Petro unlocked the door and stepped inside. At first nothing seemed out of the ordinary. "Sister, are you there?" he called out. No one answered.

"There were these two rooms to the left of where I was and I didn't know which one Sister was in so I unlocked the first one and there was nobody there; actually it was open, I think, and then I approached the other door and I knocked again. I tried it and it was locked so I opened the door with the key."

Immediately he saw the bloody body on the floor. He never even crossed the threshold.

"Once I saw the body, that was it," Petro said. "I tried to get out of the house. I didn't even look around because my immediate impression was that somebody could be in the house. So I left the door open where the body was and then I exited the same way, through the main door, and I locked the door behind me and ran as fast as I could to the candidates' house."

Petro broke the stunning news to the priests, who were sitting on a couch in the living room. "I told Father Abbot that something bad had happened, and I described what I saw," the young monk-to-be recalled, adding, "I said that I saw Sister's body on the floor naked. I said I wasn't even sure if it was Sister's body because I was always used to seeing Sister, you know, in her dress, in her habit, and I said maybe it's not even Sister. I wasn't even sure myself, so I said there's a body in one of those rooms, and there's a deep cut, looks like the body is dead, and I said something terrible had happened and then Father Abbot called 911 immediately."

While Wendt was on the phone speaking with the 911 operator, Mykhaylo Kofel walked into the room. He was still wearing the white altar boy's gown he had donned earlier for the service. Mykhaylo asked what had happened.

"I didn't want to be the one to give him bad news," Petro said, "so I said, 'Nothing.'"

• • •

Using the same key he had given to Petro minutes earlier, Wendt, his hand shaking, now unlocked the front door and directed Gonzalez to the left, to the bedroom on the southwest side of the house. The paramedics followed the cop in while Wendt remained outside.

The house felt warm and stuffy. The air-conditioning was off and the windows were closed. As they crossed the threshold, Gonzalez and the paramedics walked into a small open foyer, passing a sunken living room on their right. The cleric told Gonzalez he'd find Sister Michelle in the second bedroom on the left, so the lawman and the paramedics headed in that direction.

Just beyond a hallway closet, the team of rescuers veered left into a short corridor, which took them to two adjoining bedrooms on the southwest side of the house. As soon as he made the turn, the cop noticed footprints on the parquet floor. They led from a bathroom on the west end of the house straight to the second bedroom.

As he turned left again into the second bedroom, Gonzalez stopped dead in his tracks. He was face to face with a crime scene so bloody and evil that even hardened investigators would be brought to tears.

Lying in the middle of the room was the bloody body of Sister Michelle Lewis. She was flat on her back. Her legs, which faced the doorway, were spread-eagled and covered with blood, as were her torso and head. The black flower-print pullover she had worn to bed had been shredded and pulled over her chest to expose her breasts. A metal wrist-watch was on her right wrist.

Blood covered the walls and the armoire. The room's wall-to-wall rose-colored carpet was soaked with it. There were bloodstains on the twin-sized bed, which stood against the west wall. Scattered on the floor were an overturned lamp, a wastebasket, and a broken lamp shade. All were bloodstained, as was the nightstand, which held a bible, a pair of nail clippers, and two boxes of over-the-counter cold medicine. Two boxes of kitty litter in the southwest corner were bloodstained, too. A black nun's habit was draped over a chair that stood to the left of the body. Also on the chair were several other items: a black leather belt with a pager, black socks, a pair of panties, a nun's head covering, and a sanitary napkin.

Body decomposition begins immediately after death, when bacteria inside the intestines begin eating away at internal tissue. Immediately, too, the body begins to change color, taking on a waxy appearance with a blue or yellow tint. It's called postmortem lividity, but with so much blood covering Sister Michelle, the rescuers couldn't tell from her appearance if she was dead or alive.

Hoping against hope that she was still alive, Gonzalez stepped aside to let the paramedics in, but it was too late. At eighteen minutes past eleven the paramedics from Rescue 9 declared Michelle Ann Lewis, Sister Michelle, dead. They listed multiple stab wounds as the cause of death. The paramedics could see that she had been stabbed and battered. She had been hit in the head by a blunt-force instrument several times and suffered dozens of similar bruises and stab wounds to her torso; there were self-defense–type cuts on her hands and it appeared that her right thumb was nearly severed.

The murder of Sister Michelle was so horrific it could only have been committed by a mentally deranged killer— or by someone possessed. According to Catholic theologians, cases of actual demonic possession are rare, but they do happen. The Church teaches that the devil was once a good angel created by God and given the gift of free will. But the devil chose to reject goodness for evil in order to satisfy his own selfish desires.

"Society needs to be defended against the devil," Father Gabriele Amorth, a Catholic theologian and exorcist in

Rome told the Catholic News Service in 2006. "The devil can possess not only individuals but also entire groups and populations."

It was Father Amorth who revealed that Pope John Paul II believed in demonic possession. The revelation came after the Holy Father performed an exorcism on a young woman in 2000, after she flew into an uncontrollable rage at the end of a general audience at the Vatican.

Forensic psychiatrists and psychologists are divided on the concept of evil, but most agree that evil lurks in the hearts of nearly all humans. How else to explain Dr. Stanley Milgram's famous electroshock experiments at Yale University in the 1960s, when participating students delivered what they thought were massive jolts of electricity to fellow students because they were encouraged to do so by an authority figure?

"Evil is endemic, it's constant, it is a potential in all of us. Just about everyone has committed evil acts," says Dr. Robert I. Simon, clinical professor of psychiatry at Georgetown Medical School and the author of *Bad Men Do What Good Men Dream*. Evil, he says, is in the eye of the beholder but the concept is of no use to forensic psychiatrists.

Dr. Michael Stone has a different view. The Columbia University professor of psychiatry has examined hundreds of killers and has created a twenty-two-level hierarchy of evil behavior. He says its time for forensic psychiatrists to give predatory behavior its proper "appellation"—evil.

But none of that mattered to Officer Gonzalez, who used his radio to report the homicide then waited for the arrival of more cops. In the meantime, he noticed that a late-model Ford Crown Victoria carrying two holy men had parked in front of the house.

They identified themselves as Father Damian Gibault and Brother Petro Terenta. Gonzalez ordered them and Father Abbot Gregory Wendt to wait nearby, explaining to the clerics that detectives were on the way and they would want to speak with each of them.

Within minutes eight more officers as well as a sergeant and a lieutenant from the Kendall District Station were at Holy Cross. They cordoned off the convent with yellow crime-scene tape and waited for the arrival of homicide detectives.

4

"Art, we've got a doozie, a major blood scene, a nun."

—Homicide Detective John King

The Miami-Dade Police Department's Homicide Bureau is divided into eight squads, each consisting of four detectives and a sergeant. Assignments are made by rotation, and Squad C was slated to lead the next homicide investigation. Within the squad, it was Detective Art Nanni's turn to be the lead detective.

With more than twenty-six years as a lawman under his belt—seventeen as a detective and twelve with the MDPD's Homicide Bureau, the fifty-two-year-old Nanni had been the lead investigator on dozens of murder cases over the years.

He began his law enforcement career in Homestead, Florida, in 1975, before joining the Miami-Dade force— in those days it was called the Department of Public Safety. Nanni worked in uniform until 1984 when he became a detective, first in the auto theft division then in homicide.

As the lead, it would be his job to oversee the processing of the crime scene, interview witnesses, and take overall charge of the day-to-day operation of the investigation including the interrogation of suspects. He would also be responsible for maintaining the case file and writing search warrants and arrest affidavits.

It's an awesome responsibility. Overlook just one clue and a case can go unsolved; violate a perpetrator's constitutional rights and a cold-blooded killer can literally get away with murder.

Nanni had been at Southwest 112th Street and US 1 when he got the call that would send him racing across Miami-Dade County. The veteran detective had been on duty since seven A.M. He was scheduled to work until three P.M., part of a team of investigators processing a murder scene until a cell phone call at ten minutes past noon directed him to the campus of Holy Cross Monastery and Academy.

The call was from Bill Gilliland, Squad C's sergeant. The sergeant informed Nanni that a white female had been found lying naked in a pool of blood inside a house located on the campus.

Art Nanni likes to get as much information as he can about a crime before he arrives on the scene. As he steered his dark blue Ford Taurus squad car north then west toward Holy Cross, another cell phone call shed a bit more light on the case. This time the call was from another Squad C detective, John King.

"Art, we've got a doozie," King said. "It's a major blood scene, a nun."

The thirty-one-year veteran of the MDPD had been on the road when he was notified of the homicide at Holy Cross by a sergeant at the communications division. The sergeant gave King, a homicide detective since 1981, a cell phone number and suggested that he speak with a uniformed sergeant already at the scene. King spoke with the sergeant then phoned Nanni.

As they talked on their cell phones, both men realized that they were about to become key investigators in what had the makings of a very high-profile case, one that would attract swarms of media as well as religious leaders, politicians, and top brass from the MDPD. Within minutes both detectives were at Holy Cross, arriving at virtually the same time. Nanni tasked King with overseeing the processing of the crime scene. King spoke briefly with Wendt and Gibault, who were sitting in their car in front of the convent.

Wendt was in the driver's seat. He never stepped out of the car. He told the detective that the victim was Sister Michelle Lewis, that she was in her thirties and had been at Holy Cross since 1992. Wendt then volunteered that he was the abbot of the monastery and the chancellor-headmaster of the academy, "the highest authority" at Holy Cross. King then asked the priest to sign an official "Consent to Search" form, which would allow MDPD investigators to enter the convent. The priest complied.

While King was talking to the priests, Nanni spoke with Officer Gonzalez. The cop briefed the homicide detective about what he'd seen inside the convent and what Wendt had told him about the events leading up to the discovery of Sister Michelle's body by Petro Terenta.

Next Nanni spoke briefly with Petro. The young monastic candidate was sitting on the grass under a tree a few feet from the front door of the convent. He recounted how he came to be the one to find the body, what he had seen inside, and what he did afterward.

Nanni was finished with Petro, at least for the time being. "I'll be getting back to you," the lawman promised. Experience told him that the murder of Sister Michelle had probably been a break-in and a rape, likely to have been committed by a worker from one of the surrounding nurseries or from Holy Cross itself, but Nanni's training told him to suspect everyone—from Wendt on down.

Nanni now wanted to interview the abbot and Father Damian Gibault, his Kris Kringle lookalike lieutenant. After speaking with King, the two clerics left the area in front of the convent and drove to the academy's main building. Art Nanni and Bill Gilliland found them in the school's administration office.

As soon as the detectives entered the school, they noticed security cameras in the hallways. Nanni wanted to know if there were videotapes they could review. There were none, the priests said, adding that the cameras worked only during school hours to monitor student activities.

The detectives did not know it then, but video cameras were pervasive at Holy Cross Academy. In addition to the hallways, they were mounted inside classrooms and in students' bathrooms. In the boys' bathrooms they were aimed at the urinals, while cameras in the girls' bathrooms were focused on areas just outside the toilet stalls.

Investigators would learn from former Holy Cross Academy teachers that Wendt kept a small video monitor on his desk in his private office. On it he could watch as the images from the cameras rotated automatically every ten seconds. If he wanted to, Wendt could halt the rotation at any time and view a scene for as long as he wanted to.

"The cameras were pretty much everywhere," former student Danelys Perera told reporters from the *Miami Herald.* "There was one stall next to the camera where none of the girls liked to go because you weren't sure whether the camera could see you when you were going to [the] bathroom."

Wendt explained that the cameras were for security.

"The school said a student had been caught smoking in the bathroom," recalled Miami-Dade Police Director Carlos Alvarez, whose son had graduated from Holy Cross several years earlier.

At first, the video cameras made perfect sense to Lucy Hernandez, whose oldest son attended the school the previous year, "but in hindsight it sounds strange." One former teacher quit after just one day at Holy Cross because the cameras made her uncomfortable.

At this point in the investigation, however, the lawmen were interested in learning more about the events that led up to the discovery of Sister Michelle's body, so they zeroed in on the hours before her bloody body was found.

The priests told the detectives about the haircuts on Saturday afternoon. Gibault related that he and two of the monk candidates, Sasha Korsak and Mykhaylo Kofel, had gone grocery shopping afterward. They had been away from the campus little more than an hour. Gibault recalled giving his set of master keys to Kofel, who helped put the groceries away. When the keys were returned to him, Gibault noticed that one was missing but did not question Kofel.

Next, they turned to Wendt who informed them that Sister Michelle shared the convent with Sister Marie, and that as far as he knew the elderly and hard-of-hearing nun was the last person to see Michelle alive.

Nanni told the priest he wanted to speak with Sister Marie. The detective was taken aback when the priest declared, "I will not allow it. She's in frail health." Besides, Wendt said, Sister Marie still did not know that her young colleague had been murdered. She believed that her colleague had died from an asthma attack.

At five feet six inches, Art Nanni is not a big man. The holy man towered over him, but the detective is a committed investigator who passionately believes that every murder victim deserves justice. There is no glamour in being a homicide detective. The hours are long and irregular. The pay is barely enough to live on, especially for a father of six like Nanni, and the job takes a terrible toll on family life. The reward comes when all the pieces of the puzzle come together and a killer is caught and convicted.

Even if Wendt was a man of God, Art Nanni was not about to allow him to stand in the way of the investigation. But according to investigators, it wouldn't be the last time the six-foot-four-inch priest would try.

5

"The crime scene was gruesome, one of the worst I have seen in my career."

—Assistant State Attorney Priscilla Prado

By mid-afternoon the Holy Cross campus was crawling with lawmen. In addition to the uniformed cops from the Kendall District Station, eight detectives from the Homicide Bureau and one from Kendall were on the scene. Ten more detectives and criminalists from the MDPD's Crime Scene Investigations Bureau responded, too.

The bureau is comprised of three sections: investigations, or CSI; forensic imaging, which includes art and photo units; and fingerprint identification.

Forensic photographers took pictures of the body and the room, shooting twenty-five rolls of film in and around the convent alone. They also took pictures elsewhere on the campus, including the interior and exterior of the candidates' house as well as the school building.

Fingerprint specialists gathered dozens of fingerprints and palm prints. Electrostatic lift sheets were used to collect the footprints inside the convent, while casts were made of foot impressions found on the concrete walkway in the rear of the convent.

Police artists drew detailed sketches of Sister Michelle's bedroom, the convent, the Holy Cross grounds, and its other buildings. Personnel from the forensic biology section of the MDPD's crime lab went about the grim task of collecting blood evidence and possible semen and saliva specimens that Sister Michelle's killer might have left behind.

Investigators found bloodstains on the doorjamb of a bathroom and on the handle of a back door. Smaller bloodstains, contact smears, were also found on a light switch, the inside and outside knobs of the bedroom door, and on the inner edge of the door near the lock. Hairs found on Sister Michelle's hands were collected. Her fingernails were trimmed and the clippings were collected, too.

Two members of the department's media relations team and its top commander, Police Director Alvarez, were at Holy Cross, too. In addition, Nanni called in two K-9 units and the MDPD's helicopter, which circled overhead with a police photographer on board, snapping dozens of aerial photos of the campus and the surrounding area.

A prosecutor from the Miami-Dade state attorney's office responded to the scene, too. Assistant state attorney Priscilla Prado was on call that weekend, ready to race to the scene of any homicide that occurred in the southern part of Miami-Dade County. Earlier she had been at the Aventura Mall on a disappointing blind date when she was contacted by Sergeant Gilliland, who told her about the murder at Holy Cross Academy.

It would be Prado's job to stand by in case detectives needed help with legal issues that might arise during the initial stages of the investigation, and she'd be taken on a walk through of the crime scene to get a firsthand look and a feel for what had happened.

It was not an easy walk-through for the thirty-three-year-old prosecutor. The sister's body was still uncovered and lying in the middle of the bedroom.

"The crime scene was gruesome, one of the worst I have seen in my career," recalled Prado, who became a prosecutor in 1991 after graduating from the University of Miami Law School. And it smelled badly, very badly.

By the time Prado walked through just after 4 P.M., the putrid stench of death had permeated the entire house. Homicide investigators know the stench all too well. It gets onto their clothes and into their skin. It can take days to wash it away no matter how many showers or baths they take, or how much perfume or cologne they splash on.

The stench of death at a crime scene is bad enough, but the rancid odor that emanates from the human body during an autopsy is even worse. There was still much work to be done, however, before the medical examiner could remove Sister Michelle's body and transport it to the morgue for autopsy.

With no known eyewitnesses and no weapons found at the crime scene, lawmen had a genuine whodunit on their hands, but they had blood—lots of blood. To the untrained eye a bloody murder scene may seem like nothing more than a bloody mess, but to forensic investigators it holds a wealth of information.

Because a murder victim's blood can leave the body in many ways—it oozes, drips, gushes, or spurts—analysis of the shapes and locations can help investigators figure out the sequence of events, the movements and the positions of the victim and the attacker, as well as the type of weapons that caused the wounds. Careful collection and accurate analysis can help lawmen find a killer, and blood evidence can lead to a conviction. That's because analysis techniques have advanced rapidly in the last twenty years.

Every human being can be classified under the ABO blood-typing system. Until the early 1990s, the best crime labs could do was to determine blood type, but with the advent of DNA analysis beginning in the 1990s, a blood source can be statistically narrowed down to one person out of several million or even one in several billion.

But not all bloodstains are visible. Some are latent, or invisible. To find them, investigators spray Luminol, an extremely sensitive chemical, over areas where they suspect they would find unseen traces of blood. It reacts with hemoglobin in blood to produce a glowing substance, which can then be photographed. In this case, however, Luminol wasn't necessary—investigators had more than enough visible blood evidence to work with.

The MDPD's blood expert, Toby Wolson, was called to Holy Cross to interpret the bloodstains and unravel their secrets. A certified bloodstain pattern expert and a DNA analyst, Wolson had been working in the forensic biology section of the MDPD's crime lab since 1982.

Unlike Art Nanni, Wolson prefers not knowing too much about a case prior to arriving at a scene. "I try not to get too much information in advance because I don't want it to bias how I look at the scene," the veteran serologist said in her deposition, explaining that she would rather view the scene first "and get some thoughts and then start asking questions, so I don't ask for a lot of input initially."

As she drove to Holy Cross, Wolson didn't know very much, only that there was a female victim who had been found on her bedroom floor. She had been stabbed multiple times.

However, Wolson doesn't only look for blood spatter. She looks for semen and saliva, too. She views the scene "from a forensic biology standpoint as well as from a plain pattern standpoint, so I go through the entire scene as much as possible to see if there's anything that catches my eye."

What caught her expert eye at Holy Cross was the position of the body—flat on its back, legs spread-eagled, suggesting the possibility of a sexual assault. The extensive blood spatter on the walls indicated that there had been a fierce struggle in the bedroom, while the large pool of blood on the carpet in the southwest corner of the room indicated that the body had been there for a long period of time.

The average human body holds about five quarts of blood, and it seemed that nearly every drop had drained from the sister's body in that corner of the room. Because it's impossible to determine the speed of blood flow as it left her mortally wounded body, Wolson couldn't say how long Sister Michelle had been in the corner, but she wasn't in the corner when found. Instead, she was in the center of the room, lying in a supine position. It was Wolson who had to figure out how that had happened. As she examined the carpet, she noticed bloodstain patterns consistent with dragging, which meant that Sister Michelle's body had been pulled from the southwest corner to the middle of the bedroom.

While bloodstains on the walls and the carpet helped investigators figure out what had happened in the bedroom, it was a tiny stain found on Sister Michelle's left thigh that had the potential to convict her killer beyond a reasonable doubt. It had been noticed earlier by John King, who pointed it out to Wolson.

The shape of bloodstain patterns can reveal the angle from which they fell. The stain in question was round, indicating that it had fallen from a ninety-degree angle. To Wolson and King, it meant that the sister's attacker was wounded and dripped his own blood on her as he stood over her. The stain was collected and labeled "Stain B-6." It and twenty-one others were sent to the MDPD lab for analysis, along with the scrapings taken from underneath the dead sister's fingernails.

An earlier examination of the sister's body turned up what appeared to be a bloody palm print on her right forearm. It was collected, too. Crime scene investigators were also looking for latent fingerprints on the slain sister's body. To expose them they sprayed areas where they would likely be found with Ninhydrin, a chemical reagent that reacts with amino acids in perspiration, turning once-invisible prints into visible ones. Dozens of latent prints were collected and sent to the fingerprint section for analysis.

But it was the news of that tiny drop of blood on Sister Michelle's thigh that gave Nanni his first eureka moment.

"As soon as I heard about it," the detective said, "I knew that sooner or later we would get the son of a bitch."

A second eureka moment came at 3:30 in the afternoon, when Holy Cross head custodian Daniel Puerto observed what appeared to be multiple footprints on the narrow concrete walkway between the monastery and the candidates' house. He reported his find to one of the uniformed cops, who notified Nanni. The detective hurried across the campus to see the footprints for himself. The custodian was waiting for him.

Puerto told Nanni that he and his four-man crew had been performing routine maintenance in that very area on Saturday. He was certain that the footprints had not been there. As he bent down to examine them more closely, Nanni noticed that they were clear as a bell, characterized by a high arch and a unique toe pattern.

They appeared to have been left by someone who was either barefoot or wearing a very thin pair of socks. Before fading out, the footprints pointed in one direction—to the two-story building just a stone's throw away from where the detective was standing—the former barn known as the candidates' house, the home of the Ukrainian monks-to-be and Father Damian Gibault.

Nanni's instinct told him that the footprints would lead to Sister Michelle's killer, but before he could go where they pointed, he was sidetracked by startling news: There was yet another crime scene at Holy Cross.

This one was in an office inside the single-story, pre-fabricated building on the northwest side of the campus. It was Sister Michelle's office, the academy's business office. It had been broken into and ransacked.

Daniel Puerto had discovered the break-in just minutes earlier. Nanni had asked him to check the other buildings on the campus and to report anything unusual. It hadn't taken the custodian long to stumble upon the burglary.

Lawmen now had two crime scenes at Holy Cross: A primary scene, the homicide at the convent, and a secondary scene, the break-in, at the modular building. Were they connected, or was it merely a coincidence?

Lawmen do not believe in coincidences. As he entered the modular building, Nanni noticed blood smears on the handle of the entrance door. Just inside were footprints. They were identical to those the detective had just examined on the sidewalk outside, and all were similar to those found inside Sister Michelle's residence.

After passing through a vestibule that students and faculty referred to as the assembly room, Nanni found himself in front of Sister Michelle's office. A fire extinguisher had been hurled through the double sliding-glass pass-through window, which separated the office from a small reception area. Papers from the sister's desk and file cabinets were scattered on the floor. It was apparent that the intruder had been looking for something, but in his search he left behind some important clues: bloodstained files, blood smears on the broken windowpane, and a single hair. Investigators also found bloodstains on a desk drawer handle, a doorknob, the fire extinguisher, and on the Levolor blinds that covered the interior side of the pass-through window.

Just before 6:30 P.M., while crime scene investigators processed the secondary scene, Nanni hurried back to the convent to meet with homicide detectives Tom Romagni and Doug McCoy. They had been canvassing area businesses, collecting oral mouth swabs for DNA analysis from their workers. Nanni had another assignment for them. He wanted the detectives to collect oral mouth swabs from Wendt and Gibault, and from the five monk candidates living at Holy Cross.

The detective was convinced that the footprints would lead him to Sister Michelle's killer, but he never imagined that the search for the truth about what happened at Holy Cross would also lead investigators halfway around the world to the western Ukraine.

6

"America is a good country. Why shouldn't we let him go there?"

—Maria Kofel

The Transcarpathian region of southwestern Ukraine is an area the size of Connecticut in a corner of the world where five countries—Hungary, Romania, Slovakia, Poland, and Ukraine—come together. It's a desperately poor region in a poor country. According to statistics released by the World Bank in 2005, the average salary in Ukraine is seventy-five to one hundred dollars a month in cities, and half as much in rural areas.

The population of Transcarpathia is ethnically diverse. The region was part of Hungary until the end of World War I, when it became part of Czechoslovakia. After World War II, it became part of the Ukrainian Soviet Socialist Republic, one of the constituent republics of the former Soviet Union. Hungarians, who are second in number to Slavs in the country as a whole, predominate over all other ethnic groups in the western Ukraine. There are also sizable numbers of Slovaks, Romanians, Poles, Armenians, Carpatho-Russians, gypsies, and nearly seventy other ethnic groups.

This mix can be heard in the languages spoken on the

streets of Uzhgorod, an ancient city of 111,000, which was founded by Slavs in the ninth century. Today it's the regional capital of Ukraine's Zakarpattia Oblast, or province. It has long been a crossroads for European and Asian traders, a battleground for invading armies, and a hotbed of ethnic and political strife.

Ukraine was the center of the first Slavic state, Kievan Rus. During the tenth and eleventh centuries it was the largest and most powerful nation in Europe. Weakened by internal feuds and Mongol invasions, it was absorbed into Lithuania and eventually into the Polish-Lithuanian Commonwealth.

During the latter part of the eighteenth century, most Ukrainian territory was taken over by the expanding Russian Empire during the reign of Catherine the Great, who called the region "Little Russia." Ukraine would enjoy a brief period of independence following the Russian Revolution of 1917, but freedom lasted only until 1920, when the country was conquered again, this time by Russian Communists, and made part of the Soviet Union.

Soviet rule was brutal. The Communists forced collectivization of farms and created famines in which more than eight million Ukrainians perished. During World War II, German and Soviet armies were responsible for some seven to eight million more deaths.

Ukraine became independent again in 1991 with the collapse of the Soviet Union, but democracy and economic reform remained elusive thanks to the long legacy of tyranny and corruption.

During their ruthless reign, the Communists did everything they could to crush religion. Worship was forced underground. Clergymen of all faiths were exiled to gulags in Siberia, but despite the brutal persecution, centuries-old spiritual beliefs proved impossible to stamp out, and many in the Transcarpathians remained steadfast and deeply religious, albeit secretly.

The majority of Ukrainians practicing a religion today belong to branches of Orthodox Christianity that follow the Byzantine Rite but are not under the authority of the Vatican. There's the Ukrainian Orthodox Church, which is under the authority of the Russian patriarch, and the independent Orthodox Church, which is headed by a Ukrainian patriarch. It has a strong following among Ukrainian nationalists.

Separate from both is the smaller Ukrainian Catholic Church, also known as the Greek Catholic Church. No church in the Ukraine suffered more at the hands of the atheistic Communists than the Greek Catholic Church, which, as part of the Byzantine Catholic Church, recognizes the authority of the Pope in Rome. It has been in full communion with the Vatican since 1596, when the Synod of Brest-Litovsk, healed the split dating back to the eleventh century. The rift, known as the Great Schism, stemmed from bitter disputes between Catholic theologians in Eastern Europe and their counterparts in Western Europe over church doctrine and the ongoing attempts of the popes in Rome to establish primacy over the patriarchs of the Eastern Church.

The final breach occurred with the sacking of Constantinople during the Fourth Crusade in 1204, under the banner of Pope Innocent III. Eight hundred years later Pope John Paul II apologized for what happened in Constantinople, but centuries-old wrongs are neither easily forgotten nor forgiven.

It was to this impoverished and strife-torn region that Father Abbot Gregory Wendt traveled in the mid 1990s. He spoke no Ukrainian, but through an interpreter he reportedly claimed that he was acting under the direct authority of the Vatican.

He said that he had "a great deal of independence

because he is the head of his order and subject directly to the Holy See in Rome," recalled Father Yuri Sabov, a Greek Catholic cleric. "He had no written recommendations, but he came into the eparchy administration, met with the bishop, and started talking about building a monastery in Ukraine."

Wendt claimed to be an archimandrite, a title bestowed on abbots of large Eastern Rite monasteries. He had come to Ukraine, he said, to open a training center where Greek Catholic boys would be exposed to the monastic life. If their parents agreed and they passed muster with Father Abbot Gregory Wendt, they would travel halfway around the world to the Monastery of the Exaltation of the Most Holy Cross in Miami where he would educate and train them for service in the monastery he planned to build in Ukraine.

Wendt didn't arrive with an empty pocket. For ninety-one thousand Ukrainian *hryvnia*—about eighteen thousand dollars—he purchased a one-story building in Konsovo that would serve as the training center.

But there was something strange about Father Gregory Wendt. "He seemed very peculiar," recalled Bishop Ivan Semediy, whose eparchy in the Transcarpathians encompassed one hundred fifty Greek Catholic churches and more than three hundred thousand faithful adherents. Normally, the bishop said, Byzantine priests who visit from outside the country participate in church services, but not Father Gregory. "His behavior was different from other priests," the bishop said. Whenever the two men met, they "would only meet for a couple of minutes and then [Wendt would] leave without relating any information about the activities at his center."

Nevertheless, the bishop agreed to write letters to U.S. Embassy officials in Kiev, Ukraine's capital, in support of student visas for Wendt's monks-to-be even though the bishop would have no jurisdiction over the monastic training center.

Wendt wasted no time recruiting for his monastery in Miami, but not all were chosen. Yevdokiya Sokolovych would have liked nothing better than to have sent her sons, already in their twenties, to America, but Father Gregory told her they were too old. The first boys Wendt recruited were Petro Terenta, a serious and studious sixteen-year-old, the grandson of a priest, and Mykhaylo "Misha" Kofel, a shy, fourteen-year-old altar boy from a backward mountain village

Petro Terenta was born on July 22, 1980, in Irshava, a small city not far from Uzghorod. He was the oldest of three children born to Petro and Maria Terenta. By the standards of the region, the Terenta family was well-off. Their two-story home had indoor plumbing, electricity, and a television set.

By all accounts, the Terentas were a loving and close family, and they were deeply religious. Petro's maternal grandfather, Vasyl Roman, was a Greek Catholic priest. The Terentas attended church every Sunday. When he was just ten years old, young Petro became passionate about religion. He mastered the melodies of the Mass and by age twelve he was able to lead the congregation in prayers. He felt he had a vocation for the monastic life "to serve God in every possible way, and the best way to do that is to become a monk," he said.

After completing the eleventh grade in 1996, Petro applied to a monastery in the Ukrainian city of Lviv, but he applied too late and he was not accepted. He heard about the new monastic center at Konsovo, however, and visited there to learn more. He met with Father Sabov, who was teaching religion at the center, and later with Wendt. It didn't take Petro long to make up his mind that he wanted to pursue a monastic life at Holy Cross, where Father Abbot Gregory Wendt would be his spiritual shepherd.

Petro's family would be very thankful that he did. His father landed a job as caretaker of the monastic center in

Konsovo while his uncle, Mikhail Roman, his mother's brother, became the center's director.

In all, there would be twenty-four Ukrainians on the Holy Cross payroll in Ukraine. According to Wendt they were paid two hundred dollars a month, a princely sum by Ukrainian standards.

Mykhaylo Kofel wasn't nearly as well off as Petro. His father was not on the Holy Cross payroll. His grandfather was not a priest. He did not live in a nice house, and he wasn't raised in a loving family.

Mykhaylo was born on July 2, 1982, the only child of Yuri and Maria Kofel. His parents called him Misha. The Kofels lived in a three-room cinder-block house in the remote mountain village of Verkhovina Bystra, House #166. The tiny home had plenty of religious icons, but no telephone or central heating. A wood-burning stove kept the family warm in the winter. They used an outhouse for a toilet. They did have electricity, but service was sporadic.

There are no paved roads into Verkhovina Bystra. The remote village is virtually inaccessible during the winter months. There is no doctor and no hospital. However, there is a house of worship, the Church of Saint Peter and Paul, and a small school that provides village children with an education up to the ninth grade.

The Kofels were a bit better off than most of their neighbors, which wasn't saying much. Yuri earned a modest salary driving a locomotive for the state railway, but because of the economic turmoil that plagued the region following the collapse of the Soviet Union, the railroad was not always able to make its payroll, which meant Yuri didn't get paid regularly. He kept on working anyway, even though it was difficult for him to support his wife, her parents, and Misha.

To help make ends meet the Kofels, like most of their neighbors, were subsistence farmers. They raised cows, pigs, and chickens, and they worked the fields tending crops without the benefit of any modern farming tools. It was backbreaking work. Early on, Misha, who was sickly and small for his age, had to work in the fields, too. He was responsible for chopping wood, planting crops, and looking after the animals.

Life was hard in Ukraine; it was even harder in Verkhovina Bystra, but villagers could always find comfort in their Greek Catholic faith. It was the foundation of life in the tiny village, and Maria Kofel was deeply devoted to it. Spiritually, Misha took after his mother, while Yuri took no comfort from religion; instead he found solace in vodka.

Misha was first introduced to church services when he was seven years old. From then on he prayed and attended services regularly. He studied the bible and eagerly looked forward to the once-a-week visits to his school by priests who would discuss God and religion with him and his schoolmates.

The visits inspired Misha who would listen attentively as the clergymen talked about the heroes of the religion, men like Metropolitan Josyp Slipiy who in 1944 became patriarch of the Greek Catholic Church. Slipiy was arrested the following year for standing up for religious freedom. The Communist authorities forced him to endure eighteen years in Soviet prisons, labor camps, and Siberian exile until he was released in 1963, thanks to the intervention of Pope John XXIII.

Until his death in 1984, Slipiy worked tirelessly from his exile in Rome for his countrymen's religious freedom. In 1992 his remains were brought to the Ukrainian city of Lviv, where they were interred in St. George's Cathedral in a stirring ceremony attended by more than one million Ukrainians. He was a national hero, a role model for thousands of his countrymen, especially young boys like Mykhalyo Kofel, who was ten years old at the time.

Misha would say that he felt the call to serve God when

he was just in the sixth grade. "He loved religion," Maria said. "He felt joyful in church."

Maria's heart swelled with pride when villagers told her they thought her son would make an excellent priest. By age thirteen, Misha had set his sights on becoming a monk at a local monastery until Father Yuri Sabov told him about Holy Cross and Father Gregory Wendt.

Sabov had known Mykhaylo since the boy was eight. He regarded Misha as serious and deeply religious, a good candidate for Wendt's monastery in Miami, so he introduced the Kofels to the six-foot-four-inch cleric at a special vocations camp Wendt held to recruit monastic trainees.

Wendt showed Maria and Misha color photos of Holy Cross and of Father Damian. Speaking through an interpreter, he told the Kofels that Misha would be educated at Holy Cross Academy and later at an American university. He would become a monk, perhaps even a priest. It was music to Maria's ears, a dream come true beyond her wildest expectations.

"America is a good country. Why shouldn't we let him go there?" Maria asked her husband.

Besides, they were compensated for allowing their only son to travel to the United States to study. They used the money—five hundred dollars, according to investigators—to buy furniture for their home.

Within a few weeks, Mykhaylo Kofel moved into the monastic center in Konsovo to begin his religious-driven life, even though Wendt had doubts about his academic abilities.

"Judging from his report card in the Ukraine, he was not a good student," Wendt would say. But Kofel was young and devout, and Wendt desperately needed candidates for the Miami monastery. He might have made a different decision had he known more about Misha.

• • •

While religion is the foundation of life in Verkhovina Bystra, it had no significance in Yuri Kofel's life. He did not attend church services, nor did he approve of the importance religion played in the lives of Maria and Mykhalyo. In fact, Maria's religious faith was a source of much tension between her and her husband, who was mostly uninvolved in his son's upbringing. They lived in the same house but didn't interact much. Yuri admits that he did not show love to his son because, he says, he felt it would be inappropriate.

As for Maria, she received no prenatal care while pregnant with Misha. She was sick for much of the time. With no medical services in Verkhovina Bystra, she never saw a doctor until the week before she gave birth to Mykhaylo.

She was unable to rest or take care of herself during the pregnancy. During that period, she maintained a full-time job, working at a radio plant in the village of Novgorod, where she soldered materials together. Her job exposed her and her unborn baby to toxic chemicals and adhesives. She also continued working in the family garden, planting and lifting heavy items in order to have food for the family. Maria was so ill toward the end of her pregnancy she spent the entire last week in a hospital suffering from influenza and high blood pressure. Consequently, Misha's birth was not without complications. Maria was in labor for three days and suffered a ruptured uterus and cervix.

After Misha's birth, Yuri continued to work long hours but was paid sporadically. There was often not enough food for the family to eat. Yuri would drown his sorrows in vodka. "It's hard not to drink here, because every occasion is celebrated," Yuri explained to a visitor through an interpreter. "A guy brings potatoes, you have to party with him, drink vodka. Another guy brings logs, you party with him, too."

Yuri would party on the way home from work, and he'd continue partying until he passed out. His drinking affected his work performance. Many times, he was too hungover to go to work. Hangovers also prevented him from working in the fields, so Mykhaylo and Maria were left to pick up the slack. Once, Yuri came home from his railroad job on payday without his money. He was so drunk he had forgotten that he had given the money to coworkers. When he arrived home, he accused Maria of stealing his money. Mykhaylo watched his father scream, hit, and slap the innocent Maria.

Drinking didn't make Yuri happy. In fact, it made him angry and violent. Mykhaylo witnessed his father's violent rages against his mother. Yuri admits hitting and kicking Maria when he was drunk. He would beat her to a pulp while she lay on the floor sobbing and begging him to stop. Maria was so fearful of Yuri she would run and hide from him when he came home drunk.

Mykhaylo was afraid of Yuri, too. At times Yuri's anger would flare for no apparent reason. Many times Mykhaylo and his mother would be sleeping at night and Yuri would come home so drunk he could not walk. He'd turn on the light and destroy anything in the house he could get his hands on. Yuri's vodka-driven rages would rouse Mykhaylo who cried and ran away from his father.

The unpredictability of his father's violence made Mykhaylo withdrawn and submissive, wracked with fear and anxiety, and left him wondering when his mother was going to be beaten by his father yet again, and when he, in turn, would be beaten by his mother. He worried, too, that Yuri would kill Maria, and he feared that his father would get into a serious accident due to his drinking problem.

While Mykhalyo was going through puberty, Yuri taunted and laughed at his son, making fun of his developing body, telling him that he was effeminate and looked like a girl.

While tiny Maria took the brunt of Yuri's beatings, there were times Yuri beat up Mykhaylo, too. But the majority of physical abuse Mykhaylo suffered was at the hands of his mother. Maria slapped and beat him up until he reached the age of ten. She hit him the most when he was around the ages of five or six. She would whack him on his head or slap his face, or she'd beat him with a belt. Maria, an impulsive and high-strung woman, admits that she hit her son on his head when he was very young as a means of disciplining him.

In 1994, at the age of twelve, Mykhaylo was injured in an explosion and suffered serious head trauma. According to eyewitnesses, Mykhaylo was playing with his cousin and a group of boys when they found a metal cylinder and filled it with gunpowder. While he was handling the cylinder, it exploded. The force of the explosion knocked Mykhaylo to the ground, unconscious. Blood gushed from his head. The other boys ran for help. Ten minutes passed before they returned with Mykhaylo's aunt, Hanna Kahanec. By then Mykhaylo had regained consciousness and was struggling to sit up. Hanna took her nephew home and cleaned his wounds.

Mykhaylo remembers feeling very different in the aftermath of the explosion. He complained of dizziness and a loss of appetite. He was less able to concentrate and he struggled at school. Before the explosion, Mykhaylo received good grades. Afterward, his grades declined. He became even more withdrawn and self-conscious. He had difficulty reading and answering questions in front of other students. He was frightened because he knew his body and mind had changed, but he didn't know why.

Maria noticed the changes, too. Her son seemed more nervous and he became very forgetful. He slept more. Maria was alarmed but did not take Mykhaylo to see a doctor. Instead, she took him to an old woman in the village whom, it was said, had healing powers. The woman prayed over Mykhaylo.

•   •   •

Yuri Kofel's drinking was at its worst just before Mykhaylo left Verkhovina Bystra for the monastic center in Konsovo. Petro was already living there. As monk candidates, the two boys took vows of poverty, chastity, and obedience to Father Abbot Gregory Wendt as Christ's representative in the monastery. A week later Petro and Mykhaylo, accompanied by Wendt and an interpreter, traveled to Kiev where they applied for the F1 student visas that would enable them to live and study in the United States.

Under U.S. law, Wendt was required to sign an affidavit declaring that Holy Cross would be responsible for their room and board and had a minimum of $10,500 in the bank for each of them. Petro and Misha were also required to obtain passports and exit visas from the Ukrainian government.

With their documents in order Wendt, the boys, and an interpreter left Ukraine. They arrived at Newark International Airport on Wednesday July 31, 1996. Wendt continued ahead to Miami, while the others spent the night in a hotel near the airport. They flew to Miami the next day. Wendt was waiting for them at the airport when their plane landed. So was his vicar, Father Damian Gibault.

They arrived in Miami on a typical South Florida summer day—blazing hot, sunlight so bright it hurt their eyes. The air was heavy, with 100 percent humidity and the threat of thunderstorms toward evening. It was the height of hurricane season, and Floridians were watching the Caribbean. A series of tropical storms were wreaking havoc in the islands and any one of them could gather strength and head for the Florida peninsula. South Florida had not yet fully recovered from Hurricane Andrew, the Category Five storm that devastated much of Kendall in 1992, where hundreds of homes were either totally destroyed or sustained major damage.

Meanwhile, the rest of America was paying rapt attention to the hunt for the terrorists who set off a bomb just five days earlier at the 100th Summer Olympics in Atlanta, killing one spectator and injuring more than one hundred others.

But what was on Americans' minds that day most likely went unnoticed by the boys from Ukraine, who spoke no English. Besides, they were too busy acclimating themselves to their new surroundings to pay attention to current events.

To Petro Terenta and Mykahylo Kofel, it must have seemed as if they'd been transported to another universe. All that Florida and Ukraine have in common is that they're on the same planet: Florida is hot, while Ukraine is cold; sleek luxury cars and SUVs are the major mode of transportation in South Florida, while in the mountains of western Ukraine people still travel in donkey carts.

Miami is "a city fueled by flagrant materialism and conspicuous consumption," the alternative weekly *New Times* observed in 2006. In the cities of Ukraine people struggle just to get by.

Then there are the steamy temptations for which Miami is world famous. In the mountains of southwestern Ukraine, women do not wear halter tops or hip-hugger jeans, their cleavage doesn't show, and there are no topless bars. But there is all of that and more in Miami.

When they arrived at Holy Cross, the young monks-to-be were shown to their temporary living quarters in the monastery, a three-bedroom, two-bath single-story residence on the western edge of the campus. The candidates' house was being renovated so Petro and Mykhalyo slept in bunk beds in the same bedroom.

Later that day, the boys met Sister Michelle. She would be their surrogate mother. She welcomed them and took them shopping for sundries and their monastic clothes— black pants, white shirts, black socks, and black shoes. Several days later she took them to a dentist who examined their teeth—Mykhalyo had never before been to a dentist and needed extensive work—and to a medical doctor, who gave each boy a thorough examination.

They both tested positive for tuberculosis, which is rampant throughout the former Soviet Union, but chest X-rays showed that their lungs were clear, which meant they were not suffering from an active infection. Nevertheless, the doctor prescribed Isoniazid, a powerful antibiotic, which they each took for six months.

Wendt kept them, and every monk candidate who arrived after them, on a short leash. He imposed a rigid schedule, which he and Gibault strictly enforced. The boys were required to wake up before 6 A.M. Morning prayers began promptly at 6:30 in the chapel. Afterward, they would eat breakfast before going to school, which didn't end until 3:30.

At 4:30, they were required to report to the chapel for afternoon prayers. Afterward they had to participate in athletics—usually basketball on an outdoor court—from 5:15 to 6, after which they would shower and have dinner. The hour from 7 to 8 P.M. was reserved for recreation. According to Kofel, that meant sitting in the monastery living room with the priests for a minimum of thirty minutes.

"During recreation it was the rule to stay in Wendt's house for a minimum of thirty minutes, and then if you wanted to leave you had to ask him for permission. Then he gave you a blessing and you had to kiss his hand." There was no recreation on Saturdays. Instead, they usually had church from 6 to 8 P.M.

The two hours from 8 to 10 P.M. were devoted to studying. The monk candidates were not permitted to talk to each other after 10 P.M., which was also their bedtime. Any deviation from the schedule, even for the most mundane reason, required permission from Father Gregory. If they wanted to take a shower at an unscheduled time, they needed his permission. If they wanted to go to their room between morning prayers and school, they needed his permission.

They were not allowed to leave Holy Cross without his approval, nor were they permitted to befriend the other students at the academy. Once they learned English they could talk with their classmates about school matters during class, but there would be no socializing with them after school, no phone calls or visits to their homes, and no participation in extracurricular activities.

The monk candidates had vowed obedience to Father Abbot Gregory Wendt. Those were his rules and he decided everything—what they read, what personal items they could keep, even if and when they could write letters home. In fact, when they wrote letters they were required to give them to Father Gregory in unsealed envelopes. The young monks knew that Father Gregory would read them before for putting them into the mail.

Those were the rules of the monastery for Petro and Mykhalyo and for every monk candidate who would come to Holy Cross after them. But Mykhalyo felt betrayed. "Wendt lied to us," he would say years later. "If he would say those things, I wouldn't [have] come to the United States."

Almost immediately he wanted to leave Holy Cross. He even packed his bags, but a letter from his mother changed his mind. "My mom wrote that my teachers and headmaster [sic] from my school say 'Hello,' and my grandfather died. It is because of this letter I changed my mind. I felt really ashamed to go back to my village because so many people said 'Hello' to me and I felt very sad because my grandfather died."

Three weeks after they landed in Miami, the new school year began at Holy Cross. Petro and Mykhalyo, wearing black pants, jackets, shoes and socks, white shirts and black ties, were assigned to the first grade.

Wendt and Gibault, their spiritual shepherds, hoped the

boys would learn English quickly so they could be moved ahead to the fifth grade. It would not be easy. In addition to having to learn to speak English, the boys had to learn a new way of writing—Ukrainian, like Russian, is written in the Cyrillic alphabet.

But by the late afternoon of March 25, 2001, more than five years after they started school at Holy Cross, Petro Terenta and Mykhalyo Kofel were fluent enough in English to communicate with the two MDPD detectives who knocked on the front door of the candidates' house.

7

"People don't shake when they open to door for us. They usually shake when they start talking to us."

—Homicide Detective Art Nanni

Homicide Detective Doug McCoy was at home enjoying a quiet Sunday afternoon when a 1:30 phone call from Bill Gilliland sent him racing to Holy Cross. After he was briefed by Art Nanni, McCoy, a ten-year veteran of the MDPD, and Detective Tom Romagni were assigned to collect oral swabs at the Gilmer Nursery just south of the convent. They interviewed employees and collected swabs from each of them.

With that done, the two detectives reported back to Nanni, who assigned them to the candidates' house to collect oral swabs from the five young monks-to-be and the two priests.

At 6:30 P.M., the lawmen were at the front door of the two-story candidates' house. Romagni knocked. "Just prior to the door opening, this detective observed what appeared to be blood on the door handle and lock," McCoy would write in his official report.

He was pointing to the blood when the door swung open. Standing before the lawmen was a short, scrawny young man with brown hair and a scraggly beard. He was dressed in black and his hands were shaking.

He identified himself as Brother Mykhalyo. Almost immediately the detectives noticed what looked like a fresh scratch on the young monk's left cheek. Looking closer, they noticed cuts, scratches, and Band-Aids on both of his hands.

"We're here to interview you and the others," Romagni told the young cleric as the two lawmen entered the house. But Romagni didn't stay. Instead, he left McCoy in the living room while he hurried across the campus to report to Art Nanni.

As he stood in the room, McCoy kept his eyes fixed on Kofel. He noticed that the young monk had put his hands inside his pant pockets. When he removed them, the Band-Aids, which had been stuck on each hand, were gone.

It was Kofel who broke the silence.

"How long have you been a police officer?" he wanted to know.

"About ten years."

"How do you like it?"

"I like it very much."

Just then Petro Terenta entered the room. He spoke briefly with Kofel in Ukrainian. Then he circled behind the detective and signaled Kofel to stop talking to the lawman by putting his right index finger to his lips.

Petro would explain later that he wasn't trying to silence his fellow monk to keep him from revealing anything incriminating. Instead, he was merely being considerate of the detective.

"I saw the detective was hesitant," Petro said. "You know, like if the other person is interested in talking to you, then if one person starts questioning, then you keep going, but the officer was just answering the questions shortly and he wasn't, you know, much into it so I just said leave him alone."

Meanwhile back at the murder scene, Detective Romagni was speaking to Art Nanni, telling him about the blood on the door to the candidates' house, the cuts on the young monk's hands, the scratch on his face, and that his hands had been shaking when he opened the door.

"I want to talk to him right now!" Nanni exclaimed, his basso voice a mix of excitement and determination.

To the detective it was looking more and more as if his team of investigators were closing in on Sister Michelle's killer.

"People don't shake when they open to door for us," Nanni explained. "They usually shake when they start talking to us."

Ten minutes later Art Nanni and Mykhaylo Kofel were standing face to face inside the candidates' house.

"I asked him if I could speak with him in regard to the death of Sister Michelle Lewis," Nanni remembered. Kofel agreed and the detective and the monk stepped outside to talk. He appeared nervous. The detective couldn't help but notice that Kofel's hand shook when he reached out to shake Nanni's hand.

Nanni began talking. First, he asked the young monk to spell his name. Then he asked Kofel where he was from.

"From western Ukraine, the village of Verkhovina Bystra, House number 166,"

"What are you doing here at Holy Cross?"

"I am training to be a monk."

Kofel went on to tell the detective that he had graduated from Holy Cross Academy the year before and was attending Barry University in Miami Shores, where he was enrolled in nursing courses.

Miami is a melting pot, and its police officers are trained to deal with people whose native languages are not English. To Nanni, Kofel seemed to have sufficient command of the English language, but the lawman wanted to make sure.

"Do you understand the way I am talking to you?" he asked.

"Yes, I can understand you. I can read and write English, but sometimes I have hard time understanding big words."

"What kind of words?"

"Adjectives."

After satisfying himself that Kofel understood English, the detective asked the monk to explain the cuts on his hands. In his official report, Nanni wrote: "While talking with Mr. Kofel and verifying that he had no difficulties understanding the way that this investigator was talking to him, this investigator also observed the scratches on his face and cuts on his hands. Mr. Kofel was then asked how he sustained the cuts on his hands, at which time he advised that on Friday night at around 10:00 P.M. while washing a glass at the monks' residence, the glass slipped out of his hands and during the attempt to catch it before it broke, he reached out and grabbed it and it broke in his hands."

But the veteran lawman wasn't buying the monk's story. It didn't pass his "smell" test. The deep cuts looked much too fresh to have been sustained nearly forty-eight hours earlier, and they were still oozing blood.

"I have a hard time believing what you are telling me," he told the monk.

Kofel just shrugged. They had been talking for about fifteen minutes.

"At that point I decided I wanted him on my turf," Nanni remembered, so he invited the monk to accompany him to the homicide bureau, where they could continue their conversation. To the detective's surprise, Kofel agreed to go.

It is a ten-mile drive from the Holy Cross campus to the MDPD's headquarters at 9105 NW 25th Street. Before starting the engine of his unmarked Ford Taurus, the law-man turned to Kofel, who was sitting beside him in the front passenger's seat. He wanted to make sure that the young monk understood that he was not in custody, he was not a prisoner, and he was free to get out of the car. In his report, Nanni wrote:

"At 7:05 P.M. Mr. Kofel sat in the front seat of an un-marked police vehicle. Mr. Kofel was then explained that he did not have to respond to the Homicide Bureau Office, that this was strictly voluntarily on his part, that this was his decision to make in regards to talking about Sister Michelle's investigation, and that he could say no, if he didn't want to go, and we would continue to talk inside the police vehicle. He was asked again if he understood every-thing that I had just explained to him, and he advised yes. He was told one more time that he didn't have to go with me, that if he was going, it was because he wanted to keep talking to this investigator. He advised yes, he had no prob-lems with going to the office.

"At approximately 7:15 P.M., this investigator and Mr. Kofel departed the parking lot of Holy Cross and re-sponded to the Homicide Bureau Office at the Miami-Dade Police Department."

As they drove away, Nanni noticed that TV news crews had taken up positions along SW 72nd Street, which is also known as Sunset Drive, and SW 123rd Avenue. Drawn by the police activity, dozens of curious passersby had gath-ered, too. Among them were Holy Cross Academy stu-dents and their parents who stood in knots wondering what had happened.

Rumors swirled—a body had been found on the cam-pus. It was a priest. It was one of the monks. It was a fe-male, a nun.

Reporters who tried to contact school authorities by telephone had no luck, as no one was picking up. Investigators remained tight-lipped until later in the evening when a police spokesperson briefed reporters, confirming that detectives were investigating a homicide, that the victim was a woman in her thirties or early forties. She was found, the spokesperson revealed, lying naked and stabbed to death inside her residence on the grounds of Holy Cross.

"We have no idea if the woman is a nun or someone else employed by the school," reporters were told. Police refused to reveal the number of times she had been stabbed or whether there had been signs of forced entry. Miami's television stations reported the sketchy details of the slaying during their late newscasts.

That was how Miami-Dade Assistant State Attorney Gail Levine learned about the brutal slaying. She joined the state attorney's office in June 1985, one year after graduating from law school. When she was hired, Janet Reno was the state attorney for Florida. She had been appointed by then governor Reubin Askew in 1978 when Richard Gerstein, her predecessor, resigned before completing his term. Voters would return Reno, the six-foot-two-inch Miami native, to office four more times.

The last half of the twentieth century was arguably the most turbulent time in the county's history. Its population exploded, increasing from 935,000 in 1960 to 1.9 million in 1990. By then it had become the cocaine import center of America.

In 1980 the county was forced to absorb thousands of refugees during the massive Mariel boatlift, when Cuban dictator Fidel Castro announced that anyone who wanted to leave Cuba could do so. Among the new refugees were criminals who were freed from the island nation's prisons and mentally ill men and women who were released from its mental hospitals. As a result Miami-Dade's criminal justice system was overwhelmed and nearly paralyzed.

Reno left Miami in 1993 when President Bill Clinton chose her to be the first woman attorney general of the United States. Then governor Lawton Chiles named Katherine Fernandez Rundle, Reno's protégé and top deputy, to succeed her. She has held the office ever since. By 2001, the Miami-Dade state attorney's office employed more than 1,100 paralegals, investigators, support staff, and assistant state attorneys, more than half of whom were women.

With a long history of women in the top job, there is no glass ceiling in the Miami-Dade state attorney's office. Like every new prosecutor, Levine began her career working on misdemeanors, but her talent and ambition propelled her into more serious cases.

"She's an alpha female," a courthouse observer said of the blonde prosecutor.

Over the years the New Jersey–born Levine proved again and again that she's a tough litigator with the guts to confront evil and the confidence to send cold-blooded killers to the death house. She had been a prosecutor for sixteen years, during which time her courtroom efforts were responsible for sending five murderers to death row.

Three thugs—Ricardo Gonzalez, Leonardo Franqui, and Pablo San Martin—were convicted of shooting to death North Miami police detective Steven Bauer during a bank robbery in 1992, while two others—steroid-addicted bodybuilders Daniel Lugo and Noel Adrian Doorbal—were convicted in the 1995 torture and dismemberment deaths of a Hungarian couple, thirty-three-year-old millionaire phone-sex entrepreneur Frank Griga and his twenty-three-year-old girlfriend, Krisztina Furton.

Lugo and Doorbal were part of a ruthless gang of bodybuilders who extorted money from rich South Floridians. When Griga and Furton resisted, they were tortured and murdered. Their body parts were found in fifty-five-gallon drums and buckets left along highways in Miami-Dade and Broward counties.

In that ghastly case, Levine stood before the jury during her opening argument to let them know what the case was all about: "Heads cut off. Hands and feet chopped away. A planned series of awful crimes." In her closing argument, Levine pointed to Lugo and Doorbal and asked rhetorically, "How could something like this happen in our society? . . . How could there be evil people like these men?"

It was a high-profile case, one that made headlines and television newscasts from start to finish. Levine's gut told her that the Holy Cross murder would be a high-profile headliner, too. She wanted it, and the next morning she got it. She would be the lead prosecutor, the "first chair," in prosecutorial lingo. Priscilla Prado and Penny Brill, an appellate attorney with an expertise in death penalty issues, were asssigned to assist her.

As Nanni steered the unmarked Ford Taurus north along the Florida Turnpike toward the MDPD headquarters complex in Doral, Kofel remarked that he was very familiar with the route—it's the same one he, Petro, and Father Wendt would take to the single-family residence Holy Cross owned near Barry University.

The house, which the clerics referred to as "the Barry house," had been purchased in December. The two monk candidates and Wendt lived there during the week while attending classes at the Miami Shores university, twenty-four miles from the Holy Cross campus.

By nature Art Nanni is friendly and affable, so it was easy for him to make small talk with the young monk, asking him about the breakup of the Soviet Union and life in Ukraine under communist rule.

Nanni was born in Erie, Pennsylvania, but he had been living in Miami since he was ten years old. He remembers the tensions of the Cold War, when the United States and the Soviet Union squared off against each in a nuclear arms race that could have killed hundreds of millions.

He was just twelve years old during the Cuban Missile Crisis of October 1962, when Soviet missiles armed with nuclear warheads and based in Cuba had Miami, home to tens of thousands of refugees from Castro's Cuba, in the crosshairs.

Kofel told the detective that life was hard in his homeland, adding that he was an only child who lived with his mother and father in an impoverished mountain village until coming to Miami. He mentioned that he spoke Russian as well as Ukrainian and English.

Twenty minutes after driving away from the Holy Cross campus, Nanni pulled into the parking lot at the police department's headquarters complex. Kofel was not in custody. There was no evidence linking him to Sister Michelle's murder, at least not yet, so he was not under arrest. Officially he was not even a suspect, merely a person of interest.

While Nanni wasn't buying Kofel's broken-glass story, it was possible that there was another logical explanation for the cuts and the scratches on his face that had nothing to do with the murder of Sister Michelle. If Kofel had asked, the detective would have made a U-turn and driven him back to Holy Cross.

But the monk never asked. Instead, he accompanied the lawman to the homicide bureau's offices on the second floor of the sprawling three-story building. Nanni ushered Kofel into a tiny windowless interview room, which held a small rectangular table and three chairs. The detective offered him a cold drink, asked if he needed to use the restroom, then left him alone while he went to get a Miranda Rights form.

The Miranda warning, a staple of every TV police drama since the late 1960s, was named for Ernesto Miranda, an Arizona man who confessed to kidnapping and raping an eighteen-year-old woman after intense questioning by detectives. The warning has been a requirement of police procedure since 1966, when a landmark U.S. Supreme Court decision overturned Miranda's conviction because he had not been advised of his rights under the U.S. Constitution.

Less than ten minutes later, the lawman was back. He sat down opposite the young monk and began speaking. It was an interview, not an interrogation, so the detective's tone was firm but friendly.

"I told him that I believed there was more to the cuts on his hands than what he was telling me," Nanni recalled. Then he showed Kofel the Miranda form, explaining that he had the right to remain silent, that anything he said could be used against him in a court of law, and that he had the right to have an attorney present during questioning.

"Do you know what an attorney is?" the detective inquired.

"It's someone who goes to court and speaks for someone else," the monk answered, adding, "I don't need an attorney."

Satisfied once again that the Ukrainian teen understood, the detective asked Kofel to read out loud the first line of the Miranda form.

" 'Before you are asked any questions, you must understand the following rights,' " the monk repeated.

Then Nanni proceeded to review the rights one by one.

" 'One: You have the right to remain silent and you do not have to talk to me if you do not wish to do so. You do not have to answer any of my questions. Do you understand that right?' "

"Yes."

" 'Two: Should you talk to me, anything which you might say may be introduced into evidence in court against you. Do you understand that?' "

"Yes."

" 'Three: If you want a lawyer to be present during questioning, at this time or any time hereafter, you are entitled to have the lawyer present. Do you understand that right?' "

"Yes."

" 'Four: If you cannot afford to pay for a lawyer, one will be provided for you at no cost if you want one. Do you understand that right?' "

"Yes."

" 'Knowing these rights, are you now willing to answer my questions without having a lawyer present?' "

Once again the young monk answered, "Yes."

As he finished each question, Nanni passed the form across the table for Kofel to initial. He wrote "MK" next to each document that his rights had been read to him, he understood them, and was waiving them. Then he passed the form back to the detective.

Nanni read the final paragraph out loud while the monk read along with him.

" 'This statement is signed of my own free will without any threats or promises having been made to me.' " Kofel signed his name at the bottom of the form. Nanni wrote in the time: 8:01 P.M. Then he left the interview room to make a phone call.

Squad C Detective Larry Belyeu wasn't scheduled to report to work until midnight. He was still at home enjoying his Sunday when his phone rang. It was Art Nanni calling. He informed Belyeu that the squad was investigating the murder of Sister Michelle Lewis at Holy Cross, and that Mykhalyo Kofel, a monk in training, had voluntarily accompanied him to the homicide office. Nanni wanted Belyeu to assist him with the interview. Could he come in earlier? He said he could.

While he waited for Belyeu to arrive, Nanni resumed

interviewing the monk. He began by telling Kofel that he needed to tell the truth about how he had sustained the cuts on his hands and the scratches on his face.

"In my opinion, you didn't get those cuts from a broken glass," the detective told Kofel.

Nanni then explained to the monk that the evidence collected at the crime scene would reveal the truth, and that at that very moment analysts in the MDPD's laboratories were busy going over the bloodstains and fingerprints found inside Sister Michelle's bedroom.

"I believe that it's your blood and your prints that we will find," Nanni said, leaning forward and looking directly into the young monk's eyes.

"I was not at the convent. I had nothing to do with Sister's death," Kofel replied, maintaining eye contact with the detective. He said he hadn't even seen Sister Michelle since the church service the previous Sunday.

Lawmen are trained to spot liars. They reveal themselves in their body language and eye contact. If a suspect looks up, he's trying to remember. If his eyes go to the side or down, chances are very good he is lying. But if he looks you directly in the eye, he could be telling the truth. Still, Nanni didn't believe Kofel, and he told him so.

"That cut on your right hand is still oozing blood. It looks to me like you did that in the last several hours rather than the last forty-eight," the detective countered.

But Kofel stuck to his story, declaring over and over again that he had nothing to do with the murder, he had not been in the convent, and his fingerprints would not be found there—all the while maintaining eye contact with the detective.

"He was believable because of his eye contact," Nanni remembered. "He wasn't going into a defensive posture," but because of the cuts on his hands the detective's instincts told him otherwise. "I mean, the wounds were still oozing blood."

The detective decided to challenge him. "Then let us fingerprint you," he dared.

To the lawman's surprise, the monk agreed, telling the detective that he was willing to submit to fingerprinting because he had nothing to hide, that his prints would not be found inside the convent.

Once again the detective asked Kofel to sign a consent form, this time a Consent to Fingerprint form, telling him that if he agreed he would be taken to the MDPD's I.D. lab, where he would be fingerprinted and photographed. After reading the form out loud Nanni passed it over along with a pen. This time Kofel hesitated.

"I'm not really sure right now," the monk explained.

"Earlier you told me your fingerprints were not inside the house," Nanni reminded Kofel. "Why are you hesitating now? If you tell me you had nothing to do with it and your fingerprints aren't in the house, then you shouldn't have any problems giving consent to having your fingerprints taken."

Then the lawman told Kofel again that he wasn't under arrest and that if at any time he wanted to stop the interview, Nanni would drive him back to Holy Cross.

As soon as Nanni mentioned going back to Holy Cross, Kofel picked up the pen and signed the form. Nanni noted the time. It was 9:38 P.M.

Art Nanni had been working nonstop since 7 A.M. He had not eaten all day and he was tired. But he had no thoughts of letting up or taking a break, at least not yet.

"The adrenaline kicked in," he remembered. He walked Kofel to the I.D. section of the MDPD's lab where technician Gil Tomaz recorded the young monk's fingerprints. When that was done, Nanni asked Kofel to remove his socks so that the bottoms of his feet could be inked and foot impressions taken of them.

Again Kofel complied. While the young monk wiped

the ink off his feet and fingers, Nanni studied the foot impressions.

"You know, they appear to match the footprints we found at Holy Cross," he told Kofel. "You have a high arch and a very unique foot impression, just like the ones at Holy Cross."

The monk said nothing. Minutes later, he was standing in front of a camera at the crime scene investigations bureau. Color closeups were taken of his face, hands, torso, and legs. Crime scene detective Victor Mazzarella documented seven cuts and scratches on Kofel's body including two small scratches on the left side of his face, one scratch and a bruise on his left shoulder, two scratches and a cut on his left forearm, and a cut on his right palm.

Thirty minutes later Kofel was back at the homicide bureau sitting inside the interview room. Nanni was beyond hungry. "I'm starved," the lawman said. "Do you want anything to eat? I'm thinking of ordering in a pizza from Domino's."

Kofel replied that yes, he would appreciate a couple of slices and a soda.

Two pizzas—one cheese and one pepperoni—arrived at 11:20. By this time Larry Belyeu had joined them in the interview room.

As the lawmen and the monk-trainee chowed down, Art Nanni reminded Kofel that he believed the evidence from both crime scenes would lead to his arrest and that the time had finally come for Kofel to tell his side of the story.

"There are only two people who can tell us what happened in the convent, and one of them is dead," the detective told the young monk. "Based on my experience, what you've told me so far doesn't make any sense."

Kofel sat silently. He took a sip of soda, then heaved a deep sigh. As he leaned back in his chair, his shoulders slumped. "Okay," he said. "I will tell you what happened, but I want to start my story from Ukraine."

"If that's where you need to start, we'll start in Ukraine," Art Nanni said. Again, he noted the time. It was 11:45.

Speaking calmly in a deep monotone, Mykhaylo Kofel began talking. He would talk for more than an hour, and before he finished he would level allegations that would, when made public, shock Miami. They would shake the Catholic Church and the faithful who entrusted their children to the clerics at Holy Cross Academy. And they would send investigators halfway around the world in search of justice.

8

"She mind-fucked me."

—Mykhalyo Kofel

Even before he left the Holy Cross campus with Detective Nanni, the thought occurred to some of the clerics there that Mykhaylo Kofel had something to do with the murder of Sister Michelle Lewis.

It occurred to Petro Terenta. After speaking with Art Nanni in front of the convent, Brother Petro joined the monk candidates. They discussed the slaying.

"We had a conversation about what was going on," Petro remembered. "We were trying to figure what had happened and who could have done it."

It wasn't long before they were all thinking the un-thinkable—that Mykhaylo Kofel had killed Sister Michelle.

Petro had good reason to suspect Kofel. At 10:30 A.M., as they prepared for church that morning, he noticed cuts on Kofel's hands.

"Misha, how did you get these wounds?" Petro asked.

"I cut my hand washing a drinking glass on Friday," was the reply.

Petro was skeptical. He recalled that the same thing had happened three years before to Ivan Kalynych, another monk candidate from Ukraine. Kalynych, who left Holy Cross in 1999 after deciding that he no longer wanted to be a monk, had to have stitches to close the wound.

Petro thought it odd that the same accident had happened again. And he was puzzled; he hadn't recalled seeing any cuts on Kofel's hands or scratches on his face on Saturday. By Sunday afternoon his puzzlement had turned to suspicion.

Petro was not the only one at Holy Cross who suspected Kofel. The other monk candidates were wondering about him, too. Kofel had been with them through most of Saturday when they left Holy Cross with Father Damian at 10 A.M. for the Miami-Dade County Fair and Exposition, an annual event also known as the Youth Fair because some of the proceeds are donated to local youth charities. It has been a Miami tradition since 1952. The main events back then were greased pig–chasing contests and cow-chip tosses. People came to show off their prize heifers and home-grown tomatoes, and to ride the Ferris wheel and merry-go-round.

By 2001, the Youth Fair had grown into a huge eighteen-day event that would draw one million visitors who came to enjoy its one-hundred ride midway, its Las Vegas–style ice show, and its concerts featuring big-name acts, not to mention its exotic treats like fried Oreo cookies, pork chops on a stick, and peach dumplings.

The four monks-to-be and Father Damian drove there in the monastery's Ford Crown Victoria. They sat shoulder-to-shoulder during the short ride, and they stayed together during the entire time they were at the fair. The boys rode the roller coaster and half a dozen other rides before heading back to Holy Cross sometime after 2 P.M. Back at the campus they played basketball from 3:45 until 4:45.

No one recalled Kofel having a problem dribbling or

shooting the basketball, and no one noticed any cuts on his hands or scratches on his face. They would not be noticed until the next morning, long before Brother Petro would find Sister Michelle's body.

Sasha Korsak was the last of the monk trainees to see Kofel on Saturday night. The nineteen-year-old Ukrainian grew up in the village of Hanychy. He arrived in Miami in December 1999. He shared a bedroom in the candidates' house with Vasyl Kopych and Yosyp Lembak, while Mykhalyo and Petro had their own rooms in the four-bedroom residence until renovations to their quarters in the candidates' house could be completed.

Sasha recalled seeing Kofel just before bedtime at 10 P.M. There were no cuts on his hands and no scratches on his face. He would not see Kofel again until Sunday morning at 9:30. At that time, he noticed Band-Aids on Kofel's hands and scratches on his face.

While Sasha was the last to see Kofel on Saturday, Vasyl Kopych was the first of the monk trainees to see Kofel on Sunday morning. Vasyl had been living at Holy Cross since the fall of 1997.

He came from a deeply religious family—his oldest brother is a priest—in the village of Bilyn, Ukraine. At age fourteen, Vasyl made the decision to devote his life to God. He lived at the monastic center in Konsovo for six months before Wendt brought him to Miami.

Konsovo, Vasyl said, was "like a little monastery where you live with other candidates like yourself, and there is a person who looks over you, who makes sure that you have food, that you go to school, that you study, that you follow the schedule, that you pray when you suppose [sic] to pray, that you got to play sports when you suppose [sic] to play."

While there, Vasyl worked in the garden planting and

harvesting potatoes, and he worked in the monastery washing floors. When he arrived in Miami, his education at Holy Cross began in the first grade.

Vasyl remembered that he was the first monk candidate out of bed the morning Sister Michelle died. He dressed and went downstairs to study at his desk before the church service. Fifteen minutes later, Kofel came downstairs, too.

"Have you seen Father Damian?" Kofel asked in English. "I want to talk to him." Vasyl replied that he had not seen the priest since the day before.

Kofel then showed Vasyl that he was wearing a Band-Aid on the palm of his right hand. As Vasyl looked, the door to Father Damian's first-floor bedroom opened. Kofel turned toward the priest and walked to him.

"I heard them talking," Vasyl remembered. "They were talking about the hand, the cut hand. I heard Misha say that he cut his hand Friday with a glass, a drinking glass."

What Kofel was saying made no sense to Vasyl. "I thought something is wrong, that since we went to the Youth Fair and we played basketball after that, it's a little hard to play basketball with a cut hand," he explained.

Later in the afternoon while police combed the campus, Wendt got wind of the candidates' suspicions. He wanted to see the cuts for himself, so he summoned Kofel. Petro remembers looking on as the abbot carefully examined Misha's right hand.

"Father Abbot was saying that the cut looks very fresh," Petro recalled, but Kofel kept insisting otherwise, adamant that he had sustained the cut on Friday while washing a glass.

The abbot changed his mind. Said Petro, "He was saying, 'Yeah, yeah, that looks like an old cut . . . it could have been done yesterday.'"

With Wendt's pronouncement, all discussion about Kofel's culpability in the death of Sister Michelle ended. The monks-to-be said nothing about their suspicions when detectives came to talk with them at the candidates' house. Neither did the priests.

For one thing, they couldn't believe that one of their own, especially one as pious and devoted to God as Brother Mykhalyo, could have committed such a ghastly crime. For another, Father Abbot Gregory Wendt, to whom they had pledged obedience, had accepted Kofel's explanation.

However, what Wendt thought did not matter to the investigators. Before Sunday faded into Monday, lawmen would know who murdered Sister Michelle.

Mykhalyo Kofel was still eating pizza when be began his confession right where he said he would, in Ukraine. His tone was matter-of-fact, icy. He showed no remorse, never even shed a tear.

Between bites of pizza and sips of soda, Kofel told the lawmen that while growing up he had been physically and sexually abused by his alcoholic father. He explained that he slept in his own bed in his parents' bedroom, or on a couch in the living room. On several occasions he awakened to his drunken father's hands "playing with my sexual organs."

He said he never confronted his father because he was falling-down drunk whenever it happened, and Yuri wouldn't remember what he'd done. He never said anything to his mother because it would not have done any good either—Maria was no match for Yuri.

"When I came from Ukraine, I thought it would be better that I escape from the abusing father, but on the other hand, Father Abbot, Father Damian, they were also sexually abusing me," Kofel alleged. "Mostly Father Damian. It's like twice a month, he would be sexually abusing me, playing with my sexual organs. And Father Abbot, he also abused me sexually. He abused me three times while I had clothes on."

"And that was over the course of the past four years?" Nanni asked. "For the four years that you've been at Holy Cross, Father Abbot has only abused you three times with your clothes on?"

"Yes."

"Did Father Damian say anything to you on the reasons?"

"On the reasons that he sexually abused me? Was [because] I come from a poor family, so he knew if I would say no, he would say 'Go back to Ukraine.' But he knew that I wouldn't want to go back, because I come from a poor family, first, and, secondly, an abusing father."

"But Father Abbot is the only one that can send you back for not following the rules of the monastery, not Father Damian?" Nanni wondered.

"That's correct. But they are together." As he answered, Kofel put the first two fingers of his right hand together to indicate just how close the priests are.

But Nanni wasn't investigating a sexual abuse case.

"He wasn't going into great detail, so I did not pursue each and every sexual abuse allegation he was making at that time," the lawman explained. Those allegations would be referred to the MDPD's sexual crimes bureau. Homicide detective Art Nanni was investigating a murder. He wanted to know what happened to Sister Michelle.

"Did she ever sexually or physically abuse you?" he asked.

"No."

"What did she do to you while going to school?"

"She was abusing me verbally, calling me names like 'Ukrainian trash' or 'freak' or 'good-for-nothing.' She mind-fucked me."

The lawman was stunned.

"Up until that time Kofel didn't curse, and I didn't curse," Nanni remembered. "And I kind of looked at him as somewhat holy because he's a monk."

Without skipping a beat, Kofel continued. He was never a student in a class taught by Sister Michelle and she never threatened or physically harmed him in any way, but she was verbally abusive to him and to the other monk candidates.

"She didn't like the idea that we were there, the Ukrainians," Kofel told the lawmen.

"Okay," Nanni interrupted, "Saturday night, March twenty-fourth—but before I get to Saturday night, let's talk about Saturday evening. Did you ask Father Damian for the master key?"

"I asked him for the whole bunch of keys, which he had because we were grocery shopping for Mrs. Wendt."

"That's Father Abbot's mother?"

"Yes."

"Okay. So he gave you his keys. After you put the groceries away, what did you do to the keys?"

"I took one key out and I gave him the rest."

"And what was the purpose of taking the one key?"

"Well, the purpose was in the assembly room, there were like pictures, so I could unlock and go and just look at them."

Kofel was talking about the graduation photos of his Holy Cross classmates, which were hanging inside the entrance to the modular building.

Under cover of darkness—there was no moon over Miami that night—Kofel slipped out of the candidates' house sometime before midnight. He was in stealth mode, dressed in black from head to toe. There were no shoes on his feet, just a pair of black nylon socks.

Using the master key from Father Damian's key ring, he unlocked the door to the modular building. He tried to use the key again to get into Sister Michelle's office, but it did not unlock the door. Kofel next made his way to the Holy Cross chapel, where he took a bottle of wine from behind the altar and began drinking from it.

"Where did you drink, outside the church? Inside the church?" the detective asked.

"Outside."

"While drinking this wine, what did you have in your possession at this time?"

"I was remembering all these bad events that happened to me. I was really depressed and so then to my mind came . . ."

The detective leaned forward. "What came?"

"I wanted to hurt Sister Michelle."

"Did you have any sort of weapons in your possession at this time?"

Kofel told detectives that he had a steak knife and a foot-long cast-iron poker, which he had removed from the faux fireplace in the candidates' house. He didn't tell the lawmen that he also had a pair of latex gloves, a flashlight, and a roll of duct tape.

"Where did the steak knife come from?" Nanni wanted to know.

"I brought it from Barry University. We have a house there."

"Now, this is the house that you stay at Monday through Thursday?"

"Monday through Friday."

"While you attend Barry?"

"Yes."

"The knife, do you remember about how long the blade was on the knife?"

"I would say approximately five inches."

"Why didn't you wear shoes that night? Why did you just go around in your socks?" Nanni wanted to know.

"I wanted to make it quieter."

There was a brief pause while the detectives tidied up the interview room and got rid of the empty pizza boxes and the soda cans. Then Nanni resumed the questioning.

"You said earlier that you went over there to do what to Sister Michelle?"

"My intention was just to hurt her."

"What happened?"

"It got out of hand."

Kofel recounted how he made his way across the campus toward the convent, drinking from the bottle and stumbling as its effects kicked in. As he approached the convent, he hurled the now-empty bottle over the seven-foot-high wooden fence that separated the convent from the street.

Using the key he had taken from Damian's key ring, Kofel unlocked a back door that led into a bathroom. He was familiar with the layout of the house, having been inside just before Christmas when he helped decorate the convent for the holidays.

"Once you were inside, what did you do next?" Nanni asked.

"Well, her room was unlocked so I went inside."

Through the darkness he was able to see that Michelle was in her bed sleeping.

"Once you saw where she was at, what took place next?"

"Well, she woke up because I made a noise with the iron stick. When she woke up she screamed and yelled."

"What did she scream?"

" 'Help.' "

"Loud?"

"Loud, yes."

It was Michelle's worst nightmare, the very thing she feared most—an intruder was in her bedroom.

"Did it scare you, the way she screamed?" Nanni asked.

"Yes."

"Did she get out of bed?"

"Yes. She jumped on her feet and she hit me first. She scratched my face, the left side."

So Kofel swung the poker. The blow caught the sister on the side of her head. He hoped it would knock her out, but it didn't. She fought back. Despite the blow, she even managed to wrestle him to the floor.

"She got the metal thing and was hitting me," Kofel would recall later. "I didn't feel anything. I was unstoppable. Crazy angry. After that I don't really remember anything—[I was] kind of not there, a dream." Although there were deep cuts on his hands, he felt no pain, "like I was drunk, high, like a dream."

Kofel recalled wielding the poker at least five more times.

"What was she wearing?" Nanni asked.

"She was wearing only a top."

"Was it a short top?"

"Yes."

"Was the bottom of her [body] exposed?"

"Yes."

"Did you ask her to take off her clothes?"

"No."

"Did you tear any of her clothes off?"

"No."

"Why were her clothes torn off?"

"Her clothes were torn off?" Kofel seemed surprised.

"Yes," Nanni responded. "Do you remember, did she voluntarily take her clothes off for you?"

Kofel seemed surprised again. "Her clothes were torn off? Maybe because of the knife. From the knife, but I never took off the clothes from her. Maybe from the knife when I cut her."

"How many times did you use the knife to hurt her?"

"Less than ten."

"Did you hate Sister Michelle?"

"Well, she was a pain in the ass for me. Only because she didn't like me. She verbally abused me and she didn't like me."

"Did you have any sexual contact with her?"

"No."

"No intercourse?"

"No."

"No anal sex?"

"No."

"No oral sex?"

"No."

"How many times did she scream [for] help?"

"About five times."

"Every time she screamed, did you stab her with the knife?"

"Yeah. I tried to make her quiet, yes."

"And by trying to make her quiet you used the knife?"

"I put my knife on her mouth, but she was still like . . ."

"Were you on top of her now?"

"I think so."

"Was she on the ground?"

"Yes."

"Did you fondle her breasts?"

"Yes, during the fight."

"All the cuts on your hands, arms, face, bruises on your back, biceps, was all that caused from the confrontation that you had with Sister Michelle?"

"Yes."

"Now, during this confrontation, how did you end up cutting your hands or getting the cuts, marks, and bruises?"

"Well, the cuts is [sic] from the knife, like it slipped and I cut myself. And with her nails she scratched me."

"Is it a possibility that you may have stabbed her more than ten times?"

"It's possible."

Covered with blood—the slain sister's and his own—Kofel said he exited the convent through the same door he'd used to enter it. Before leaving he locked Sister Michelle's bedroom door.

At some point, though he didn't recall when, he realized that he'd lost Damian's master key, so he returned to the modular building.

"Sister Michelle's office, did you break into that?"

"Yes."

"And for what purpose?"

"Because I lost my key, so I wanted to replace the key."

"When you say you lost your key, you're talking about the key from Father Damian?"

"Yes."

"And in order for Father Damian not to discover that his key was missing, you went to find another key?"

"Yes."

"How did you break into her office?"

"I took a fire extinguisher and broke through the glass and opened the door."

"In order to open her door, what did you do?"

"Put my arm like through the broken glass and opened it, unlocked it."

"The inside doorknob?"

"Did you ever find her keys in the office?"

"There were keys," Kofel said, "but not the one that I needed."

"The key you had from Father Damian, you told me that it opened up the doors to the modular building?"

"Where the office is, Sister Michelle's office," Kofel said.

"Why didn't you use it to open Sister Michelle's office?"

"It didn't open it. I tried, but it didn't open it."

Afterward, Kofel returned to the candidates' house and went directly to his room. He thought it was about 5 A.M. Kofel recalled undressing and tossing his clothes into the washing machine. He showered and went to bed, but he couldn't sleep. His hands were hurting from the cuts he sustained during the attack on Sister Michelle.

•   •   •

It was now a little before 1:00 A.M. Nanni was tired. He
had been working nonstop for nearly eighteen hours without a break, but if he was hoping for a brief respite until a
stenographer could arrive to formally record and transcribe
the young monk's statement, he would be disappointed—
Father Abbot Gregory Wendt was in the first-floor reception area. The priest had not come alone: Petro Terenta and
a lawyer named James McGuirk were with him. Wendt demanded to speak to Art Nanni. He demanded Kofel's release. He demanded to know what was going on.

9

"The purpose of this corporation shall be to operate an independent, self-governing preparatory school in the educational tradition of the Catholic faith, which school shall not be under the jurisdiction or control of the hierarchy of any church."

—Amended Articles of Incorporation of Holy Cross Academy

In the early morning hours of Monday, March 26, Father Abbot Gregory Wendt found himself sitting on a chair in the first-floor lobby at Miami-Dade police headquarters waiting for attorney James McGuirk. The holy man had become furious hours earlier when Petro told him that Kofel had left the campus with one of the MDPD detectives.

"They were supposed to let me know," the cleric fumed. "They can't take any of us from the grounds without my knowing."

Wendt put in a call to the homicide bureau, raising hell with the watch commander because Nanni had dared to drive away from the campus with Kofel without clearing it with him first. He demanded Kofel's release.

Father Abbot Gregory Wendt was not a well man. The fifty-six-year-old cleric was battling diabetes and high blood pressure, and he had difficulty walking—a serious ankle injury several years earlier had necessitated surgery. Lately he had been hobbled by knee trouble. In addition to his medical woes, there was a skeleton in the Holy Cross closet that could jeopardize the very existence of the monastic community and the school if parents found out.

Wendt was embroiled in a long and bitter controversy with Bishop Andrew Pataki of the Eparchy of Passaic, the successor to Bishop Michael Dudick. The feud had gone beyond the eparchy. It reached across the Atlantic Ocean, all the way to the Vatican in Rome. Bishop Andrew had expressed grave doubts about the legitimacy of Holy Cross, both the monastery and the academy. He considered them rogue operations headed by a pair of holy men whose religious qualifications he found questionable at best. What's more, he doubted the validity of Wendt's and Gibault's monastic vows as well as Wendt's right to call himself an abbot. Bishop Andrew was very angry. He learned that in December 1996, Holy Cross Academy's articles of incorporation had been amended "as an independent self-governing school . . . not under the jurisdiction or control of the hierarchy of any church."

On May 14, 1997, Bishop Andrew summoned Wendt and Gibault to a sit-down in the Pocono Mountains of Pennsylvania during the eparchy's Presbyteral Days, an annual meeting during which members of the clergy gather together to study, reflect, and pray. With the bishop were five priests from the eparchy: Father Gerald Dino, Father Peter Lickman, Father Robert Evancho, Father Robert J. Hospodar, and Father Benedict DeSocio. By all accounts it was a tense encounter.

According to the official minutes of the meeting, the purpose of the confrontation was "to provide Bishop Andrew with the opportunity to personally communicate to Fathers Wendt and Gibault, in the presence of eparchial officials . . . irregularities which had been found and required correction."

Bishop Andrew began by announcing that he had recently discussed the issues with Bishop Michael, "the former residential bishop." Their conversation, he said, confirmed his concern that "canonical irregularities existed." They were "very serious" and "needed to be addressed promptly and effectively."

The bishop branded the monastery "the monastery so-called" and the academy "*contra legem*" (against the law). And he questioned Wendt's and Gibault's spiritual credentials, pointing out "that a proper novitiate is required prior to religious profession." Bishop Andrew declared that he had determined that Fathers Wendt and Gibault had not satisfied "this essential requirement."

Wendt was defiant and evasive. According to the official minutes of the meeting, "Father Wendt interjected that he understands and 'sees' the Bishop's viewpoint and appreciates any assistance from the Bishop and his staff because it has been made in good faith and continues in good faith. He added that there can be no questioning if the Law declares certain actions to be illicit or invalid. Those instances are closed cases. However, Father Wendt added, those canonists with whom he consulted (here he identified the Reverend Victor Pospishil) do not agree with Bishop Pataki's conclusions."

When Father Wendt admitted that he had gone over the Bishop's head by writing directly to Cardinal Silvestrini at the Sacred Congregation for the Eastern Churches in Rome "for protection" from Bishop Andrew, the Bishop could barely contain his anger.

He scolded Wendt for acting "so prematurely," and he reminded the cleric from Miami that he "had not received any directives from the Bishop until the present moment because the facts were under careful investigation and review." A decision, Bishop Andrew said, "could not be made until all aspects of the matters at hand were properly discovered."

Wendt replied that a monsignor he consulted "had proposed . . . that only Rome could resolve the issues of the canonical status of the Miami community and academy," and that he, Wendt, "had decided to refer the matter to Cardinal Silvestrini" in Rome.

Gibault chimed in: "The Cardinal did not object to our request," whereupon Wendt claimed that "he had recently received a response from His Eminence. He refused, however, to share its contents with the Bishop and the others present when requested to do so."

At this point, the confrontation grew even more heated. "Fathers Hospodar and DeSocio expressed their concerns with regard to the conduct of Father Wendt. Father Hospodar asked Father Wendt for the reason why he had not inquired of Bishop Pataki when a decision or directives would be forthcoming rather than writing to Cardinal Silvestrini first. Father Hospodar also noted that the nature of the issues properly required careful investigation which would unavoidably preclude an immediate decision or directive from the Bishop. It seemed, Father Hospodar remarked, that Fathers Wendt and Gibault were unusually nervous and did not have a clear understanding of proper administrative procedure."

Bishop Andrew and his aides wondered if Wendt had any understanding whatsoever of church law. "Father DeSocio questioned Father Wendt's reference to the Miami community as a 'monastery *sui juris*.' Fathers Hospodar and DeSocio noted that if a monastery had indeed been established in Miami it would have been of eparchial right and not autonomous or independent of the local hierarch. Neither Father Wendt nor Father Gibault appeared to understand the notion of 'eparchial right' in canon law. Bishop Pataki noted that whatever manner of house the priests were occupying in Miami, it was not a properly constituted monastery because Bishop Dudick had not properly consulted with the Holy See."

And they accused Wendt of attempting to hoodwink officials at the Archdiocese of Miami.

"Father DeSocio drew attention to certain discrepancies with regard to the establishment and identification of the academy. Presenting a letter from the superintendent of schools, Father DeSocio explained that evidently Father Wendt has managed to posture the academy in such a way that school officials of the Archdiocese of Miami have presumed the school belongs to the Eparchy of Passaic. Legal documents, however, clearly demonstrate that the academy is vested in the hands of Father Wendt and a board of lay trustees. The house (aka 'monastery') in which the two priests were residing, moreover, has been determined to be on land owned by the independent academy (whose charter of incorporation rejects any hierarchical authority). This arrangement contravenes the norms of the law for ecclesiastical property.

Next, one of the clerics who accompanied Bishop Andrew, Father Hospodar, asked Father Peter Lickman, pastor of St. Basil's, a Byzantine Catholic church in Miami, "if he was aware that (1) Father Wendt had executed a change of the charter of incorporation which declared the academy independent of episcopal authority, and (2) that Father Lickman's name [was] listed in the revised charter as a trustee." Lickman responded that he was unaware of the revision, or that his name appeared on it. Turning to Wendt, Father Lickman demanded that his name be removed.

Before the meeting ended, Wendt told Bishop Andrew what he thought of the eparchy: "At this time Bishop Andrew asked Father Wendt if he was satisfied to know that he could not convince any of the officials present that the state of the community and academy was according to the norms of canon law. Father Wendt replied that he is willing to do everything according to the canon law but will receive such directives from the Sacred Congregation.

"Bishop Andrew then stated that Father Wendt's remarks had only served to confirm his doubts concerning the regularity of the Miami community and academy. He expressed his serious disappointment that there did not seem to be any accountability to anyone except Father Wendt."

Bishop Andrew announced that he would notify Wendt and Gibault of his decision in writing. In the meantime, he ordered that Wendt and Gibault "make arrangements to enter novitiates as soon as possible and satisfy this essential requirement," and he directed Father Wendt to "no longer present or declare himself as an abbot and he is not to wear the insignia of this office. The academy, moreover, is no longer to describe itself as a Catholic school."

Subsequently the bishop had Holy Cross Academy removed from the list of approved Catholic institutions. The following month, Bishop Andrew wrote a letter to the Vatican's prefect for the Congregation for the Eastern Churches, Achille Cardinal Silvestrini. In it he declared that "neither a valid monastery nor valid institute of consecrated life ever existed" at Holy Cross.

In the lengthy missive dated July 31, 1997, the Bishop laid out his case against the Holy Cross priests, explaining why he'd ordered them to "cease and desist" from calling themselves monks, and why he had prohibited them from wearing monastic habits: Neither cleric had served proper novitiates under canon law.

As for the academy, the Bishop cited 1984 correspondence to Wendt from his predecessor. In it, Bishop Michael denied Wendt's request for permission to expand Holy Cross Academy beyond the eighth grade. Wendt and Gibault defied him.

"Bishop Dudick," Pataki wrote, "specifically denied permission for the establishment of a senior high school. Nevertheless, Holy Cross Academy now encompasses grades nine through twelve. There is no record extant that

Bishop Dudick rescinded his decision prohibiting the establishment of a senior high school."

And, Bishop Andrew noted, the academy's articles of incorporation had been amended in 1996, as had its promotional literature, to declare the school a "self-governing preparatory school in the educational tradition of the Catholic faith, though not under the jurisdiction or control of the hierarchy of any church." The Bishop was especially incensed because the eparchy had guaranteed a $1.4 million bank loan from Suntrust Bank to Holy Cross Academy just two years before.

An investigation—a canonical visitation—was ordered to establish the facts of the dispute. A tribunal of church law experts convened at the Holy Cross campus on September 22 and 23, 1998. At the time, nervous South Floridians were keeping a wary eye on Hurricane Georges, whose 115 mph winds were battering the Caribbean and threatening South Florida. The visitors packed three days of work into two.

The tribunal was headed by Father Michael U. Thomas, Judicial Vicar of the Eparchy of Saint Maron of Brooklyn. He was assisted by Father Andrew Anderson, Judicial Vicar of the Archdiocese of Miami; Sister Elizabeth McDonough, Canonical Consultant to the Cardinal Archbishop of Washington; Attorney J. Patrick Fitzgerald, civil legal counsel for the Archdiocese of Miami; and Jerome Lucas, the accountant for the Byzantine Eparchy of Passaic.

Representing the monastery and the academy were Wendt and Gibault; attorney Daniel Blonsky, legal counsel for the monastery and the academy and a trustee of the academy; and his father Joseph Blonsky, an attorney and also a member of Holy Cross Academy's board of trustees.

At the conclusion of the inquiry, the tribunal issued a blistering report. Among the findings:

- the Monastery of the Exaltation of the Holy Cross had been established without following proper procedures as prescribed under canon law;

- Wendt and Gibault defied their bishop when they added grades nine through twelve to the academy;

- the elementary and high schools could not be considered Catholic schools because they were never established by the bishop;

- Wendt had "divorced" the academy from the eparchy in 1996 when he amended the articles of incorporation to state that Holy Cross Academy was "independent, self-governing and not under the jurisdiction or control of the hierarchy of any church;"

- neither Wendt nor Gibault had completed a canonical novitiate in any sense of the word: "Father Wendt stated that his novitiate lasted two months and Father Gibault's novitiate lasted an indeterminate period of time and had Father Wendt, a novice, acting as his novice master. [Canon] law is clear in that the novitiate, in order to be valid, must last for three full and continuous years and that the director of novices must be professed for at least ten years;"

- there is one woman [Sister Michelle Lewis] affiliated with the community living in a separate residence. "Father Wendt made it clear however, there was no canonical establishment of a monastery of women."

The report blasted the two clerics: "In other documents church officials in the Vatican and the eparchy reportedly expressed reservations about the the monk candidates who were living at Holy Cross. Among other things, they worried that the Ukrainian boys had been brought to the United States without proper guardianships, which could expose the eparchy 'to grave liabilities' should something happen."

Now Wendt found himself at police headquarters waiting to speak to one of those candidates who had just confessed to the brutal murder of Sister Michelle Lewis. It must have seemed that the situation could not get any worse, but it would.

10

"Let me change my hat, detective, and ask if Mykhaylo was making any statements that would embarrass the Holy Cross Academy?"

—Attorney James McGuirk

A few minutes after the desk officers in the lobby notified them that the priest was in the building with an attorney, detectives Nanni and Belyeu left the interview room and reported to the reception area to meet them. In his report of the incident, Nanni wrote:

At approximately 1:00 A.M., this investigator was advised that Attorney James McGuirk as well as Father Gregory Wendt, were in the lobby of the Miami-Dade Police Department Headquarters Building. This investigator, along with Detective Belyeu, responded to the lobby and met with Mr. McGuirk and Father Wendt

McGuirk advised this investigator that he was an attorney and wanted to speak with Mr. Kofel. This investigator asked if Mr. McGuirk was Mr. Kofel's attorney, at which time Mr. McGuirk advised that he represented Holy Cross Academy and Church. Mr. McGuirk further advised that he had an attorney on standby if Mr. Kofel wanted an attorney. It was explained to Mr. McGuirk and Father Wendt that we would respond back to the interview room and explain to Mr. Kofel that there was an attorney in the lobby who would like to speak to him.

At approximately 1:10 A.M., this investigator and Detective Belyeu responded back to the interview room inside the Homicide Bureau office and spoke with Mr. Kofel about Mr. James McGuirk being in the lobby and wanting to speak to him. Mr. Kofel was further advised that he had the right to speak to Mr. McGuirk if he wanted to do so and also that they had an attorney standing by for him if he wanted one. Mr. Kofel advised this investigator that he did not need an attorney and that he was still willing to talk to me even after knowing that there was an attorney waiting in the lobby to speak with him.

Mr. Kofel advised that he did not want to speak with Father Wendt [saying], "He would be the last person I want to talk to."

While Nanni remained with Kofel, Larry Belyeu returned to the lobby to tell the priest and the attorney what Kofel had said. In his report of the incident, Detective Belyeu wrote:

Kofel was contacted in the interview room, at which time he stated he did not wish to meet with either Wendt or McGuirk. This investigator responded back to the first-floor lobby area and relayed Kofel's message to both Wendt and McGuirk.

Wendt appeared to be puzzled and stated in a questioning manner, "He doesn't want to speak with me?" at which time he was told again of Kofel's wishes. McGuirk stated to this investigator, "Let me change my hat, detective, and ask if Mykhaylo was making any statements that would embarrass the Holy Cross

Academy?" Both Wendt and McGuirk were told that any statements made by Kofel would not be made public at that particular time. Both departed and this investigator returned to the Homicide Bureau.

Back at the Holy Cross campus, staffers from the medical examiner's office were about to remove Sister Michelle's body from the crime scene. Associate medical examiner Ray Fernandez was at Holy Cross, too. He had gone there to review the crime scene before Sister Michelle's body was removed so that he would have a better understanding of what had happened. It would help when he performed the post mortem.

Even before her killer had finished confessing, the slain sister's body was tagged, put into a bag, placed on a gurney, and wheeled to a van for the eighteen-mile trip to the morgue at the Joseph H. Davis Center for Forensic Pathology. The three-building facility occupies eighty-nine-thousand square feet adjacent to Miami's Jackson Memorial Hospital/University of Miami Medical School Center.

The morgue itself takes up more than twenty-three-thousand square feet on a ground floor. There is a main morgue with twelve autopsy rooms and a separate "decomp" morgue with two autopsy rooms that handles decomposed bodies or bodies known to have infectious diseases.

Bodies brought to the morgue are stored in massive refrigerated rooms called coolers. The main morgue has four; each has a capacity of 120 bodies, while the "decomp" morgue has a cooler capable of handling seventy-five bodies.

In all, the Miami-Dade County Medical Examiner's morgue can store 555 bodies, a number that the building's designers deliberately chose: They based it on the combined passenger and crew capacity of a 747 jumbo jet.

It's a very busy facility. Each forensic pathologist conducts more than two hundred post mortem procedures yearly, while the examiner's office handles more than three thousand annually.

Autopsies, or post mortems, are smelly, dirty, and gruesome. They are performed by forensic pathologists—medical doctors whose specialty is pathology and whose subspecialty is medicine as it relates to the law, most often criminal law. There is a standard protocol for autopsies: After arriving at the morgue, a body is removed from the body bag and placed on a stainless-steel autopsy table. The bag isn't discarded; instead, it's sent to the crime lab, where criminalists will examine it for trace evidence—fibers, dirt, hair, paint chips, for example, that may have been transferred to it from the body.

The first phase in the actual post mortem procedure is the external examination. The pathologist will examine the corpse while it is still clothed—damaged clothing should correspond with wounds to the body. After carefully removing the clothing, the pathologist sends the garments to the laboratory for processing. After that, the corpse's height and weight are recorded.

Next, the pathologist will perform a careful external examination. X-rays may be taken in order to find broken bones or unseen evidence, such as bullet fragments. The pathologist will also search for additional trace evidence, which may have become embedded in the body. If found it, too, will be collected and sent to the lab for processing.

If there are indications that there had been a struggle, a homicide victim's fingernails will be clipped and processed because the assailant's hair, blood, or tissue may have gotten under them. If a sexual assault is suspected, the pathologist will comb the corpse's pubic hair, looking for hairs from the attacker that may have become entangled with the victim's. In addition, the pathologist will check for semen by obtaining anal and vaginal swabs.

Next, the pathologist will painstakingly examine each

wound and injury, measuring them one by one for length and depth. Their locations will be precisely marked on an anatomical diagram. In addition, each will be photographed. If weapons have been found that investigators believe are connected to the corpse, they will be compared to the wounds and injuries on the body.

The second phase of the post mortem is not for the faint of heart. It involves dissecting the corpse. The pathologist makes a Y-shaped incision on the front of the body from the shoulders in a downward direction toward the breastbone, then a straight incision down toward the pubis. Using a saw, the pathologist will cut the ribs and collarbone in order to remove the breastplate, exposing the heart and lungs. They will be removed and weighed and sent to the toxicology lab for testing.

Next, the pathologist will examine the abdomen, weighing each organ and taking tissue samples for microscopic examination. The contents of the stomach will be examined along with other body fluids including urine, bile, and liver samples, all of which may be sent for toxicological testing.

The pathologist will look for brain injuries, too, by opening the skull with an incision from behind one ear, crossing over the top of the head to a point behind the other ear. Using a saw, the pathologist then removes a section of skull to expose the brain, which will be removed and weighed, and from which tissue samples will be taken.

Finally, each removed organ is returned to the body and the incisions are sutured. Once all the results are in from the toxicology lab, the medical examiner will write and file an official autopsy report.

Sister Michelle's autopsy was scheduled for 1:00 P.M. the afternoon of March 26. In addition to Dr. Fernandez and his assistants, Detective John King was on hand along with

Detective Tommy Charles from the MDPD's crime scene investigations bureau. He was there to take photographs during the procedure.

King, a veteran of more than one thousand autopsies, had supervised the processing of the crime scene at Holy Cross, which meant that he also was responsible for the body aspect of the investigation. He was there to witness the post mortem and to assist the pathologist by filling him in on details of the crime scene as the procedure was performed, and to immediately take custody of any evidence found on or in the body.

Dr. Fernandez followed the post mortem protocol. He began by measuring and weighing the sister. In his report he wrote: "The body is that of a 5-foot-5-inch, 162-pound, well-developed, well-nourished, adult white female appearing about the reported age of 39 years. The scalp is covered by long, black hair which is 12 inches in maximum length. The eyes are brown . . . The lower lobe of each ear has two remote piercings. The oral cavity contains native teeth in fair state."

Dr. Fernandez reported that Sister Michelle had not been raped: "The external genital and anal areas are atraumatic."

The medical examiner confirmed what crime scene investigators had observed: Sister Michelle had been repeatedly struck with a blunt-force instrument, stabbed, and kicked. Most of the injuries were to the front of her torso and to her head, which was severely bruised and battered.

By bashing her with the fireplace poker, Kofel fractured her skull and broke her right hand and left wrist. He inflicted five blunt-force injuries to her left leg, four to her left forearm, seven to her right forearm, two to the back of her right hand, and eighteen to her head and face.

Wielding the steak knife, he stabbed Sister Michelle a total of ninety-two times. Twenty-five stab wounds were to her chest while twenty-four were to her abdomen. She also had fifteen stab wounds on her arms and nine on her legs. On her neck, Dr. Fernandez found ten stab wounds; three more were on her back.

The knife had sliced her nose open—"a partial transaction of the lower half of the nose," is what the medical examiner called it. There were self-defense–type cuts on Sister Michelle's hands and forearms and on her right thumb, which was nearly severed. The knife had pierced her lungs, her liver, and her heart. She had also been stomped six times. Kofel had left "bloody shoe-like impressions," the medical examiner said: two were located on the lower right side of her chest, two on her upper abdomen, and two on the front of her right thigh.

In all she had been hit with the fireplace poker thirty-six times. One of the blows caused her brain to hemorrhage. Surprisingly, there were no post mortem wounds, indicating that Sister Michelle was still alive the entire time Kofel stomped, stabbed, and pummeled her, and that she had fought desperately for her life right up until the very end with nothing more than her bare hands.

Because of the number and extent of her injuries, Dr. Fernandez would need two days to complete the post mortem examination. His written report would not be finished until April 25, and it would not become public knowledge until May 1, when the state attorney's office released it to the press.

While the medical examiner was performing the post mortem, Art Nanni phoned Beverly Lewis at her home in Ohio to tell her that her daughter was dead. Before making that call, Nanni contacted the local sheriff's office to request that an officer be with Mrs. Lewis when he phoned. The Portage County Sheriff's Department dispatched a deputy. When the cop arrived at the address, Nanni was notified that the officer would stand by while he spoke with Mrs. Lewis.

Whether in person or on the phone, notifying next of

kin is never easy. Mrs. Lewis broke down when Nanni gave her the bad news. Before hanging up the phone, Nanni promised he would call again with more details. In the meantime, he left his phone number and invited Mrs. Lewis to call him if she had any questions.

"What appears a homicide at first glance is not always the case."

—Assistant Public Defender Edith Georgi

By seven o'clock Monday morning, Art Nanni was bone-weary and dog-tired. He had been working nonstop for twenty-four hours. The lawman had been able to catch a couple of catnaps, but he hadn't been home in more than a day and would have welcomed a hot shower and a change of clothes.

Mykhaylo Kofel was dog-tired, too. He was still confined to the interview room. The cut on his right hand continued to ooze, and it hurt. He had been able to get some rest by putting his head down on the table. He had even closed his eyes but could not fall asleep. Now he was about to give another statement, this one to investigators from the MDPD's sexual crimes bureau (SCB).

Nanni had called them to report Kofel's allegations of sexual abuse at the hands of Wendt and Gibault. Less than an hour after he called, SCB Detective Steve Signori and Detective Jose Cabado were at the homicide bureau to interview Kofel. Signori recalls being taken aback by the way Kofel looked.

"What caught me mostly was his shiny appearance," the sex crimes investigator remembered. "He looked like most guys after sweating and drying."

Kofel repeated the allegations he had leveled against the priests when he confessed to Nanni and Belyeu, adding one that he hadn't mentioned before: Father Damian, he said, had ejaculated on him.

He would reveal more later on, but that would be all for now.

Sex crime investigators say it's not uncommon for victims to withhold details. If they reveal them at all they do so little by little over time. Besides, Steve Signori had been a cop for twenty years, the last five with the sexual crimes bureau. His experience, he said, told him that Kofel was telling the truth.

"He was sincere, believable," Signori declared, noting that as Kofel repeated the allegations, he maintained eye contact with the lawmen, and spoke in a manner that was "matter of fact."

The SCB investigators opened two case files. One identified Wendt as the subject of a sex crimes investigation, while the other named Gibault. SCB Sergeant Kimet Pomes wrote a memo and a narrative summary of the accusations for Major Karin Montejo, the bureau's commander:

"Detective A. Nanni of the Homicide Bureau contacted the Sexual Crimes Bureau (SCB) and advised that the victim, a monk-candidate and the subject of a homicide investigation, was alleging that he was sexually assaulted by the subjects. The victim resides at Holy Cross Academy and the subjects are both priests at the academy. The victim told SCB detectives that Subject #1 [Frank Wendt] fondled his penis, chest and buttocks area over his clothing on three different occasions between 1997 and 1998.

"He also advised that from the age of 17 until about two weeks ago, Subject #2, James Gibault, W/M/48, 12425 SW 72 Street, also fondled his genitals and buttocks on numerous occasions. The allegation against Subject #2 is a battery and is documented under Miami-Dade Police Department Case Number 16765-Z. The subjects will be contacted later in the week. The investigation continues."

Later that morning, Miami-Dade Police Director Carlos Alvarez held a press conference to announce the arrest of Mykhaylo Kofel. He revealed that homicide detectives questioned the monk candidate late Sunday and he had confessed. Kofel, Alvarez said, was charged with first-degree murder, armed burglary, and using a weapon to commit a crime. He said nothing about Kofel's allegations of sexual abuse.

Assistant State Attorney Gail Levine proved prescient: The murder at Holy Cross did grab headlines. Local media covered the story like white on rice. When the residents of South Florida awoke Tuesday, their newspapers carried banner headlines.

MONK HELD IN MURDER OF NUN, blared the *Miami Herald*, while the South Florida *Sun-Sentinel* trumpeted MONK, 18, ARRESTED IN MURDER OF NUN.

The newpapers reported the arrest and the charges. There was no mention of Kofel's allegations of sexual abuse—investigators remained tight-lipped on details about that aspect of the case. Readers also learned that Kofel had been brought back to the crime scene to help investigators locate evidence that he'd tossed away.

The papers reported two items incorrectly: Mykhaylo Kofel was not a monk and Sister Michelle was not a nun. She had been laboring at Holy Cross for nearly a decade, sweating profusely in the South Flordia heat under the oppressively heavy black habit she was required to wear, living a life of poverty, chastity, and obedience to Father Abbot Gregory Wendt, yet she was not a nun in the eyes of any church. No woman, in fact, had ever attained the status of nun at Holy Cross, and no woman ever would.

In order to become one in the Byzantine Catholic Church, she would have had to have been tonsured, a ritual that is usually performed by a bishop, but Holy Cross had been at odds with its bishop since 1997, and Sister Michelle was caught in the crossfire.

As for Kofel, "he's a candidate to become a monk," Joseph Blonsky, a lawyer on the academy's board of directors, told reporters. "There are a number of stages. He's a learner, in the early stages of candidacy."

While Blonsky faced the media, the man who referred to himself as "the highest authority" at Holy Cross, Father Abbot Gregory Wendt, declined to speak to reporters who were clamoring for him to answer their questions. Detectives were clamoring for him to answer their questions, too, but the priest wasn't about to talk to them either.

It was 11:00 A.M. on Monday when an unmarked MDPD police car carrying Kofel and two detectives drove onto the Holy Cross campus. Kofel was a prisoner now, so he sat in the back, in shackles. He still wore the same black clothes he'd had on when he left the campus with Art Nanni the evening before.

An hour earlier Larry Belyeu asked Kofel if he would be willing to return to the campus to help investigators locate the knife, the fireplace poker, and the wine bottle he'd thrown away during his murderous rampage. Kofel said he would. Before leaving the homicide bureau with Belyeu and John King, Kofel signed a Consent to Search form. Less than an hour later he was back at Holy Cross.

With Kofel's help, investigators found what they were looking for within minutes. The wine bottle was located on a grassy patch on the opposite side of Southwest 123rd Avenue, almost directly across from Holy Cross. It was unbroken and empty. The label read MAVRODAPHNE OF PETROS, a sweet wine from Greece. The bloody knife and the fireplace poker were located lying next to each other on the Holy Cross side of Southwest 123rd Avenue, just beyond a hedge on the north side of the property. Crime scene personnel photographed each of the the items as they were found, then collected them and took them to the MDPD's crime lab for analysis.

During their search, investigators stumbled upon a bloody latex glove and a half-empty roll of gray duct tape. At first Kofel denied that he had anything to do with either the glove or the tape, but when pressed by Belyeu he admitted that he had but said that he didn't use them. He then told detectives where to look for the second latex glove.

While Kofel was helping investigators recover the murder weapons, uniformed MDPD cops directed traffic in front of Holy Cross. Incredibly, school had not been cancelled even though the entire campus had been sealed off while investigators continued to process the scene, but no one had told the five hundred students and teachers who began arriving for school at 7:30 that morning only to find that they were barred from the campus. After checking with Art Nanni, cops decided to allow them to enter the parking lot on the south side of the campus but kept them from going anywhere else.

Reporters weren't so lucky. They were still being kept away from Holy Cross, but from their vantage points they could see students, parents, and faculty members milling about, sharing hugs and trying to make sense of the tragedy. They even managed to elicit comments from some of them.

"She was probably the smartest math teacher I ever had," Freddie Middelstaedt told the *Miami Herald*.

"She ran the place," said his mother, Elaine. "I think that's why there was school today, because nobody else had enough sense to call it off."

Sunita Balani, a 1999 graduate of Holy Cross, said Sister Michelle "was a very disciplined person. She was constantly reading math and education books, trying to learn as much as she could. She had high expectations of herself and others."

Claudia Negrette, the valedictorian of the class of 1999, recalled attending school with Kofel, but said she never got to know him or the other Ukrainian monk candidates. "We weren't allowed to communicate with them," she told the *Sun-Sentinel*. "They were just to themselves because they knew each other and they spoke the same language. They never, ever socialized with us."

The fact of the matter was they couldn't, because they were prohibited from doing so by Father Abbot Gregory Wendt. From the first day of their arrival on campus, school officials made it crystal clear to students, parents, and to the monk candidates, too, that the boys from Ukraine had not been brought to Miami to socialize.

Mykhaylo Kofel and the other monk candidates lived by a set of rules that permitted them to rub elbows with their classmates but kept them a world apart. For example, the boys from Ukraine were outstanding soccer players—it's their country's national pastime—but they weren't allowed to play for the Holy Cross team.

"I always wanted to play sports for Holy Cross," Kofel recalled. "Especially during my senior year. Holy Cross had a soccer team for the first time. In Ukraine, I grew up playing soccer. I wanted to play, but Wendt didn't allow me. I even cried." And they were among the smartest kids in their classes, but they weren't allowed to study with their classmates or partner with them in classroom projects.

By all accounts Mykhaylo was the friendliest and the most outgoing of the candidates, but friendship with his schoolmates was forbidden. He couldn't talk to them about movies they had seen or about the music they were listening to. He could not go to their parties. And he wasn't allowed to go with them on the senior class trip to Disney World in Orlando. "I felt very isolated," Kofel said.

He was, however, allowed to attend his class prom, but he had to sit at a separate table with Wendt and Gibault, unable to interact with his classmates. "They were dancing, but I only watched them. I wanted to join them, but I couldn't. I felt like a total loser," he remembered.

Despite the isolation, during his time at Holy Cross Cupid's arrow found its way to the monk-in-training's heart. He fell in love with a schoolmate named Maria. She was nice to him and gave him presents. "I loved her a lot, but I couldn't do anything about it," he said. Eventually he got over Maria, only to develop strong feelings for other girls, too.

After Kofel helped detectives locate the wine bottle, the knife, and the poker, they brought him back to the homicide bureau. Later, Belyeu and Detective Rom Nyberg drove Kofel to Jackson Memorial Hospital. They took him directly to Ward D, the hospital's prison ward, where he was examined by medics.

"We have to take a prisoner to Ward D whenever there are signs of injuries," Nanni explained. "Ward D needs to clear them before they can be booked into the county jail."

At 1:30 P.M., an intake nurse noted the scratches on Kofel's face and the cuts on his hands. The physician on duty asked if he suffered from any mental illness, or if he had ever been diagnosed with a mental disorder. Kofel answered no to both questions. The doctor examined him and asked questions about the injuries.

"How did you injure your hands?"

"With a knife."

"Was it an accident?"

"No."

"What happened?"

"Don't you know the story?"

The medic didn't answer. Instead he cleared Kofel for admission into Miami-Dade County Jail, noting that he was "coherent" and appeared to be "neurologically intact." The doctor also noted that Kofel "denies suicidal thoughts or ideas of self-harm." Nevertheless, the doctor recommended a full psychological evaluation and ordered jailers to put Kofel on a suicide watch.

An hour after they first arrived at Ward D, detectives drove Kofel four blocks to the county jail, where he was booked and photographed and issued inmate number 01-25383. After booking he was taken to the ninth-floor psychiatric unit, where he could be watched around the clock. Jailers took away his clothes and gave him a special padded garment, a Furgeson gown, to wear instead of the standard prison jumpsuit. Then he was led to a one-man, ten-by-seven-foot cell where, exhausted, he fell into a deep sleep.

Assistant public defender Edith Georgi doesn't recall when she first learned about the murder at Holy Cross, but when she did she knew that the case would be coming her way.

Georgi is one of two hundred attorneys at the Miami-Dade County Public Defender's office. By 2001, they were handling more than one hundred thousand cases annually. A passionate opponent of capital punishment, Georgi concentrates on death penalty cases. It's a hallmark of American justice that every criminal defendant is entitled to a defense and to their constitutional rights, no matter how heinous the crime or repulsive the defendant. It's a concept that Georgi has fought for throughout her professional life.

"I've always worked for the underdog," said the lanky blonde marathon runner, who joined the public defender's office in 1981 after graduating from law school. She signed on to represent indigent men and women who face the loss of their liberty and have been determined by the court to be unable to afford a private attorney. Her longtime boss, public defender Bennet Brummer, is a former Peace Corps volunteer. He joined the office in 1971 in the appellate division. Five years later he was elected the county's public defender. He had been reelected seven times since then.

As for Georgi, the Kentucky native taught English in Hong Kong, lived on a kibbutz in Israel, and managed a bookstore in Arkansas before moving to Florida to study law at the University of Miami. In her twenty years as an assistant public defender, she had been involved in more than one headline-grabbing murder trial. In 1987, an enraged Alberto Farinas was convicted of stalking and chasing down his common-law wife, Elsidia Gonzalez, and pumping two bullets into the back of her head. The jury voted to send Farinas to death row, where he would be strapped into "Old Sparky," the nickname given to Florida's electric chair, and executed. Before the judge passed sentence, Georgi argued that a once-in-a-lifetime murderous rage did not warrant a trip to the electric chair or to the lethal injection room.

"One day of his life he lost total control of his actions," she told the judge as she pleaded for mercy for her client. "A few moments out of a person's life do not merit death."

Georgi was disappointed when the judge did not agree.

He followed the jury's recommendation and sentenced Farinas to death, but the condemned man's sentence was commuted to life in prison by an appeals court.

In 1995, Georgi defended Roy Conde, a serial killer who murdered six prostitutes. He went to the death house, where he's been awaiting execution ever since. That year, too, Georgi won an acquittal in the case of a Miami teen who confessed to shooting a woman in the head after a tryst and stealing her car.

She was able to persuade the jury that the teen fell asleep after having sex with the woman. When he awoke the woman was lying dead next to him. Fearful that the real killer would come back, he drove away in her car. As for the sixty-five-page confession, Georgi argued that it had been coerced by investigators.

Now the fifty-one-year-old attorney would take on a case that, on the surface, seemed to be strikingly similar— the brutal murder of a woman at the hands of a teen who had given a full confession to police. But appearances can be deceiving. As Edith Georgi once told a reporter, "What appears a homicide at first glance is not always the case."

12

"If the police ask you any questions about your personal life, tell them you do not want to talk with them anymore and ask for an attorney to be present."

—Father Abbot Gregory Wendt

The murder at Holy Cross wasn't the only school violence to hit Miami that week, and it wasn't the only murder case grabbing headlines in South Florida. At Miami Jackson Senior High, a student stabbed a classmate in the neck with a homemade knife. The victim survived and police arrested the stabber. In Fort Lauderdale, the case of Lionel Tate was still in the news even though the young killer had been tried in January and sentenced on March 9. The fourteen-year-old was convicted of murdering a six-year-old family friend by tossing her tiny body around the living room of his home. Tate was only twelve years old at the time, but that didn't stop the judge from sentencing him to life in prison.

Over the weekend an outraged Johnnie Cochran, one of O. J. Simpson's "dream team" attorneys, flew into South Florida from Southern California. At a morning press conference, the controversial attorney, who had won acquittals for Simpson and hip-hop performer and record producer Sean "Puffy" Combs, announced that he would either appeal Tate's sentence or demand the governer grant clemency. It was a miscarriage of justice, Cochran declared, to put someone in prison for life for a crime committed at age twelve. "O. J. got the dream team. I got the miracle team," gushed Tate's mother, a Florida state trooper.

In the evening Cochran went to South Beach, whose residents that day were reliving the July 1997 murder spree of Andrew Cunanan, a crazed killer whose nationwide rampage ended in Miami where he gunned down Italian fashion designer Gianni Versace on the steps of his Ocean Drive mansion. Newspapers reported that furnishings and artwork from the Versace mansion would be auctioned at Sotheby's in New York on April 5 to raise money for the fight against gun violence.

Meanwhile in Tallahassee, the state capital, a committee of the Florida House of Representatives was about to hold hearings on a bill that would prohibit the execution of mentally disabled criminals. A similar measure was ready for final passage in the state senate. Florida governor Jeb Bush announced that if a bill reached his desk, he would sign it. It was welcome news to death penalty opponents.

Two days had passed since the murder of Sister Michelle and the wheels of justice were spinning. On Tuesday, March 27, a bond hearing was held in the Richard E. Gerstein Justice Building, the massive and unmajestic nine-story courthouse just south of the county jail. All that stands between the two facilities is a narrow roadway that runs for one block between Northeast 13 Court and Northeast 13th Avenue. An enclosed skyway connects the jail to the justice building, which means prisoners can be brought to court without ever having to walk outside.

Kofel chose not to attend the hearing. Edith Georgi stood in for him. In addition to deciding that Kofel would be held without bail, circuit court judge Manuel "Manny" Crespo declared him indigent and officially appointed the public defender to defend him. Kofel's first court appearance would come soon enough—his arraignment was set for April 5 before Judge Crespo. Until then there was lots of work for Georgi to do to prepare, and there were still loose ends for investigators to tie up.

At the top of their list were the other monk candidates. Lawmen had spoken with the boys from Ukraine the day of the murder, but now they wanted to question them away from Holy Cross, and they wanted to take their sworn statements, which would be recorded and transcribed by a stenographer.

At 3 P.M. on March 27, four detectives from Squad C—Art Nanni, John King, Larry Belyeu, and Bill Gilland—were at Holy Cross. They came armed with subpeonas for Vasyl Kopych, Sasha Korsak, and Yosyp Lembak. The boys knew the detectives were coming and were waiting for them in the candidates' house along with Wendt and Gibault. In his report, Nanni wrote: "Prior to departing the Holy Cross campus, Father Wendt instructed Mr. Lembak, Mr. Korsak and Mr. Kopych to 'remember what we had discussed earlier and that if the police ask you any questions about your personal life, tell them you do not want to talk with them anymore and ask for an attorney to be present.'"

The lawmen didn't take kindly to Wendt's words. Detective King warned the abbot that he was dangerously close to obstructing the investigation, and if he continued he would be arrested.

Forty-five minutes later the detectives and the boys were at the homicide bureau. They were separated from each other and put into interview rooms. As soon as they were sworn in, the interviews began. Larry Belyeu interviewed Lembak, John King interviewd Korsak, and Tom Romagni interviewd Kopych. In accented English, the three boys repeated what they had told detectives on Sunday: They had not noticed any cuts on Kofel's hands prior to Sunday morning. Both Lembak and Korsak told investigators that Kofel told them he had sustained the wounds when he cut his hands while washing a glass on Friday, while Vasyl Kopych stated he had overheard Kofel giving that explanation to Father Damian on Sunday morning.

Belyeu had a difficult time communicating with Lembak. Lembak had been in Miami only seven months and his English skills were not as advanced as the others. Nevertheless, the detective learned that for as long as he had been at Holy Cross, he had never seen Kofel angry.

"He was quiet, a nice person who got along with everyone," Lembak said in broken English. As for Sister Michelle, the monk candidate said that he "never knew her to be mean or mean-spirited, or show any anger toward anyone, not even toward Kofel."

The detective asked Lembak if he knew what sexual abuse was. The seventeen-year-old said he did not, so Belyeu explained it to him. Lembak then said that he had never been sexually abused by Father Wendt or Father Damian. When asked if he knew if any of the monk candidates were being abused by the priests, Lembak said he did not. Finally, Belyeu wanted to know if Kofel had ever said anything to him to indicate that he had been a victim of sexual abuse by the priests. Lembak said he had not.

During his interview with Sasha Korsak, John King delved into living and sleeping arrangements at Holy Cross. In his report King wrote: "He advised that he and the three other monk candidates live in the candidate house with Father Damian. He advised that the candidate Petro sometimes stayed in the candidate house and sometimes in Father Wendt's residence. He also advised that Petro and Misha (the subject) stayed in the residence by Barry College when they were going to school."

King wanted to know about Kofel. In his report, the detective wrote:

Mr. Korsak was asked what, if anything, he knew about the subject in this case, Mykhaylo Kofel. Mr. Korsak advised that he only knew this individual as Misha, since he arrived from Ukraine. He advised that Misha was already living at the academy. He related that although they were from the same country, they were from different areas and that he did not know him prior to coming here. He described Mykhaylo as being a quiet individual that pretty much stayed to himself. He related that he never indicated to him that he was having any problems. He was also unaware of Mykhaylo ever being the subject of name-calling or verbal abuse by anybody at the Holy Cross Academy. Mr. Korsak also advised that Mykhaylo and Petro were the two senior monk candidates and, therefore, had their own sleeping quarters.

Mr. Korsak advised that he never saw Mykhaylo angry or involved in any aggressive behavior, like fighting. He advised that kind of conduct at the monastery would not be tolerated.

Mr. Korsak was asked if he was aware of a fireplace poker that was bent at the end in the candidates' house by the fireplace. He advised that there had been one there, but was not aware of it still being there.

And King wanted to know about sexual abuse at Holy Cross—specifically, had Sasha ever been a victim, was he aware of any sexual activity between any of the monk candidates and the fathers who operated the monastery and school?

He advised that there has never been any sexual activity that he is aware of. He advised that he was never approached and was not aware of anybody else. He also advised that had that occurred, he would have requested to be returned to Ukraine.

Afterward, the lawmen got together and compared notes, which Nanni summarized in his report:

At the conclusion of the interviews, it was learned that the [monk candidates] knew of no sexual abuse allegations made by Mr. Kofel. They also stated that they were not sexually abused by the priests. They further advised they never heard [of] Mr. Kofel or any of the other candidates having problems with Sister Michelle Lewis.

While the monk candidates told investigators that Sister Michelle had never been verbally abusive toward them, at least one of the Holy Cross students they interviewed told a different story.

"She was mean to Mykhaylo and the other Ukrainian boys," said Danelys Perera. "She would humiliate him because he didn't speak English. She hurt his feelings."

Kofel, she said, confided in her, telling her "that whenever the Ukraine boys would ask her a question or something, she would make them feel stupid, all of them, and that [Sister Michelle] would embarass them." Perera said she had seen that herself more than once, when Sister Michelle scolded Kofel.

"I would see her talking to him, and [he'd look] sad, put his chin in, and just go to school because it was usually in the passageway on the way to school from where the monks live."

Danelys and Mikhalyo were in the same classes in ninth grade, and they often ate lunch together even though they both knew it was against the rules. But Perera was curious about the monk candidates so she struck up a friendship with Kofel even though it meant risking "big trouble," with the priests.

"We were really not allowed to socialize with them, but I didn't really care because I felt sorry for them," she told investigators several days after the killing. "We were not allowed to give them any notes saying they were cute or any party invitations or ask for their phone numbers or socialize with them, because they are going to work for God."

Another Holy Cross student told investigators that Kofel revealed to him how he felt about Sister Michelle. "He didn't like her. He hated her," said Badi Sheffey.

Later that evening, assistant state attorney Gail Levine was at the MDPD's homicide bureau helping detectives tie up loose ends. She was there when Wendt made yet another unannounced visit to police headquarters.

Almost every one of the detectives who worked the Holy Cross murder case were products of Catholic schools. Art Nanni had even attended the same Miami seminary as Wendt had—St. John Vianny—but unlike the priest the lawman left after only one semester. "I liked girls too much," he explained. The cops were accustomed to treating men of the cloth with respect and reverence, so when the call came from the desk officer on duty that Father Abbot Gregory Wendt was once again demanding to speak to investigators, the lawmen appeared somewhat flustered—at least that's how it seemed to Gail Levine, who rode the elevator to the lobby floor where she introduced herself to the six-foot-four-inch cleric.

"He demanded to know what was going on," the prosecutor remembered. "I told him that I could not comment on an ongoing investigation, but I invited him to tell me anything he liked."

Instead of cooperating, the clergyman turned and walked away in a huff. As for Levine, she rode the elevator up to the homicide bureau and went back to work. There was still much work to be done. Lawmen had Kofel's confession. Fingerprints and blood evidence would put him inside the sister's bedroom, but they weren't buying everything Kofel had told them.

13

"Upon turning on the computers, in order to find any letters or diaries, a document was listed as Death Penalty Thesis—Mykhaylo Kofel."

—Amended Search Warrant, March 27, 2001

Mykhaylo Kofel had been the ideal monk-in-training, or so it seemed. He was devout and obedient, a young man completely dedicated to serving God. As a reward, the priests honored him. They chose him to carry the staff during Mass, leading the way in front of the abbot.

He had made remarkable progress since arriving at Holy Cross in 1996, a fourteen-year-old who could neither read nor write English. He proved to be a fast learner. After graduating from high school, he enrolled at Miami-Dade Community College for the fall semester. He took classes in chemistry, anatomy, microbiology, and math, earning As and Bs. For the spring semester Kofel transferred to Barry University.

"He was an excellent student, polite, punctual, and quiet," said Professor Servando Munoz, Kofel's chemistry lab professor at Miami-Dade. His work, he said, was "impeccable." Munoz remembered Kofel from Holy Cross, the school his children attended. "I can tell you all of his teachers are puzzled over what happened. No one had any indication."

Neither did his teachers at Barry University, where the monk candidate was enrolled in freshman courses. When he first applied for admission to Barry, Kofel told school officials he was planning to study nursing at the Roman Catholic university. One of the courses he enrolled in was Introduction to Microbiology. Father Abbot Gregory Wendt was in the class, too. Kofel would carry the abbot's books as well as his own to and from the class.

Mykhaylo Kofel had come a long way, and he was on the verge of achieving an impossible dream for a poor Greek Catholic from Ukraine, but by 2001 he was seething. He was angry because Wendt reneged on a promise to let him return home for a visit the summer before. He was angry because he wanted to live the life of an American teen—he wanted to go to parties and have girlfriends. He was angry because he was, he said, being sexually abused by Father Damian Gibault. And he was angry because when Petro graduated from Holy Cross, Wendt offered to bring his parents to the United States, but they didn't get their visas. But for his graduation one year later, Wendt said nothing about bringing Yuri and Maria Kofel to Miami.

Instead, on his next visit to Konsovo, Wendt traveled to Verkhovina Bystra to bring the Kofels a videotape of the graduation ceremony. They were able to see their son receive his diploma and a slew of awards and medals for academic excellence and service to the school.

By then, however, Mykhaylo hated his life at Holy Cross, and he was looking for a way out. At least that's what Kofel told Ricky Hernandez, another former Holy Cross student. But Kofel had no money, Wendt held his passport, and he didn't know where he would go.

He thought of joining the air force, even contacted a recruiter, but he was told he would not be able to enlist because of his immigration status. He had lost the spiritual passion that had originally brought him to Holy Cross, claiming it had been drained away by sexual abuse. He blamed Wendt and Gibault, and he was angry with Sister Michelle.

Kofel told the lawmen that he brought the knife he used to kill her from the Barry house where he lived during the week with Petro Teranta and Father Gregory. Detectives wanted to search the house. Art Nanni prepared the warrant. It read:

On 3/25/01, Sister Michelle Lewis was found stabbed to death at their residence at 6950 SE 123rd Avenue. She was a nun who lived and taught on the campus of Holy Cross Academy. The Academy also houses and educates monastic candidates. These candidates reside in a dormitory on the property at Holy Cross Academy. While investigating the crime scene located at Holy Cross Academy, a blood trail was located. Detectives began to interview monastic candidates who resided at the property.

Detectives came into contact with Mykhaylo Kofel. When Kofel opened the door to the monastic candidate's residence, detectives noticed that Kofel had cuts to his hands. He agreed to be interviewed by detectives and, after Miranda, confessed to killing Sister Michelle Lewis.

Subsequent investigation has led to information that Kofel resided not only at the dormitory on the property of Holy Cross, but on Monday through Thursday he lived at 92 NE 117 Street, at or near Barry University where he took courses and studied. During Kofel's statement, he told detectives about frustrations and concerns that he had living at the Holy Cross Academy. In addition he told detectives that the knife he used to murder Sister Michelle Lewis was taken from his residence at 92 NE 117 Street.

It was about 4 P.M. on March 27, when Art Nanni brought the warrant to Judge Crespo's courtroom for his signature. One hour later, the lawman was in front of the Barry house along with Bill Gilliland and John King. Crime scene detectives were there, too, but the house was locked and no one answered their knock.

Nanni phoned James McGuirk, the attorney who was with Wendt at the homicide bureau in the wee hours of Monday morning. "I advised him that we were at the house and asked for someone from Holy Cross to meet us there with a key," the detective recalled. An hour and a half later, another lawyer showed up. He brought a key. After he read the warrant, the lawmen entered the house.

Detectives quickly found three steak knives in the kitchen sink that matched the knife Kofel used to stab Sister Michelle. They photographed the knives, bagged them, and took them into custody. In a bedroom they learned was Petro Terenta's, the lawmen found an un-monklike pink-and-white Valentine's Day card. It was addressed to "Blue Eyes." The card read:

> *The times we spend together*
> *talking and laughing*
> *listening and sharing*
> *are some of my favorite*
> *times of all.*
>
> *No matter what we do,*
> *I always enjoy myself*
> *because I enjoy*
> *your company so much . . .*

On the bottom, the sender penned a personal note. It read:

My Dearest BE;

Words can't explain what you mean to me. The only thing that I am certain of is that you bring a lot of joy into my life and for that I am thankful. Thank you for making me smile and I hope our friendship lasts a lifetime.

Claudia

Claudia's signature was surrounded by two hand-drawn hearts, each with an arrow running through it. Investigators interviewed the sender of the card, a twenty-one-year-old Barry University coed named Claudia Guido. "We're just friends," she said. They met as classmates and lab partners at Barry, where Petro was enrolled in nursing classes. They often ate out together and went to the movies together.

When questioned several months later about his relationship with Claudia, Petro declined to answer. But when asked by investigators how Wendt reacted, he said they had a conversation. "He asked me what was really going on and whether there's anything he should know, or whether I have changed my mind about being a monk."

Petro promised Wendt that, "I still had my purpose," but there was a consequence: "The abbot prohibited me [sic] to communicate and he said to make sure that whatever friends you have, make sure that they understand that you're a monastic candidate and that you cannot be friendly with them to such an extent."

In another room the lawmen came upon a desktop computer. When switched on, it opened to a window that revealed that the last document worked on was entitled

"Death Penalty Thesis Mykhaylo." They wanted to impound it, but there was a problem—the warrant did not authorize them to do so. They would need an amended warrant.

"At this time," Detective Nanni wrote in his report, "Assistant State Attorney Gail Levine was notified and requested that we amend the warrant to take the computer for further analysis."

The lawman then drove to the state attorney's office, where he picked up the amended warrant, and drove to Judge Crespo's home in South Miami. The judge read it and signed it at 8:45 P.M. Nanni then raced back to the Barry house. The lawmen impounded the steak knives and the computer, which they turned over to the U.S. Secret Service. A forensic computer expert would download its contents for analysis.

By Thursday, March 29, there was still one monk candidate investigators wanted to take a sworn statement from: Petro Terenia. It was late in the afternoon when he showed up at the homicide bureau. Art Nanni, Gail Levine, and a stenographer were waiting for him in a second-floor conference room. Like the other monk candidates, Terenta had been subpoenaed, but unlike the others, Petro showed up with an attorney.

His name was Clark Mervis, and he was one of at least fourteen lawyers hired by the Church Mutual Insurance Company, Holy Cross's insurance carrier. Father Abbot Gregory Wendt wasted no time calling the Wisconsin-based company, the nation's largest insurer of houses of worship and religious institutions. "I called them immediately," he admitted.

Lutheran ministers founded the company in 1897. Over the years Church Mutual battled thousands of sexual misconduct cases in civil court and dozens more in criminal court. One of those cases was in Miami. In 1990, Bobby Fijnje (pronounced FEEN-yea), a fourteen-year-old helper at the Old Cutler Ridge Presbyterian Church nursery school, stood trial as an adult for sexually abusing three preschoolers. When arrested, Fijnje confessed to police but later recanted. Church Mutual hired Miami criminal defense attorney Mel Black to defend the teen. After a lengthy trial, Fijnje was found not guilty.

Now the insurance company retained Black to represent Father Abbot Gregory Wendt. It also hired Richard Hersch, a former prosecutor-turned-defense attorney, to represent Father Damian Gibault. And they hired attorneys for the monk candidates and every Holy Cross employee who had been subpoened by investigators, including a janitor and Sister Marie.

No one at Holy Cross knew Mykhaylo Kofel better than Petro Terenta. They were the senior monk candidates, the first to come to Miami from Ukraine. They had been together since the summer of 1996. They were in classes together at Holy Cross, prayed together, and shared a room when they first arrived in Miami. If anyone could fill investigators in about Kofel's relationship with Sister Michelle and his mental state on the day of the slaying, it was Petro.

After he was sworn in, Terenta stated his name, address, date of birth, and occupation. "I'm an apprentice training to be a monk and a student," he declared.

Nanni began the questioning by asking Petro to review what had happened when he discovered Sister Michelle's body and what he did next after opening her bedroom door: "I ran over to Father Abbot and I told him what happened."

Next, the questioning turned to the week prior to Sister Michelle's death. "Where did you and Mykhalyo stay?" Nanni wanted to know.

"We stayed at the house at Barry the whole week."

"Did Father Abbot stay with you?"

"Yes."

Then Nanni inquired about the evening before the murder. "Going back to the Holy Cross Monastery, on Saturday, March 24, do you remember seeing Mykhalyo at the monastery?"

"I saw him twice. It was when they came from the Youth Fair in the early afternoon. It was around one or two o'clock. And I saw him again before they went grocery shopping, and again when he came back, so actually three times."

"During those three times that you saw him, did he ever complain to you about any sores that he had on his hand, any cuts?"

"No."

"The last time you saw him on Saturday, March 24, did he seem angry about anything?"

"No. He seemed fine."

"Did he seem depressed?"

"No."

Next, the detective wanted to know how the monk candidates got along with Sister Michelle. Terenta and Kofel had known her since the first day they arrived at Holy Cross, August 1, 1996.

"During those four and a half years, has Sister Michelle ever treated anyone from Ukraine badly?" Nanni asked.

"No."

"Did she ever call anyone derogatory names?"

"No."

"Or make fun of your accent?"

"No."

"Call anyone stupid?"

"No."

"Did you ever witness her specifically pick on Mykhaylo, in reference to the name-calling that we just talked about?"

"No."

"Did Mykhalyo ever confide in you that she would call him names and make him feel inadequate?"

"No."

Next Nanni inquired about one of the murder weapons. Had Petro seen Kofel with a steak knife at the candidates' house the night of March 24?

"I never saw him with a knife," the apprentice monk replied. "But what I noticed was that when we moved into [the Barry house] we bought a set of knives, so they're all the same, with the black handle."

It was a set of three or four, but Petro could not recall exactly how many.

"Did you take any knives?" Gail Levine asked.

"No."

"Did you notice whether any knives were missing?"

"No, I didn't notice."

Next, the prosecutor wanted to know about sexual abuse at Holy Cross. "Did Mykhaylo ever tell you that his father sexually abused him in Ukraine?"

"No."

"Did Mykhaylo ever tell you that anyone at the monastery sexually abused him?"

"No."

"Do you know whether anyone sexually abused him?"

"No."

The prosecutor wanted to be absolutely certain that Terenta knew what she meant by sexual abuse, so she asked him, "Do you understand the term that I'm using, *sexual abuse*? I'm not just talking about intercourse. I'm talking about good touching and bad touching, specifically about bad touching. Did he ever tell you that someone was touching him inappropriately?"

"No."

"Did he ever complain about the abbot?"

"No."

"Did he ever tell you the abbot wanted to have sex with him?"

"No."

"Did the abbot ever touch you in an inappropriate way?"

"No, never."

"Has the abbot ever touched you sexually?"

"No."

"Has the abbot ever hugged you in an inappropriate way?"

"No."

"What about Father Damian?" Detective Nanni asked.

"No."

"Did Mykhaylo ever tell you any of those things about Father Damian inappropriately touching him?" Levine asked.

"No."

"Did you have any reason to know, or do you know, of any reason why Mykhalyo would kill Sister Michelle?"

"I don't have any reason. It's unbelievable to me that he did it."

Finally, the questioning turned to Kofel's mental state and his demeanor the day of the murder. "Did he say anything to you to make you think that something was wrong with his mind?" Levine asked Terenta.

"No."

"Did he answer you appropriately?"

"Yes."

"Did he appear coherent? Do you know what that word means?"

Terenta shook his head, indicating that he did not.

"Did he appear like he was following along with what was going on?"

"If he could follow along? Yeah, I think so. Like, what do you mean? What would be an example?"

"Like he didn't know where he was or he didn't know what day it was."

"If he was oriented?" Terenta asked.

"Yes," Levine replied.

"Yes, he was."

"Have you dealt with patients?" the prosecutor asked Terenta, a second-year nursing student.

"Yes."

"Have you seen patients who were not oriented?"

"Yes. In fact yesterday I went to patients who have Alzheimer's, so I saw lots of that."

"Did Mykhaylo, at any time on Sunday that you saw him prior to finding Sister Michelle, did he appear disoriented in any way?"

"No."

"Did you see him later that day before he was questioned by the police?"

"Yes."

"How was he acting?"

"He was studying at his desk. He was writing flash cards, you know, to study."

"Is there anything else that you want to tell us about Mykhaylo?" Levine asked.

"All I can say is that, to me he appeared always a little selfish and like, I couldn't really trust him. I had this sense that I couldn't trust him for some reason. That's all."

The prosecutor pressed him. "What does that mean?"

"Like, he was always kind of strange. Like, I mean, if I told him something that I wouldn't want anybody to know, I wouldn't trust him, because he would say it to other people."

There was one more thing Terenta wanted investigators to know: Kofel's mother and father were pressuring him to leave Holy Cross. Mykhaylo had gone back home the year before to renew his visa. Yuri and Maria did not want him to leave Ukraine.

He implored them to permit him to return to Miami so that he could finish his education, Terenta said. When he returned to Holy Cross, one of the priests—Terenta didn't recall if it was Wendt or Gibault—asked Kofel what he would have done if his parents insisted he stay.

"He said, 'Over my dead body,'" Terenta recalled. "That there was no way he would go home. It would be over his dead body."

The entire session lasted forty-seven minutes. When it was over, the apprentice monk and his attorney left the building.

While Petro Terenta was answering questions, Sister Michelle's body was on its way to Ohio. It had been re-leased from the medical examiner's office and driven to Miami International Airport, where it was put on a com-mercial flight to Cleveland's Hopkins International Airport. It was met there by a hearse, which took the slain sister's body forty miles to Short's Funeral Home in Ravenna.

Earlier that week the local daily, the *Akron Beacon Journal,* carried news of the murder. Retired high school English teacher Christine Nines told the paper that she re-membered her former student: "She was just a very nice girl. I remember her being quiet and very intelligent." The paper also reported that Lewis had been the valedictorian of her graduating class in 1979 and had been chosen "most intellectual."

On Friday evening, mourners paid their respects to the Lewis family at the funeral home. Gary Salmon, Michelle's ex-husband, sent flowers. There was no view-ing of the body; it had been battered beyond recognition so the casket remained closed.

At 10 A.M. on Saturday, mourners gathered at Ravenna's Immaculate Conception Roman Catholic Church for a funeral mass. Afterward, Michelle Lewis was laid to rest at St. Mary's Cemetery under gray skies. A Catholic priest comforted the mourners by declaring that she "had remained true to her vow of chastity even in the face of death." Sister Michelle, the priest said, "had died in the arms of God."

14

"He was pale and thin. He looked like a prisoner of war"

—Assistant Public Defender Edith Georgi

It's a short walk from the five-story building that houses the offices of the Miami-Dade public defender to the Miami-Dade county jail. The two buildings sit next to each other on the same block.

Edith Georgi had made the walk thousands of times since beginning her legal career in 1981. She took it again on March 27, this time to visit her newest client, Mykhaylo Kofel.

She was struck by Kofel's appearance—"He was pale and thin. He looked like a prisoner of war," she said. "He is scared, confused, and shell-shocked" but "faring as well as any child could, having been separated from his family, having no local support or friends, and immersed now in a foreign legal system."

Georgi feared that Kofel was suicidal, and she worried that his jailers would be unable to keep him alive.

She had good reason to be concerned. There had been too many prisoner suicides over the years in the chronically overcrowded facility. In one year alone, three prisoners managed to hang themselves. An eighteen-year-old prisoner in a "psych cell" hanged himself with a bedsheet even though guards were looking in on him every fifteen minutes. Earlier that same year another inmate managed to string himself up with a pair of socks only forty minutes after guards stopped his previous suicide attempt.

"In the early stages of incarceration, the client may suffer tremendous pain, and even be suicidal," Georgi warned in an article she wrote for *Champion* magazine, the official journal of the National Association of Criminal Defense Lawyers. Although the article was entitled "Defending the Accused Child Killer," it laid out a road map for defending those accused of other heinous crimes as well, such as the brutal murder of a nun.

It could be summed up this way: Act quickly—there may be only "a brief window of opportunity in the early stages of a case, a window which will be closed as the client begins to heal and face the future." Listen closely "for clues which can lead to mitigation; these will be found in the worst experiences of his childhood, but it may take weeks or months of intensive interaction to unpeel the layers." Consider the insanity defense—"the client's actions may be part of a delusionary, or other psychotic, episode, even when there is no history of mental illness." What's more, Georgi wrote, "there may be elements of a post traumatic stress disorder (PTSD) defense as well."

Finally, Georgi wrote that defense attorneys should be prepared to explain to jurors "how physical violence to an individual at an early age affects the soul and integrity of the person, and leads to the warped development or even death of self-esteem."

The article, written in 1998, set the stage for Georgi's defense of Mykhaylo Kofel.

•   •   •

From start to finish, *State of Florida v. Kofel* would be presided over by Circuit Judge Manuel "Manny" Crespo, a gregarious and highly respected jurist who, at five-foot-six and 415 pounds, had been a larger-than-life presence in the Miami-Dade legal community for years. He began practicing law as a solo practitioner in Miami in 1979, handling personal injury and criminal cases. In 1991 his son, Manny Jr., graduated from law school and the once solo practice became Crespo and Crespo. Five years later, the elder Crespo became the Honorable Manuel Crespo when the voters of Miami-Dade County elected him to the circuit court bench.

He was born in Havana, Cuba, in 1945, the son of a medical doctor. When he was five, his physician father decided to open a medical practice in Florida. The family moved to Miami, to the area now known as Little Havana. A Roman Catholic, Crespo attended parochial schools, graduating from Archbishop Curley Senior High School in 1967. He went on to earn a degree in history from Florida Atlantic University, marry his childhood sweetheart, work for a moving company, and study law at Memphis State University in Tennessee.

He was a man of many interests, active in his church and active politically as a Democrat, a rarity among South Florida's Cuban-Americans. He liked rock and roll and big band music—especially Glenn Miller and Harry James, the music GIs listened to during WWII. He was also a history buff, an expert on the Second World War. He even dedicated an entire room in his house to mementos and books about WWII. His chambers at the courthouse and the walls behind the judge's bench in his courtroom held dozens of photographs of WWII ships and planes. A favorite memento, a statue of the marines raising the American flag on Iwo Jima, occupied an honored place directly in front of him when he was on the bench.

Over the years, Judge Crespo made frequent pilgrimages

to World War II battle sites, visiting the beaches of Normandy nine times, as well as Pearl Harbor, Okinawa, and Iwo Jima. But by 2001, the fifty-five-year-old was not in good health. He was suffering from diabetes, arthritis, and a severe case of chronic psoriasis. Nevertheless, his medical problems never kept him from performing his judicial duties. "He loved the law," his son, Manny Jr., said.

Crespo had handled high-profile death penalty cases before. In 1998, he presided over the trial of Labrant Deshawn Dennis, who was convicted of using a rifle butt to brutally murder University of Miami football player Marlin Barnes and Timwanika Lumpkins, Dennis's ex-girlfriend and the mother of his daughter.

The jury voted the death penalty and Judge Crespo followed their wishes. It wasn't an easy thing for him to do. He had his doubts about the effectiveness of the death penalty as a deterrent, but he had taken an oath to follow the laws of the state of Florida. With the defendant standing before him, Crespo declared, "Labrant Deshawn Dennis had a cold, calculated, and premeditated plan to kill both victims without any pretense of moral or legal justification. By his actions, the defendant has forfeited his right to live."

Judge Crespo took the bench promptly at 9 A.M. on April 5. Mykhaylo Kofel, wearing a prison-issued jumpsuit and shackles, was escorted into the courtroom by a beefy department of corrections officer. Edith Georgi was already there. The state was represented by assistant state attorneys Gail Levine and Penny Brill. James McGuirk, the attorney for Holy Cross, was also in the courtroom. Crespo ordered Kofel's shackles removed.

He had been indicted by the grand jury two days before. The indictment, which Judge Crespo had before him, read:

IN THE NAME AND BY THE AUTHORITY
OF THE STATE OF FLORIDA:

The Grand Jurors of the State of Florida, duly called, impaneled and sworn to inquire and true presentment make in and for the body of the County of Miami-Dade, upon their oaths, present that on or about the 25th day of March, 2001, within the County of Miami-Dade, State of Florida, MYKHAYLO KOFEL did unlawfully and feloniously kill a human being, to wit: SISTER MICHELLE LEWIS, from a premeditated design to effect the death of the person killed or any human being and/or while engaged in the perpetration of, or in an attempt to perpetrate any burglary, by stabbing the said SISTER MICHELLE LEWIS with a weapon, to wit: A knife and/or a metal rod, in violation of s. 782.04(1) and s.775.087, Florida Statutes, to the evil example of all others in like cases offending and against the peace and dignity of the State of Florida.

COUNT II

The Grand Jurors of the State of Florida, duly called, impaneled and sworn to inquire and true presentment make in and for the body of the County of Miami-Dade, upon their oaths, present that on or about the 25th day of March, 2001, within the County of Miami-Dade, State of Florida, MYKHAYLO KOFEL did unlawfully enter or remain in a structure, to wit: A dwelling, located at 6950 Southwest 123 Avenue, Miami-Dade County, Florida, the property of SISTER MICHELLE LEWIS and/or RT. REV. ABBOT GREGORY WENDT and/or PRIEST-MONK J. A. GIBAULT and/or HOLY CROSS MONASTERY AND ACADEMY, without the consent, of SISTER MICHELLE LEWIS and/or RT. REV. ABBOT GREGORY WENDT and/or PRIEST-MONK J. A.

GIBAULT and/or HOLY CROSS MONASTERY AND ACADEMY, as owner or custodian, the same being occupied by SISTER MICHELLE LEWIS; the defendant having an intent to commit an offense therein, to wit: Attempted Murder and/or Aggravated Battery, and in the course of committing said burglary, the defendant made an assault or battery upon SISTER MICHELLE LEWIS, by stabbing the said SISTER MICHELLE LEWIS, and during the commission of said burglary the defendant carried, displayed, used, threatened, or attempted to use a weapon, to wit: A knife and/or a metal rod, in violation of s. 810.02(2) (a) and s. 775.087, Florida Statutes, to the evil example of all others in like cases offending and against the peace and dignity of the State of Florida.

The proceeding began with a brief discussion about providing Kofel with a translator, prompting the judge to promise that "this court will do whatever it takes to secure an adequate interpreter for Mr. Kofel." Georgi thanked the judge.

"With that out of the way let's now proceed with the arraignment," the judge commanded. From his perch on the bench, he then turned toward Kofel, who stood before him.

"Mr. Kofel, through your counsel, we will inform you that you have been indicted in this matter in the charge of murder in the first degree, count one, and burglary with an assault or battery while armed in count two. Are you entering a plea at this time?"

"Enter a plea of not guilty," Georgi said.

With the arraignment over, the judge ordered the corrections officer to put Kofel's shackles back on, and he directed the defendant to take a seat at the defense table. There were three defense motions for him to consider. One of them was a "Motion for Material Witness Bond and or Alternative Assurances of Appearance."

It concerned the four Ukrainian monk candidates, Petro Terenta, Vasyl Kopych, Sasha Korsak, and Yosyp Lembak. Georgi believed they could provide exculpatory or mitigating evidence, but, she said, her efforts to interview them were being blocked at every turn by officials at Holy Cross. What's more, she feared that Wendt would order them to return to Ukraine, which would put the monk candidates beyond the reach of the court.

Before ruling on the motion, Judge Crespo asked Georgi to "enlighten the Court further on this matter."

She began by explaining that she had attempted to contact the monk candidates through the school but was unable to reach them. "It is a very strange situation," she said. "Normally, if there is a witness in the community, we can contact them through a normal address and normal procedure. But here, we must go through the school personnel. We have been denied access through the school."

The judge wanted to hear from the prosecutor. Gail Levine agreed with Georgi.

"You have had a chance to review these four names here?" Judge Crespo asked.

"I have them also on my witness list."

"What is the State's position as to Ms. Georgi's request to make these witnesses available? Does the State have any objection or position as to that now?"

"The problem really is, and in some ways I understand Ms. Georgi's concern," Levine said. "I do have a concern that these individuals who are housed at the monastery, on a visa through the monastery, could be sent back to the Ukraine at any time. I don't necessarily have any current information that I can report to the court that I know this to be true. I know that one individual has been already sent back prior to this homicide. And I have no access to him."

"He is not one of the four?"

"He is not. He is someone we would want to speak to. And the State Department has told me it is going to be difficult because of the Soviet policies that remain in place, like it or not. The only analogy I can give you is if these people were sent back to Cuba. That is the only analogy that I have."

"I have been through that," the judge remarked.

"I have similar concerns with keeping them here. Not for the same reason that Ms. Georgi does, but for trial purposes," Levine said.

Next, the judge heard from Holy Cross attorney James McGuirk. "I will tell you that their passports are not in their own custody. They are in Father Wendt's custody."

Levine jumped to her feet. "And that is a concern," she exclaimed. "I have actually spoken with Ms. Georgi about that, so Ms. Georgi was aware of that, I am aware of that. When we interviewed them, they told us they had no access to their passports. They are locked in an office by the Father, which raises my concern, which I understand raises Ms. Georgi's concern."

Judge Crespo agreed. He called the possibility that the monk candidates could return to their homeland "a very real issue." As a Catholic himself and a product of parochial schools, he was well aware that the student monks answered to a higher authority.

"They have taken the vows that I know they honor, and one of them is obedience. And if they are ordered to leave the United States and go back to Ukraine, under penalty of a higher authority . . . they must abide," the judge said.

To prevent that from happening, he ordered McGuirk, as counsel for the monastery, to seize their passports and hold them until he was ordered to do otherwise by the court.

Judge Crespo issued two more rulings: He ordered Holy Cross to allow defense investigators access to Kofel's bedroom, and he ordered lawmen to preserve all physical evidence in their custody, including DNA evidence, so that the defense could conduct its own independent tests. He also set a date for the trial. It would begin on July 21.

Swift justice is a cornerstone of American jurisprudence; every defendant is entitled to a speedy trial, but that would not happen in *State v. Kofel*. Instead, the case would drag on for four years, and for that, prosecutors, lawmen, and Kofel's attorneys would point the blame at the Holy Cross priests and their attorneys.

Meanwhile, Edith Georgi arranged for a priest whose church had participated in recruiting boys for Holy Cross to come to Miami from Ukraine to provide spiritual counseling to Kofel. At the end of April the priest, Father Taras, visited Kofel at the county jail, where he prayed with the young man. He was also concerned about the well-being of the other monk candidates and spoke briefly with the three of them at the state attorney's office.

15

"I trust Father Damian and Father Abbot. They've never given me any reason not to trust them."

—Parent of Holy Cross Academy student

Homicide detectives do not look kindly on witnesses who don't cooperate. They arouse suspicions; they give investigators reason to believe that something sinister is being hidden. As far as the lawmen were concerned, that's what Father Abbot Gregory Wendt and Father Damian Gibault were doing—being uncooperative—and that made detectives suspicious.

"They were stonewalling us," said John King. He said he felt that way from his first encounter with the priests the day of the murder, when Wendt didn't even get out of the car to talk to him.

Art Nanni felt that way, too. At one point he and Wendt got into a verbal altercation. "I called him a fucking son-of-a-bitch," the lawman recalled. "In most cases people who were close to a victim can't wait to talk to us, but these priests were aloof; they seemed more concerned about a possible civil suit or a scandal than about what happened to Sister Michelle."

And that was even before Holy Cross's insurance car-

Holy Cross Academy was founded by Father Gregory Wendt.
Initially headquartered in a three-bedroom single-story house,
by 1994 construction had begun on this much more
impressive building in Kendall.

(Photo courtesy Miami-Dade Police Department)

AT RIGHT:
Michelle Lewis and her brother, Tim, were brought up in a devoutly Catholic family in Akron, Ohio.
(Photo courtesy Beverly Lewis)

BELOW:
Michelle and her father, Don, on the day of her wedding to Gary Salmon.
(Photo courtesy Beverly Lewis)

Sister Michelle Lewis
(Photo courtesy Fox-Mar Photography)

Father Abbot Gregory Wendt
(Photo courtesy Fox-Mar Photography)

Mykhaylo Kofel in a photo taken the day of the murder. Two fresh scratches can be seen on the left side of his face.
(Photo courtesy Miami-Dade Police Department)

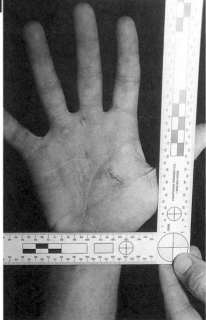

Kofel said that these suspicious cuts on his hand were caused when he broke a drinking glass he was washing.
(Photo courtesy Miami-Dade Police Department)

The convent at Holy Cross
(Photo courtesy Miami Dade Police Department)

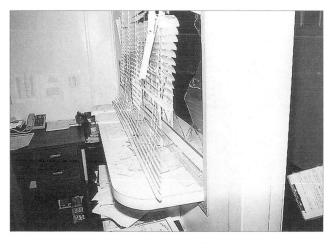

Police were shocked to discover that Sister Michelle's office
in the school building was ransacked as well.
(Photo courtesy Miami-Dade Police Department)

ABOVE:
Sister Michelle's bedroom was a bloody mess.
(Photo courtesy Miami-Dade Police Department)

AT LEFT:
Kofel stabbed Sister Michelle ninety-two times with this knife.
(Photo courtesy Miami-Dade Police Department)

BELOW:
Lead Detective Art Nanni persuaded Kofel to confess.
(Photo courtesy author)

Monk trainee Vasyl Kopych (L) with Father Damian (R)
(Photo courtesy author)

The prosecutors: (L-R) Penny Brill, Gail Levine, and Priscilla Prado
(Photo courtesy author)

ABOVE:
Miami-Dade Homicide detective Larry Belyeu in the Ukraine
(Photo courtesy Miami-Dade State Attorney)

AT RIGHT:
Mykhaylo Kofel's mother, Maria, makes a point.
(Photo courtesy Miami-Dade State Attorney)

rier assembled a team of prominent criminal defense lawyers and a public relations agency. And it was before Mykhalyo Kofel's explosive allegations of sexual abuse made headlines in South Florida.

When the MDPD's top cop, police director Carlos Alvarez, announced Kofel's arrest, he revealed nothing about the young monk's allegations of sexual abuse. But on Friday, April 6, the official day of mourning for Sister Michelle at Holy Cross, the *Sun-Sentinel* broke the story. The paper reported that police were looking into allegations of sexual abuse at Holy Cross.

The paper did not reveal who Kofel's alleged abusers were, but the priests would have known as soon as monk candidates Lembak, Korsak, and Kopych returned from their interviews with detectives the week before. If they didn't tell the priests, then Petro Terenta did, after he was questioned at the Homicide Bureau on March 29. "I informed him of these claims that Misha made, and how terrible it is, and how could he even come up with such a thing," Petro recalled.

The rest of Miami would find out in two days, but on this sunny Friday morning, one thousand people—students, parents, and teachers—had come to the Holy Cross campus for an outdoor memorial service for Sister Michelle. Wendt led the traditional Byzantine liturgy for the dead while Father Damian assisted, and the four Ukrainian monk candidates chanted.

"We have come to pray together in this memorial liturgy for the repose of Sister Michelle," the abbot told the gathered mourners. "Many of us are asking 'Why did she have to die in this terrible way?' God never abandoned Sister Michelle. Rather, he was with her when she died." The murder, the abbot said, was inexplicable, but he reminded the mourners that "God gave humans free will to do what is good or what is evil."

He said he had spoken to Beverly Lewis, the slain

sister's mother. She told him that her daughter phoned a week before she died and said that she was "very happy at Holy Cross." Mrs. Lewis, the abbot told the mourners, "asked me to pray for the young man who committed this deed. I, in turn, ask you to pray for him so that he might turn back to God and beg his forgiveness."

He spoke about Sister Michelle's duties at Holy Cross, recalling that she tutored a student in math all summer. She did not like doing it, he said, but she did it anyway. She loved teaching calculus and had an "abiding love for the monastic way of life."

For the first time since the murder, reporters were permitted onto the campus. Attorney Joseph Blonsky decried the allegations of sexual abuse, calling them "absolutely untrue" and "unbelievable." Referring to the murder of Sister Michelle and the arrest of Mykhaylo Kofel, he said Holy Cross "had already suffered two incredible blows. Now comes this third one, out of the blue, supposedly from the young man involved."

Blonsky didn't know it then, but in just two days Holy Cross would receive blow number four.

Initially, most Holy Cross parents rallied behind the priests. "No such thing could ever have occurred or will ever occur in a place like this," said Bernard Ortega, whose daughter was a student at the academy.

"I believe one hundred percent they are good people and people of God. They have always been here to serve our community and our kids," said his wife, Marta.

"We have confidence in the school," said Marta Pappas, whose son and daughter attended the school. "I trust Father Damian and Father Abbot. They've never given me any reason not to trust them."

Others had their doubts, and they began looking to enroll their children elsewhere, influenced in part by the revelations of sexual misconduct that had been rocking the Church for years as well as the emerging scandal at Holy Cross.

The Catholic Church was under siege, hammered by a steady drumbeat of revelations detailing sexual abuse, cover-ups, and defrockings that began in the 1990s. In Boston, defrocked priest John J. Geoghan was charged with molesting more than seventy children over more than four decades as a Catholic priest. The church paid millions to settle claims against Geoghan. The scandal even brought down a cardinal, Boston Archbishop Cardinal F. Bernard Law, who, it was alleged, knew about Geoghan's pedophilia for years but did nothing about it. He resigned as archbishop in 2002.

In 1998, the head of the Diocese of Palm Beach County, Bishop Joseph Symons, resigned in disgrace after admitting that he had sexually abused five boys earlier in his career. Church officials did not learn about the abuse until a man in his fifties came forward and revealed that he had been molested by Symons when he was thirteen. The abuse, the man said, had gone on for three years. Symons wasn't the only high-ranking clergyman forced to leave the Church because of sexual misconduct in the 1990s. Two other bishops—one in Santa Fe, New Mexico, and the other in Dallas, Texas, were forced out, too.

Closer to Holy Cross, a priest in the Archdiocese of Miami, Father Joseph Cinesi, was relieved of his pastoral duties after a man in his thirties alleged to police that he had been abused by the clergyman dozens of times between the ages of twelve and fifteen. The man kept the abuse secret for years, he said, because he was ashamed and embarrassed. He decided to come forward on the advice of his therapist. The scandal grew when others came forward, too, and the archdiocese made financial settlements with the priest's accusers.

A study of sexual misconduct by John Jay College of

Criminal Justice in New York City found eleven thousand allegations of sexual abuse by priests over a fifty-two-year period. According to the study, 78 percent of those abused were between the ages of eleven and sixteen, 16 percent were eight to ten years old, and nearly 6 percent were seven or younger.

The scandals were about more than sex abuse, said Tom Roberts, editor of the *National Catholic Reporter*. They were "about abuse of power and trust, and a breach of faith with the people."

Sunday, April 8, was another picture-perfect day in South Florida: blue skies, temperature in the eighties during the day dropping to the seventies at night. A drought had been plaguing the region for months, and the *Miami Herald* carried the story on its front page that morning, along with another story about a crisis in U.S.-China relations; an American military plane and a Chinese jet fighter had collided over the South China Sea. The U.S. plane was forced to land at a Chinese airbase, where the crew of twenty-one was being held while the two countries shook their fists at each other.

Closer to home, the *Herald* revealed that Mykhaylo Kofel had named the Holy Cross priests as his abusers. "Mykhalyo Kofel told homicide detectives after he was arrested that Father Abbot Gregory Wendt and Father Damian Gibault sexually abused him during a period of years at Holy Cross Academy," the paper reported.

Through their lawyers, the holy men denied the accusations. "He is emphatic that this is not true," declared Wendt's attorney, Mel Black. "He did not sexually abuse [Kofel]. We are confident that at the end of the investigation, there will be no basis for these allegations." Gibault's attorney called Kofel's accusations bizarre. "They are absolutely unfounded," said Richard Hersch.

According to the *Herald*, detectives questioned Holy Cross maintenance man Daniel Puerto, who recalled seeing one of the monk candidates inside the convent a couple of months before the murder. It was at a time when neither Sister Marie nor Sister Michelle were there. Puerto could not identify which of the candidates because he was too far away, looking into the house through a sliding glass door. "He was walking across from the kitchen to the bedroom at a fast speed, you know, like he didn't want to be seen," Puerto remembered. He thought it looked like another trainee besides Kofel.

Puerto was under subpoena and appeared at the state attorney's office on the morning of April 4 along with an attorney. Homicide detective John King took his statement in a second-floor conference room. A stenographer recorded what he said.

Puerto told King he had been working at Holy Cross for six years. He recalled talking with Kofel at 3:30 P.M. on Friday, March 23, at the Barry House. Puerto was there refurbishing one of the bathrooms. Kofel had finished classes and was waiting for Wendt and Petro Terenta to arrive at the house before heading back to the Holy Cross campus for the weekend.

"Did you communicate at all with Mykhaylo at that time?" King asked.

"Yes."

"And if you would, just tell me what type of communications you had with him, how he approached you?"

"He was going to the nearest bathroom there, that is his bathroom, and I remembered I had a soda in the fridge. I asked him to put it out, and he brung it to me."

"You don't know if he handed it to you with his right or left hand?"

"Right hand."

"When he handed it to you, did you notice anything unusual about his hand?"

"Nothing."

"See any cuts on them at all?"

"No."

"Bandages on his hands at all?"

"No."

"Complaining of any injuries to his hands?"

"No."

"Did you see blood on his clothing?"

"No."

"How long did you stay there on that Friday?"

"I got there at, I think I got there like at 7:30."

"What time did you leave?"

"I leave around 4:00. On that . . . last time I saw him was when he came in through the bathroom. Other than that, he went back out that way."

"On March 25, when Sister Michelle was found deceased, did you see him on campus?"

"Yes."

"Did you notice anything about his hands at that time?"

"They were cut. They were scratched."

"Notice anything about his face at that time?"

"Scratched."

"Was that the same condition that you saw him on Friday?"

"No."

Puerto told King that over the years he had spoken with Kofel about the young man's hopes and dreams for the future.

"Did you ever ask him about his desires or what his goals were as it pertained to being a monk?" King wanted to know.

"I didn't ask," the custodian replied. "I told him that soon he would be a priest, and he said that he didn't want to be a priest."

Before the interview ended at 11 A.M., King asked Puerto if he had "ever observed anything that would cause you to believe there was improper sexual activity going on between the staff and candidates or other students?"

The custodian replied, "No."

On Monday, April 9, three investigators from the MDPD's sex crimes bureau—Signori, Cabado, and Pomes—went to Holy Cross to interview Wendt and Gibault, but the priests weren't there. They happened to be elsewhere, their attorneys said. In the aftermath of the murder, the clerics had moved away from the Holy Cross campus and had been living at the Barry house, where they remained until seventeen-year-old Yosyp Lembak turned eighteen— the age at which he would no longer be considered a minor under Florida law.

"We will be talking with the state attorney's office to discuss providing information to prove these allegations as false," attorney Richard Hersch told the *Herald*. Prosecutor Gail Levine invited the two priests to meet with her voluntarily at the state attorney's office on Monday, April 16, but Wendt and Gibault didn't appear. Through their lawyers, the two priests announced they would not talk to investigators unless granted immunity. In a joint statement, Black and Hersch explained the priests' position: "If the state continues to believe that Father Abbot and Father Damian are under suspicion of wrongdoing, then it would be malpractice for an attorney to allow them to answer questions that might be misused against them."

Levine wasn't about to do that, and she would not subpoena the priests either because under Florida law that would have automatically granted them immunity. As far as investigators were concerned, the priests' demands for immunity were a deliberate tactic to stymie the investigation. "They were close associates and friends of Sister Michelle, yet they threw obstacles at us at every turn," Gail Levine observed. She wondered why, if there was no basis for the allegations, would they need immunity?

Her boss, Miami-Dade state attorney Katherine

Fernandez Rundle, promised to leave no stone unturned in the investigation. "This is a very complex case," she said. "We're investigating it thoroughly."

While the state couldn't subpeona the priests without immunizing them from prosecution, the defense could, and eventually the priests would have to appear to answer questions. But that was still a long way off. In the meantime, the defense assembled a team of forensic psychologists to evaluate Kofel's mental state. Even though Georgi had entered a plea of not guilty for Kofel, she was already laying the groundwork for an insanity defense.

The idea that criminally insane defendants should not be held responsible for their actions by reason of mental illness has been a part of Anglo-American law since the nineteenth century, ever since Daniel McNaughton, a woodcutter from Scotland, attempted to assassinate Great Britain's prime minister Robert Peel in 1843 because he believed the prime minister was conspiring against him.

McNaughton killed the prime minister's secretary, Edward Drummond, by mistake. He was tried, found not guilty by reason of insanity, and sent to a mental institution where he would spend the rest of his life.

Insanity is a legal term, not a medical condition. It can only be determined by a judge or a jury. Mental-health experts can diagnose mental disorders and advise the court as to their findings, but the final say comes from the law, not from medicine.

Even though Kofel had entered a plea of not guilty at his arraignment, with due notice prior to the case coming to trial, Georgi could notify the court and the prosecution that she was invoking the insanity defense. If successful, Kofel would most likely be committed to a mental hospital where he would receive treatment until cured. If and when that day came, he would be freed.

In order for that to happen, Georgi would have to prove that, at the time of the murder, Kofel suffered from a mental infirmity, disease, or defect, and that because of this condition, he either did not know what he was doing or was unaware of the consequences, or he did not know that what he was doing was wrong. It would be a difficult mountain to climb, especially if the question of Kofel's sanity ever went to a jury. For one thing, even though he might have been out of his mind the night of the murder, Kofel did not look like a crazed killer. What's more, he had no history of mental illness that would explain the unspeakably savage attack on Sister Michelle. He had not been prescribed psychotropic medications, and there was virtually no history of psychosis or mood disorder.

At the public defender's request, forensic psychologist Dr. John Quintana paid his first visit to Kofel on April 9. The psychologist would meet with him over the next four days, evaluating him clinically, observing his behavior, his body language, and his reactions. The New Jersey psychologist would also take a medical and psychological history and administer a battery of standardized psychological tests designed to reveal psychological disorders as well as his mental state before, during, and after the murder of Sister Michelle.

When he was done, Dr. Quintana sent a report to Georgi. In it he wrote: "Mr. Kofel appears alert, oriented and coherent . . . calm, friendly and cooperative. He can make eye contact and is articulate with goal-directed thoughts. He has a slight accent but has a good command of English. He appears capable of using good judgment. He appears to have fair concentration and can recall at least six digits forward."

But he seemed depressed, the psychologist said. Kofel admitted to having had suicidal thoughts, but insisted he was not having them any longer. He explained that one month prior to the murder of Sister Michelle, he felt depressed "and that the actions of Father Abbot and Father Damian caused him mental and physical pain, anger and led him to drink alcohol and take drugs." It was then, Kofel said, that he wanted to commit suicide. He cut himself on the left side of his chest with a knife, the one that he used to murder Sister Michelle. It was not the first time that he attempted to hurt himself; on at least seven other occasions Kofel said he had deliberately cut himself, hoping that feeling physical pain would somehow ease his mental suffering.

Quintana administered ten objective tests, among them the highly regarded MMPI-2, the Minnesota Multiphasic Personality Inventory, the most widely used test of adult psychopathology. The original, the MMPI, was developed in the 1940s at the University of Minnesota. It was designed to help identify personal, social, and behavioral problems in psychiatric patients and to speed diagnosis and psychiatric treatment. The MMPI was redesigned in the 1980s. The current version, the MMPI-2, is for adults eighteen and over. Released in 1989, it consists of more than five hundred true/false items. There are no right or wrong answers. The psychologist evaluates the subject's personal characteristics by comparing the responses to those given by various groups of personality types.

By analyzing Kofel's patterns of responses, Dr. Quintana was able to reach conclusions about Kofel's mental state. He painted a picture of a depressed, anxious, and insecure young man suffering from low self-esteem; someone who is shy and inhibited in social situations, "emotionally alienated from others," and who sees the world as "a threatening place," someone who "feels he's getting a raw deal in life," is "passive and dependent in interpersonal relationships," and allows others to take advantage of him.

"Individuals with this passive and withdrawn lifestyle are unable to assert themselves appropriately and are frequently taken advantage of by others," Dr. Quintana said.

In May, a forensic neuropsychologist, Dr. Leonard F. Koziol, from Arlington Heights, Illinois, was called in to evaluate Kofel as to his competence to stand trial—the doctor found him competent—as well as his sanity at the time of the murder. In his December 3, 2001, report, Dr. Koziol wrote: "This individual's cognitive profile is unlike what is observed within the general population of his age-matched peers. His attentional system adjusts to new information very slowly, and his thinking tends to be perseverative   once he has an idea about something or someone, he does not easily change it and he is likely to ruminate by thinking about the same thing over and over again. These aspects of his functioning are important because they relate to his level of impulse control."

Even though Kofel is "oriented, alert, cooperative and can seem knowledgeable about social standards in routine conversation, logic does not guide his behavior." Kofel's thinking, Dr. Koziol said, "tends to be rigid and obsessional," not by choice "but by nature of his cognitive (frontal system) make-up."

Regarding the night of the murder, Dr. Koziol explained: "This murder was brutal according to the autopsy, numerous hittings and stab wounds. This I can attempt to explain on the basis of his apparent type of loss of control. His poor decision-making was his drunken decision to hurt the nun. The first hit or stab wounds were initiated in the heat of anger, while all the other wounds were behavioral perseverations. His pattern of functioning reflects frontal system involvement in which thought fails to guide action."

At trial, Dr. Koziol said, he would argue that Kofel was unable to control his obsessive thinking, "He was similarly unable to control his horrific behavior, particularly under the influence of alcohol. He had a bad idea, he lost control with the booze, and the rest was uncontrollable passion."

In his report, he wrote: "It is likely that this individual was quite preoccupied with his circumstances, with his ruminating about his situation over and over again. He indicated he had been drinking alcohol the evening of the offense, and that he was thinking about his past and about wanting to hurt the victim. In other words, he was experiencing obsessive preoccupations out of his control. Given the known disinhibitory effects of alcohol, his controls were further affected. He soon lost control, and logical, rational thinking was no longer able to guide his behavior. Therefore, his behaviors can be understood as the effects of alcohol impacting upon already compromised frontal systems. A certain proportion of individuals with this type of profile exhibit abnormalities on neuroimaging studies such as PET and MRI scans. These would be useful in providing supplementary evidence for further understanding his condition."

It was an opening for the insanity defense. Kofel, Dr. Koziol said, was obessive and his obsessiveness was beyond his control. He raised the possibility that his mental problems had been caused by damage to the frontal lobe, the portion of the brain that controls reasoning, planning, emotions, and problem-solving. Koziol recommended further neuroimaging studies such as PET and MRI scans. At the time of his evaluation, Dr. Koziol may not have known that Kofel had suffered serious head trauma on more than one occasion, the result of repeated blows to his head.

But was Kofel telling the truth about having been sexually abused by the priests at Holy Cross? To find out, Georgi arranged for Kofel to take a lie detector test.

On April 18, polygrapher Warren D. Holmes administered the test. Prior to beginning the actual examination, Holmes elicited some background information from Kofel in what the polygrapher called a "pretest" interview.

According to Holmes, Kofel said that Wendt "initiated the sexual activity by fondling his penis outside his clothing," on at least four separate occasions. He also said that "Gibault engaged in sexual activity with him on at least fifteen separate occasions." On at least four separate occasions Gibault masturbated on his stomach, and "inserted his penis in his (Kofel's) rectum on at least four separate occasions."

Kofel said these acts made him angry and despondent to the point where he was driven to attempt suicide in the weeks prior to the murder of Sister Michelle.

With the pretest over, Holmes attached Kofel to the polygraph and asked him the following four "pertinent" questions:

Q. *On at least four separate occasions, did Abbot Gregory Wendt fondle your penis from outside your clothing?*

A. *Yes.*

Q. *On at least three separate occasions, did Father Gibault insert his penis in your rectum?*

A. *Yes.*

Q. *On at least four separate occasions did Father Gibault masturbate on your stomach?*

A. *Yes.*

Q. *Are you now lying about the sexual acts committed by either Abbot Wendt or Father Gibault?*

A. *No.*

Less than one week later, Edith Georgi received Holmes's written analysis:

"An analysis of the polygraph charts from the polygraph examination administered to Mr. Kofel revealed, in the opinion of this examiner, no physiological reactions indicative of deception at the points on the polygraph charts where the pertinent test questions were asked. It is therefore the opinion of this examiner that Mr. Kofel did not lie in his verbal responses to the pertinent questions."

On April 26, the results of the polygraph made headlines in South Florida. The article in the *Sun-Sentinel* read:

LIE TEST BACKS ABUSE CLAIMS

The confessed murderer of a nun at Holy Cross Academy has passed a lie-detector test in which he was questioned about being "subjected to sexual acts" by the school's two top clerics, according to a copy of the report obtained by the *Sun-Sentinel*.

The paper also revealed that Kofel, in his confession to police, had accused his own father of sexually molesting him about five times. Kofel, the paper said, "told detectives he was molested by Abbot Gregory F. G. Wendt, Holy Cross's headmaster, and by the Reverend Damian J. A. Gibault, the school's supervising principal, during his almost five years at the academy."

Through their attorneys, the paper said, the priests denied the allegations. The lawyers wasted no time firing back. Attorney and Holy Cross board member Joseph Blonsky put out a prepared statement.

"We are shocked to read in a newspaper that Mykhaylo Kofel accused his own father of sexually abusing him. The accusation was made in the same murder confession in which he also accused two highly respected local priests of the same offense."

Gibault's attorney fired off a letter to Georgi. In it Richard Hersch said that he found the report that Kofel had passed a polygraph "as unbelievable as the sexual abuse allegations." He demanded that Georgi turn over the videotape of the session as well as the charts from the test to an independent expert for evaluation.

Edith Georgi fired back, demanding that Wendt and Gibault take lie detector tests. Their lawyers, the public defender said, should provide her with the results. She labeled remarks by Blonsky and Hersch as "intimidation designed to prevent the real truth from coming out."

Even Wragg and Casas, the public relations firm hired by Church Mutual, put out a statement declaring that they were "shocked that the public defender would try to test the truthfulness of the defendant's allegations against the priests while knowing and omitting for a month the fact that this obviously troubled defendant also accused his own father in the same statement. . . . The public conscience should be appalled by this manipulation of facts."

But Georgi was undeterred. "By releasing the polygraph, we may in fact encourage witnesses who have corroborating evidence to come forward," she said. What's more, she said, release of the results could provide mitigation for her client if and when the case came to trial.

Whatever her reasons, the polygraph results could only help Kofel. Only time would tell what effect they would have on Wendt and Gibault and on Holy Cross Academy. As for the monastic program, Wendt announced it was being put on hold.

In a press release issued through Wragg and Casas—his first since the murder—Wendt said: "One of the many casualties of this tragic murder is that our training program is seriously disrupted because of the murder and, even more, because of the completely false allegations that the confessed killer has made against Father Damian Gibault and myself.

"It is extremely difficult to maintain our proper schedule of worship and religious training under these circumstances, and we would not even consider introducing new monastic candidates into this unusual environment.

"For now, the four young men who are already here will continue their prayers and education in the Monastery to the best extent possible. Of course, Holy Cross will continue to provide a classical education in the monastic tradition of Catholic education to hundreds of local students."

Meanwhile, lawmen continued to investigate the two priests, and what they were turning up raised eyebrows.

16

"Terenta has not been honest with us."

—Assistant State Attorney Gail Levine

In the weeks after Sister Michelle's murder, no less than four agencies were investigating Holy Cross: the Miami-Dade Police Department, the state attorney's office, the Florida Department of Children and Families (DCF), and the U.S. Immigration and Naturalization Service (INS).

Lead prosecutor Gail Levine was just as passionate about pursuing Mykhaylo Kofel's claims of having been sexually abused by the holy men as she was about prosecuting him for the murder of Sister Michelle. If Kofel's allegations of sexual abuse were true, she had a duty to prosecute his abusers. With Kofel facing a possible death sentence, mitigating circumstances that could explain what drove him to commit such a heinous act were just as important to her as they were to Edith Georgi, Kofel's defense attorney.

Levine believed that the other monk candidates at Holy Cross could corroborate Kofel's allegations, but none of them had. So in early May, the prosecutor and Detective Larry Belyeu flew to New York to interview former monk candidate Ivan Kalynych.

The investigators from Miami picked him up where he worked, at a restaurant in Brooklyn's Brighton Beach, the section of the borough known as "Little Odessa," after the storied seaside resort in southern Ukraine. They took the former monk-in-training to the Brooklyn homicide bureau for questioning. By the time the investigators from Miami got to him, Kalynych had been questioned by an investigator from Church Mutual, and he had been interviewed by a reporter from the *Sun-Sentinel*. He let the Miami investigators know that he was not happy about being questioned yet again.

He was indignant and defiant. Nevertheless, the twenty-one-year-old restaurant worker told Levine and Belyeu that he learned about the slaying of Sister Michelle in an e-mail from Wendt, who warned him that lawmen would want to talk with him. He was at Holy Cross from November 1996 until June 1999, when he decided to return to his home. He first learned about Holy Cross from Petro Terenta, a schoolmate in Ukraine. Kalynych said he wasn't very religious, but his mother was, and his family received money—he didn't know how much—from Wendt for him to go to Holy Cross. Kalynych said his primary reason for becoming a monk candidate at Holy Cross was the opportunity it gave him to travel to America.

As for Sister Michelle, he told Levine and Belyeu that she had never been mean to him, nor could he recall her ever being mean to Mykhaylo Kofel. What's more, he was never sexually abused by the priests, and Kofel had never complained to him about being sexually abused by Wendt and Gibault.

While the four government agencies continued their investigation of Holy Cross, Church Mutual had launched an investigation of its own. The insurance company sent private investigator Michael Zoovas, a former Miami Shores cop, to Ukraine where he interviewed Yuri and Maria Kofel and another former Holy Cross monastic trainee, Illya Hrytsak. Illya had become a monk candidate at Holy Cross at age sixteen upon the recommendation of Father Vasyl Roman, Petro Terenta's grandfather. He arrived at Holy Cross in November 1999 and stayed until August 20, 2000. His cousin, Vasyl Kopych, was already there.

Zoovas left Ukraine with signed statements from Yuri and Maria Kofel and Illya Hrytsak. Each statement bore the signature of a Ukrainian notary and the official seal of Ukraine's Ministry of Justice, and each had been translated into English.

In her statement Maria Kofel said, "My son, Mykhaylo Kofel, never complained in his letters he has been writing to us or during our personal conversations while meeting, of the fact that he was sexually abused in the monastery and forced to monosexual (homosexual) connections. Any suspicions that his father had sexually abused him are wrong."

In his statement, Yuri vehemently denied abusing his son. "Never in my life I had sexual (homosexual) connections with my own son. I never strived to obtain him sexually either," he declared.

As for Illya, the former monk trainee declared, "Neither Father Gregory nor Father Wendt never [sic] did me something that was wrong from the moral or physical point of view. They never told me things that made me feel uncomfortable. I never was a witness of moral or physical abusing displayed by Father Gregory or Father Damian towards candidates of the Monastery."

Sister Michelle, Hrytsak said, "was very polite to all of us and deserves only respect for her honorable job." He explained that he left Holy Cross of his own volition because he realized that "I have no real vocation to go into [the] church."

On his way back to Florida, Zoovas made a brief stop

in Brooklyn where, on April 23, he took a statement in English from Ivan Kalynych. "Father Abbot and Father Damian never did anything to me morally wrong or asked me to do anything to them. I was never sexually abused by Father Abbot or by Father Damian."

But as far as investigators were concerned, where there's smoke there's fire, and there was plenty of smoke blowing across Miami-Dade County. It was coming from Holy Cross, whose leaders refused to talk to them without immunity. Even Joseph Blonsky, the school's attorney and a member of its board, refused to answer their questions.

"Do you decline to answer any question in connection with the murder of Sister Michelle Lewis?" Gail Levine wanted to know.

"Yes. That's right. Yes, I do," Blonsky replied.

The Holy Cross lawyer refused to reveal how long he had been acquainted with Father Abbot Gregory Wendt, if he knew Father Damian Gibault's legal—as opposed to religious—name, and whether or not Ukrainians were studying at Holy Cross.

Their reluctance—"intransigence," Levine called it— was more than enough to raise investigators' eyebrows, but there was much more.

There was the hiring of Mel Black, a well-known criminal defense attorney who had experience defending sexual abuse cases, and there were the cameras at Holy Cross that were focused on stalls and urinals in the students' bathrooms.

During their investigation, lawmen learned that the families of the monastic candidates and others in Ukraine received money from Holy Cross. Was it a bounty? the lawmen wondered. Meanwhile, theologians the investigators consulted told them that recruiting teenage boys for monasteries was a virtually unheard-of practice.

"Maybe in their twenties, or older men," said the Right Reverend Gerald Dino, the vicar general of the Eparchy of Passaic. As far as he knew, however, no other Byzantine monastery in the United States recruited teenagers as monk trainees. Other theologians told the lawmen the same thing: Catholic monasteries do not accept monks until after they've completed high school.

The sleeping arrangements raised eyebrows, too. Kofel told investigators that on trips to Sanibel Island on Florida's Gulf Coast and to the Great Smoky Mountains in North Carolina, Petro shared a room with Wendt and Kofel shared a room with Gibault, while the other monk candidates stayed together in a single room. In North Carolina, Kofel said, he and Gibault even shared the same bed. Those arrangements were corroborated by Vasyl Kopych, who said he did not think they were strange.

What's more, even though Petro had his own bedroom in the candidates' house, he hardly ever slept there. Instead, he slept at the monastery, under the same roof, and at times in the same bedroom, as Wendt, even though the two buildings were only about ninety feet apart.

And there was the adoption of Petro Terenta at age seventeen by Wendt.

"Terenta was not honest with us," Levine said. Through all the questioning up to and including March 29, when he gave his sworn statement, Terenta did not reveal his true legal name. When asked his name, the young cleric said, "My name is Petro Terenta."

He did not reveal that he was the legally adopted son of Father Abbot Gregory Wendt. The cleric had adopted him in June 1998. The decree was signed by a judge in Miami who declared that Reverend Frank G. Wendt was "a fit and proper person to adopt the minor." And she declared Petro's full given name to be Petro Terenta Wendt, "by which name he shall be known hereafter."

The adoption came to light when investigators did a

routine search of court records. It couldn't have happened without the consent of Terenta's parents. If Wendt's adoption of Terenta seemed bizarre, investigators were in for another surprise. Gibault had tried to adopt Kofel.

That was in 1998. Mykhaylo was visiting his parents in Ukraine, but he wasn't alone. Gibault was with him, and he brought adoption papers for the Kofels to sign. He told Yuri and Maria that the adoption was for immigration purposes, to make it easier to get visas, but they refused to sign.

"What does a monk need a child for?" Yuri wondered.

Church officials wondered, too. "Very strange," said Bishop Ivan Semediy in Uzhgorod. He had never heard of a priest adopting a monastic candidate, but there was nothing he could do—neither Wendt, Gibault, nor Holy Cross were under his authority.

The Bishop learned about the murder of Sister Michelle two days after it happened. Wendt telephoned Father Sabov in Konsovo, who relayed the dreadful news to Bishop Semediy. It took a bit longer for the Kofels to find out, and it wasn't until April 20 when Yuri learned that his son had accused him of sexual abuse. The shocking allegation was delivered in person by investigator Mike Zoovas, with the aid of an interpreter.

The news stunned Yuri. "I almost had a heart attack," he said. He admitted he got drunk and yelled at his son, spanked him at times, but "no sexual abuse, never." Despite the violence in their home, Yuri and Maria loved Mykhaylo very much, and they were heartbroken to learn that their only child was a confessed killer. After the meeting with Zoovas, Maria Kofel spoke on the telephone for the first time with Edith Georgi.

"They apparently got her to a notary and she signed some kind of papers that she didn't understand," the assistant public defender explained. After assuring Maria Kofel that Mykhaylo was well, Georgi promised to arrange a phone call so that she and Yuri could speak to their son, and she informed them that she would be traveling to Ukraine soon and would meet with them then.

Meanwhile, the priests engaged in damage control with parents, meeting with them individually to persuade them to keep their children enrolled at Holy Cross Academy. While they would not talk to lawmen, Wendt and Damian assured parents that they were cooperating with investigators and there was no truth to Kofel's allegations of sexual abuse at the priests' hands. But despite their efforts, many parents were looking to send their children elsewhere. By one estimate, half the parents were planning on pulling their children out of Holy Cross.

Had the priests gone before reporters and vehemently denied Kofel's accusations or met with lawmen and answered their questions at the outset, they might have stemmed the exodus. After all, their accuser was a confessed murderer while they were men of the cloth. But by refusing to do so, a cloud of suspicion hung over them and Holy Cross, and parents weren't about to take any chances. A joint statement from the Eparchy of Passaic and the Archdiocese of Miami didn't help the priests. It read:

The Byzantine Catholic Eparchy of Passaic and the Archdiocese of Miami have issued this joint statement in response to the latest allegations of misconduct at Holy Cross Monastery and Holy Cross Academy. Both the Most Reverend Andrew Pataki, Bishop of the Eparchy of Passaic, and the Most Reverend John C. Favalora, Archbishop of the Archdiocese of Miami, express their deepest concern for the alleged victims. They ask that you keep all concerned in this matter in your prayers.

This statement is being issued to clarify the relationship of Holy Cross Monastery and Holy Cross Academy to the Roman Catholic Church. Both the

Eparchy of Passaic and Archdiocese of Miami are in communion with Pope John Paul II. Each is a diocese in its own right. The territory of the Eparchy of Passaic and Archdiocese of Miami includes Miami-Dade County.

The Articles of Incorporation of Holy Cross Academy Inc., as filed with the Secretary of State in Florida, provide in Article II that "The purpose of this corporation shall be to operate an independent, self-governing preparatory school in the educational tradition of the Catholic faith, which school shall not be under the jurisdiction or control of the hierarchy of any church." Holy Cross Academy is not affiliated with the Catholic Church and is governed by an independent Board of Directors. The independent Board of Directors is not accountable to the Catholic Church in any manner.

"There was something very strange going on at Holy Cross," Art Nanni said. In order to find out what it was, Gail Levine decided she would travel to Ukraine, and she would take Nanni and Larry Belyeu with her.

17

"I want my son back."

—Yuri Kofel

Levine and the lawmen couldn't just hop on an airplane and fly to Ukraine. They would need visas, and there was a treaty, the "Treaty on Mutual Assistance in Criminal Matters" between United States and Ukraine. It was signed in 1998 and it spelled out the protocol investigators would have to follow before they would be allowed to conduct their investigation in Kofel's homeland.

Levine started the ball rolling in May when she contacted the U.S. Department of Justice in Washington, D.C., where an official in the DOJ's criminal division helped her draft an official request to Ukrainian authorities. It stated the facts of the case and explained why investigators from Florida needed assistance from their counterparts in Ukraine, listed the names of the Ukrainian nationals under investigation—the "persons involved," cited the alleged offenses including the applicable statutes, and provided a detailed list of the Ukrainian citizens they wanted to interview. It read:

Pursuant to the Treaty on Mutual Assistance in Criminal Matters between the United States and Ukraine, the United States requests assistance on behalf of the Miami-Dade State Attorney's Office and the Miami-Dade Police. Mykhaylo Kofel, a Ukrainian national in the United States on a student visa, has been indicted on charges of First Degree Murder and Armed Burglary in the Eleventh Judicial Circuit in Miami-Dade County, Florida. The Florida authorities need help with, among other matters, claims of child abuse Kofel made when he confessed to committing the murder.

The request went on to explain that there were four other Ukrainian nationals living at Holy Cross Academy in Miami, where they were studying to be monks. They were living there on March 25, 2001, when Sister Michelle Lewis was murdered. It also stated that Mykhaylo Kofel confessed to the crime and told police that he had been sexually abused by the priests in Miami and by his own father in Ukraine.

Mykhaylo Kofel stated that he was brought to the United States at the age of fourteen by Rt. Reverend Gregory Wendt, the priest in charge of Holy Cross Academy. Kofel also claimed that he had wanted to leave his home in Ukraine because he had been sexually abused by his father. Kofel claimed, however, that Rt. Reverend Wendt and Father Damian Gibault, another priest at the academy, also sexually abused him when he came to Miami and had prevented him from leaving the academy premises.

The document explained why it was important for investigators from Miami to travel halfway around the world to the Transcarpathian Mountains of western Ukraine.

The Academy has prevented the Florida authorities from gaining meaningful access to the other students at the academy. For that reason, the Florida authorities have been unable to form an opinion, regarding the credibility of Kofel's allegations. Therefore, in order to proceed with this investigation, the Florida authorities need to interview persons in Ukraine, including persons who know Kofel and those who have worked with the Holy Cross Academy as well as other young men who came to the Academy but have since returned to Ukraine.

Levine provided the Ukrainian authorities with a list of people she wanted to interview. After sending off their official request, all Levine and her team could do was wait while it worked its way through diplomatic channels. In the meantime, they continued to investigate closer to home.

On Tuesday, June 26, Edith Georgi was able, finally, to get into Kofel's bedroom in the candidates' house. While an attorney for Holy Cross looked on, Georgi lifted a rug and found money inside three plastic bags.

At first it was estimated that no more than two hundred dollars had been found, but when the money was counted, the total came to $1,307. It was a startling discovery. It left investigators scratching their heads, wondering how Kofel had accumulated the cash.

Besides the hidden money, searchers also found contact cards for forty juniors and seniors who attended Holy Cross Academy. Cell phone records indicated Kofel had been phoning female students.

One of them, a twelfth-grader named Vanessa, had been in a French class with Kofel the year before. He was, Vanessa said, "extremely smart." She was waiting for basketball practice to begin one day in November 2000, when Kofel walked by. Vanessa casually said hello.

"That's when he came up to me and he asked how I was," she recalled. They started talking. Kofel told Vanessa that he was enrolled in college and was doing well because he was studying hard. He asked for her phone number.

"The first thing I said was no," Vanessa remembered. "You're a monk. You're not supposed to go out of your path of religious things and talk to girls," she admonished him.

But Kofel told her that he just wanted someone to talk to, that he just wanted to be friends. Convinced, Vanessa gave him her number. Later that evening Kofel called and asked her to the movies. Vanessa turned him down then and several more times before he stopped calling.

Investigators tried to figure out how Kofel managed to accumulate more than one thousand dollars. The truth of the matter was he had been stealing money for more than a year. He would steal from Gibault's room, which he was required to clean every Saturday, and from other school offices whenever he could. He planned to use the money to finance his getaway from monastic life at Holy Cross. A check of Kofel's cell phone records indicated that he had been calling a travel agency in New Jersey, which specialized in travel to Ukraine.

While investigators wondered about Kofel's money stash, they were also wondering about Petro Terenta. He drove a late-model Acura and carried an American Express card. More often than not, his monthly charges exceeded one thousand dollars.

"When we interviewed Terenta, he said he led a completely monastic life that included celibacy, poverty, and prayer," prosecutor Levine said. "We are not sure what a monastic life would be in light of what we have found out."

Clark Mervis, Terenta's attorney, insisted the American Express card was not an extravagance. "Mr. Terenta was issued a credit card by the school for authorized expenses, and that's what it was used for."

Prosecutors had other questions about monastic life at Holy Cross. Along with the two priests, the candidates took trips to Naples and Sanibel Island, where they went to the beaches and stayed in expensive hotels.

"How can monks go to the beach?" one of the investigators asked rhetorically. "Girls in bikinis all around. What about the vow of chastity?"

While Kofel's defense team was moving ahead with their investigation, Gail Levine had a problem: The MDPD's Sex Crimes Bureau was shutting down its investigation of Kofel's sex abuse allegations. She learned about it on June 27, when Detective Jose Cabado delivered his report to her office.

"Cabado was very specific and stated that since no one but the murder defendant would tell them anything, their investigation was over," Levine noted in a memo she wrote for her files.

When she asked the detective if he was concerned about money going back to Ukraine for the boys, he said "he did not find that relevant." When she asked about Wendt's adoption of Petro Terenta, Cabado said he had read about it in the newspaper, but he never went back to question Petro on the subject.

On Monday, July 2, Levine met with seven MDPD lawmen: Lieutenant Tom Gross, Sergeant Kimet Pomes, detectives Steve Signori, and Jose Cabado from the sex crimes bureau, and Bill Gilliland, Art Nanni and Larry Belyeu from the homicide bureau. In her memo, the prosecutor wrote:

Gross was annoyed and he began the meeting telling me in no uncertain terms that these were basically adult men, that they chose not to come forward, they had a right to privacy and their investigation was over. He did not care to hear about the adoption or any other information I had gathered including the large sums of unexplained cash which may be funneled to Ukraine in exchange for the boys. That, he said, was an Economic Crimes case. He didn't care that the defendant had passed a polygraph. . . . He also cared less that the men (now) were boys when they were brought over here at fourteen. . . . Detective Nanni did try to appeal to his interest by saying don't you think there are things going on there. To which he replied yes, but he had investigated churches before and they block you from getting the information. He and the others left the meeting after about 12 minutes.

It wasn't that the sex crimes bureau cops didn't believe Kofel—virtually every investigator who talked to him found his allegations credible; it's that they were stymied in their efforts to corroborate them.

Levine ended her memo with a promise:

I will continue to investigate this case until I am clear about the circumstances of the defendant's state of mind as well as [his] home life at Holy Cross are made clear to me.

Earlier in the month two other agencies, the INS and the Florida Department of Children and Family Services, had announced they were closing their probes, too. Neither agency had uncovered evidence of wrongdoing.

The INS probe focused on whether or not the monk candidates had been brought to the United States for "immoral purposes."

"All leads pertaining to this investigation have been exhausted," an INS spokesman declared. "The immigration status of all the foreign-born monastic candidates attending Holy Cross is bona fide. Holy Cross Academy is a bona fide INS-approved school for attendance by nonimmigrant alien students."

The announcements, however, were too little and too late to stem the exodus of students from Holy Cross Academy. School officials had expected the dropoff in enrollment, a school spokesman said. He wouldn't reveal how many had left or how many teachers had been laid off. "There were parents who felt the negative publicity made it impossible for them to come back next year," the spokesman said.

Gail Levine kept her promise to continue investigating. On Saturday, July 14, the prosecutor and two MDPD homicide detectives, Larry Belyeu and Joe Malott—Art Nanni couldn't make the trip because of illness in his family— boarded American Airlines Flight 96 for Chicago, where they connected to a LOT Polish Airlines flight to Warsaw. From there they flew to the Ukrainian city of Lviv, then drove two hours to Uzhgorod.

Despite the grueling journey, the investigators from the United States were in the Uzhgorod prosecutor's office bright and early on Monday morning, July 16. They were there to meet with Yuri and Maria Kofel. As they had requested before leaving Miami, the local prosecutor had scheduled the appointment, but the Kofels didn't show up. It was an inauspicious beginning for the Americans; they didn't have a lot of time—they were scheduled to return home on Friday. In his official report, Detective Belyeu wrote that the Uzhgorod prosecutor reported that the Kofels explained why they did not appear: "Public Defender Edith Georgi . . . had contacted them over the weekend and told them not to."

The assistant public defender had been in Uzhgorod in early May along with investigator Ronald Cason and an interpreter. They arrived in the Kofel's village, Verkhovina Bystra, on May 4, in time to witness the annual Blessing of the Sheep. They met with the Kofels at their home, which was brimming with fairly new furniture purchased, Georgi learned, with money Wendt had given the Kofels when Mykhaylo first left for Miami.

The Americans brought with them a tape-recorded message from Mykhaylo. He assured his parents that he was well, that he was eating, and that he loved them very much. Afterward, they spent the remainder of the day interviewing the Kofels.

Yuri and Maria told the visitors that they had second thoughts almost as soon as Mykhaylo left for America at the end of July 1996. Their doubts increased when Wendt visited them the following November during one of his semiannual trips to the region.

"He said that Misha had a problem," Maria remembered. "He had headaches. He had high blood pressure. His blood pressure was jumping up and down."

"I didn't like him right away," Yuri said of Wendt. He asked the cleric, "How is my son? How is his health? Does he eat well? And he says, 'He and Petro, they eat a lot. They eat in a garden. They eat bananas.'"

Yuri told the cleric, "Quit eating bananas, because you will become a monkey." Yuri was serious, but Wendt couldn't stop laughing.

In 1998, Maria recalled, Misha returned home to renew his visa accompanied by Gibault. Maria and Yuri gave their bedroom to the priest and their son, who slept together. At the time they didn't give it a second thought. They also thought nothing about Misha and Gibault sharing a private compartment during the twenty-hour train trip to Kiev, where Mykhaylo went to renew his visa, while the Kofels slept in another compartment.

Maria said, "When he came in 1998, he told me

'Mother, it's not the way Wendt promised us it would be. He didn't tell us everything.'"

Misha had been writing to his parents, telling them that everything in America was wonderful. Now he confessed that he had not been truthful. He explained that Wendt read letters before they were mailed, and the truth of the matter was that he was under a lot of pressure to do well in school, and the rules he was forced to live by were very strict.

To Maria, Misha seemed frightened and jumpy. He wouldn't hug her and would pull away if she tried to touch him. When he returned again to Ukraine in March 2000, this time with Wendt, he wasn't jumpy and he didn't seem frightened. Instead, he was stoic, "thoughtful," Maria said.

"He didn't want to talk to us. Like [he was] thinking over something."

To Yuri, Misha seemed like a "zombie." To Maria's brother Ivan, Misha seemed "programmed."

The Kofels wanted him home, and they told him so on each of his two visits and during their infrequent phone calls.

"What am I going to do in Ukraine?" Mykhaylo asked his mother during one of those transatlantic calls.

As far as Maria was concerned, "He could milk a cow and work around the house." It would be better than studying; Maria feared that "hard studying would damage his head."

Before they left the Kofels, Georgi and Cason wanted to know about Yuri's drinking. He had been on the wagon, he said, since just after Misha departed for America in 1996. He was deeply sorry for all the trouble he had caused, and he especially regretted that Misha had been a witness to his violent behavior.

By the time the defense team had returned to Miami, prosecutor Gail Levine's plans to travel to Verkhovina Bystra, too, were well under way.

* * *

The meeting with the Kofels wasn't all that was on Gail Levine's agenda that warm July day in Uzhgorod. At 11:00 A.M., twenty-one-year-old Mykola Varhulych reported to the prosecutor's office. He had been a monk candidate in Konsovo, but he never made it to Miami. He told the American investigators that he and Kofel grew up in the same village. They were both deeply religious Catholics who regularly attended services at the village church where Father Yuri Sabov served as the head priest.

In 1997, Sabov asked Varhulych if he would be interested in becoming a monk at Holy Cross in Miami. Varhulych decided to give it a chance. He moved into the monastic training center in Konsovo. He recalled seeing Kofel in 1988, when Misha stayed there with Gibault during a visit home. Varhulych said he was taken aback by Kofel's appearance.

"It was zombielike," he told the Americans. Misha was also thin and sickly-looking.

"Why are you so skinny?" Varhulych wanted to know.

Kofel told him that he was not eating, and that Holy Cross "was much like a prison." The monk trainees, he said, were not permitted to leave the campus without Wendt or Gibault.

"Misha, why don't you come back home?" Varhulych asked his old friend.

"Because there is nothing to come back to," was the reply.

Kofel explained that he loved his mother but his father drank all the time. Varhulych told investigators that Yuri did indeed drink a lot and was the village drunk.

After about a year, Varhulych had had enough of monastic life. There were too many rules and his mother was not allowed to visit him there. But before he could leave on his own, Wendt kicked him out after he had gotten into a fight with another monk candidate.

In looking back on his experience in Konsovo,

Varhulych told the Americans that he felt he was being "brainwashed," and that Wendt was "confusing the boys or leading them on."

Later that afternoon, the three investigators from Miami decided that if the Kofels wouldn't come to them, they would go to the Kofels, so they and their interpreter piled into a minivan and set out for Mykhaylo Kofel's remote mountain village.

The drive was harrowing, two and a half hours on unmarked, winding, and narrow dirt roads that took them deep into the Transcarpathian Mountains. There were no rest stops along the way, and there was no WELCOME TO VERKHOVINA BYSTRA sign to mark their arrival in the out-of-the-way village sometime after 7 P.M.

They found the Kofel home—house number 166—easily enough, but Yuri and Maria were still working in the field, as were most of their neighbors. While they waited for the Kofels to return, a group of about two dozen angry, fist-shaking villagers confronted the Americans.

"They were shouting and very agitated," Belyeu remembered.

"You're no good," screamed one.

"Liars," yelled another.

"Evil people from America, we were warned about you."

Maria Kofel was among them. She shook her fists and pointed angrily at the Americans, and she implored her neighbors not to speak to them.

"They did a wrong thing to my son," she shouted furiously. "Father Sabov promised a better life, promised he would be a monk. You Americans let me down. You lie, you evil people from America. Our attorneys said you were evil."

But Levine and the detectives stood their ground. They remained outside the Kofel home, hoping their interpreter could persuade Yuri and Maria to change their minds. After a while, a short, balding man introduced himself as Yuri Kofel.

"If you would be in my shoes, you would die," he said through the interpreter. He told them about Michael Zoovas, the insurance company investigator who had been there in April.

"Zoovas asked me if I sexually abused my son," Yuri said. "He said not to talk to anyone without his authorization. He said he would take care of everything."

It was after 11:00 P.M. when the Kofels finally relented and invited the Americans and their interpreter into their tiny home for an interview. Yuri did most of the talking.

"I want my son back," he said. "He's our only son. I'm not poor. I have a job. The priest cheated me. They told me lies. I wanted my son to be a priest. He is very smart."

The interview turned to Gibault's attempt to adopt Misha in 1998. "I refused to let the church adopt my son," Yuri said. Afterward, he and Maria rarely heard from Misha; communication was cut off, except for one or two brief phone calls.

Asked if Misha told him that he had been sexually abused by the priests, Yuri shook his head.

"Did you ever sexually molest him?" one of the investigators asked.

"This is nonsense!" Yuri snapped.

He had a question for the investigators: "What is going to happen to my son?" he asked as the Americans were leaving.

"He's probably going to spend the rest of his life in prison," one of them said.

The answer enraged Yuri. He produced a photograph of his son with Wendt and another monk candidate, which he ripped in half and threw at the Americans. Larry Belyeu collected the pieces and impounded them.

18

"In a death penalty case we have to gather as much information as we can about a defendent's background."

—Assistant State Attorney Gail Levine

The next day, Tuesday, July 17, was another hectic day for the three investigators. They spent the morning at the Uzhgorod prosecutor's office, where they interviewed Mikhail Roman, the thirty-three-year-old director of the monastic training center in Konsovo and Petro Terenta's uncle. Roman admitted that he received money from Wendt—seven to eight thousand dollars, twice a year. He did not live at the monastic training center, he just supervised the property and the candidates living there.

In the afternoon they interviewed Bishop Semediy and Father Sabov together. In his report, Belyeu wrote:

Bishop Semediy related he met Father Wendt in 1996 at the four hundredth celebration of the Byzantine Rite in the Ukraine. He does not know Father Damian. Bishop Semediy related that Father Wendt seemed very peculiar to him, indicating that he would only meet for a couple of minutes and then leave without relating any information about the activities at his center. Bishop

Semediy continued by saying that Petro was with Father Wendt and always remained within eye contact of him. Normally when priests arrived in the Ukraine, they would have services, but Father Wendt would not and continued by saying that his behavior was different from other priests. Father Sabov related that he met Father Wendt in 1997 and knew him to take children to America as monk candidates. Both were asked if Petro's family ever received funding from Father Wendt, to which they both indicated they did not know.

Father Sabov shook as he recalled that he first learned about the murder of Sister Michelle from Wendt, who had phoned him after the slaying. Sabov was stunned and saddened when Wendt told him that Mykhaylo Kofel had been arrested. Wendt asked the priest to notify Kofel's parents.

Before the clergymen left the prosecutor's office that afternoon, a Ukrainian official strongly suggested they sever their connections to Holy Cross.

The next day, the investigators visited the monastic training center in Konsovo, where they were met by Mikhail Roman and a local attorney. They were allowed inside on condition that they take no photographs. Afterward, Belyeu sketched the building, which consisted of a chapel, a kitchen, a living room, and an office.

Later that day, they met with Petro Terenta's parents, Petro Sr. and Maria, at the Uzhgorod prosecutor's office. The Terenta's were angry about being summoned to meet with the Americans.

In his report, Belyeu wrote:

The Terentas were explained briefly certain facts about the homicide to which Maria Terenta stated that she did not believe a single word. The Terentas were asked why they allowed Father Wendt to adopt their son, Petro, to which they stated to avoid immigration problems, and that it was an honor for a man of God to be in their family. The Terentas never met Father Wendt prior to Petro leaving for the United States.

The Terentas were asked if they were aware that their son received money from Father Wendt, of which they indicated that would never happen. When told about the benefits that Petro received while living at the monastery, again Maria Terenta stated that these are lies.

Petro Terenta indicated that he received pocket money from Father Wendt for his responsibilities as a caretaker at the monastic training center in Uzhgorod. . . . Mr. Terenta was asked if he ever received the sum of five thousand dollars from Father Wendt or the Holy Cross Academy in February, to which he stated, "No." He was shown paperwork revealing a five-thousand dollar transfer to him. Mr. Terenta simply shrugged his shoulders. . . . The Terentas seemed agitated with these investigators and advised they could provide no further information concerning the homicide at that particular time.

On the day before the investigators were to head for home, they interviewed Illya Hrytsak at the airport in Lviv, in a VIP room reserved for foreign dignitaries. He had just returned from a week in Miami where his expenses had been paid for by the public defender. While there, Hrytsak visited Kofel in the county jail. They never discussed the murder, he said. He also met with a psychologist on two successive days. Each session, Hrytsak recalled, lasted three to four hours.

Illya Hrytsak, from the village of Rosishka, was sixteen years old when he arrived at Holy Cross in October 1999. Vasyl Roman, Petro Terenta's grandfather, had recruited him for Holy Cross.

Hrytsak, Vasyl Kopych's cousin, said his family was religious and, like the monk candidates who had gone to

Miami before him, he viewed the chance to train there as a once-in-a-lifetime opportunity.

Hrytsak said he was immediately drawn to Kofel. "I wanted to be like him. He was calm, reserved, avoided conflicts. He was happy with life, didn't worry about things, and he gave good advice."

Wendt, he said, was strict, "a typical American, very strong." The candidates couldn't go anywhere alone, and Wendt let them know that once they completed their monastic training, they would be allowed to return to their homeland only if he built a monastery there.

"Even if it was built, we were told that Father Wendt would decide who was to go back to Ukraine," Hrytsak recalled. He found the prospect of spending the rest of his life at Holy Cross terrifying.

"When I went there, I was just sixteen years old," he explained. "Then I grew up, saw more of life, and started thinking, 'Should I stay here?' Can't get married, can't leave the monastery; if you're a priest, you can only serve in this monastery. The thought that I was to live my life and die in that place was frightening."

He left Holy Cross at the end of the school year. As soon as Hrytsak informed Wendt that he wanted to return to his homeland, the cleric prohibited Kofel from speaking to him. Misha, he said, was told that if he was caught talking to Illya, "he would not pass the ninth grade."

Hrytsak said he was "absolutely shocked" when he heard about the murder of Sister Michelle, and he couldn't imagine his friend committing such an unspeakable crime.

"I think something must have happened to him from the time I left Miami, something that completely changed his way of thinking," the former monk trainee said.

Hrytsak assured the American investigators that he had never been sexually abused by Wendt or Gibault, and that Kofel never told him that he had. But the former monk candidate did suspect that something sinister was going on.

Kofel, he explained, was the only one of the monk candidates allowed to enter Gibault's bedroom, which was located on the first floor of the candidates' house, and the only one who had a key. He recalled one occasion when the priest ordered Mykhaylo to his room. Kofel, Illya said, remained there for about an hour. When he emerged, he seemed depressed.

He also recalled several occasions when he heard footsteps coming from Kofel's bedroom then proceeding down the stairs. Each time it was after 11:00 P.M. Hrytsak assumed it was Kofel, and he assumed he was going to Gibault's room.

When asked why, he said that the only other room to go to on the first floor was the kitchen, but "the light did not go on in the kitchen during that time." Illya remembered the light coming on in Kofel's bedroom about an hour later.

Once he left Miami, Hrytsak said he had no further contact with Kofel, and he knew nothing about the murder of Sister Michelle until he learned about it from the insurance company's investigator in April. Before the interview ended, the investigators asked Hrytsak what he knew about Kofel's relationship with the slain sister.

"He did not like her," the former monk trainee said. Kofel would mock her and make fun of her, as did Gibault and Wendt and the other monk candidates, but it seemed to him that Kofel mocked her more than the others. When asked if Sister Michelle was verbally abusive toward Kofel or any of the other monk candidates, Hrytsak said that as far as he knew she was not.

The Hrytsak interview was the last the investigators from Miami would conduct in Ukraine. They left for home the very next day. The first leg of their return trip took them to Warsaw, where they connected with a British Airways flight to London. The next day they boarded a British Airways 747 for a direct flight to Miami. It had been a whirlwind trip. In all, they had spent more than thirty hours in the air, flying in coach all the way. Within less than a week, the intrepid investigators conducted thirteen interviews, faced down an angry mob in Verkhovina Bystra, and visited the monastic training center in Konsovo.

Although they left without a smoking gun—none of the former monk candidates admitted to having been sexually abused by the Holy Cross clerics, or to having witnessed the priests committing an act of sexual abuse—the grueling journey had been worthwhile.

"In a death penalty case," Levine said, "we have to gather as much information as we can about a defendant's background."

19

"Monks should be obedient to God and to Abbot."

—Sasha Korsak

On Friday, July 13, the day before Gail Levine left for Ukraine, Judge Crespo agreed to a joint motion from the prosecution and the defense to postpone the start of the trial from July 23 to February 11, 2002. Then at a hearing on October 25, the jurist set a forty-five-day deadline for prosecutors and defense attorneys to complete the taking of statements from the monk candidates. As material witnesses, they were not free to leave the United States. After forty-five days, the restrictions would be lifted and the boys from Ukraine would be free to leave the country.

In the aftermath of the September 11, 2001, terrorist attacks, Levine warned, "Once they leave this country it's going to be very difficult for them to come back."

Thirty days later, the monk candidates and their attorneys were in Judge Crespo's sixth-floor courtroom. It was 9:00 A.M. on November 26, 2001, and they were there to be deposed and to testify. Their appearances would be videotaped and perpetuated, which meant that if and when the case went to trial, the jury would view their testimony on a TV monitor.

Also in the courtroom that day were the defendant, Mykhaylo Kofel, his lawyers, Edith Georgi and Ray Taseff, and prosecutors Gail Levine and Penny Brill. An interpreter was on hand, too.

The monk candidates were the prosecution's witnesses. They had been subpoenaed by the State, which meant they would be questioned by Gail Levine during direct examination, then cross-examined by the defense. Vasyl Kopych would be the first to take the witness stand. He had a unique job at Holy Cross: He was the designated snitch, the one who would report candidates' transgressions to Father Abbot Gregory Wendt. The cleric, Kopych would explain, "asked me to look at the candidates and myself, at the way we follow [the] schedule and the rules, and tell him if we are not doing something, so he would ask me to come and report."

Before Kopych took the stand, Judge Crespo ordered the two other monk candidates to wait outside the courtroom until they were called.

"Do not discuss the case or your testimony with anyone," the judge warned them before they left. "Do not allow anyone to discuss this testimony with you, particularly anyone who may be a witness in this case."

Levine was on her feet. "Your Honor, just so we are clear with the witnesses, that means anyone including Father Abbot, including Father Damian, or they will be subject to possible contempt."

"I think I was pretty clear, but I will repeat it," the judge said. Then he looked directly at the boys and very sternly said, "No one means no one, gentlemen, except your own attorney."

After Kopych was sworn in, Levine began the questioning by asking the eighteen-year-old about his background and how he came to be a monk at Holy Cross. Then she asked him to step down from the witness stand and, using a pointer, identify various locations on the Holy Cross campus from a blown-up diagram. After pointing to the school, the convent, the candidates' house, the chapel and the guest house, the young monk trainee went back to the witness stand. Levine then established that the Ukrainian boys were free to contact their families, and free to leave if they wanted to.

"Have you kept in touch with your parents since you've been here?" the prosecutor asked.

"Yes," he replied.

"Has anybody prevented you from doing that?"

"No."

"When you first got to Miami, who did you share a room with?"

"Ivan [Kalynych]."

"Is Ivan still a candidate?"

"No. He decided he doesn't want to become monk."

"So what happened to him?"

"He went home to Ukraine."

"Was there any fighting or anything you remember going on in the candidates' house when Ivan said he wanted to return home?"

"No."

Next, Levine wanted Kopych to identfy Mykhaylo Kofel. "Do you see that person in the courtroom here today?" she asked.

"Yes, I do."

"Do you want to tell us where he's sitting?"

"Yes, he's sitting in front of me, a little bit to the right, in between Ms. Georgi and another man."

Levine asked him to describe his relationship with Kopych.

"We were in the Holy Cross monastery for more than three years together. I met him in Ukraine about six months, approximately six months before I came here. We went to school, Holy Cross Academy for two years, we had some classes together, and we were the candidates so we had sports sometimes together, sometimes we had dinner prayers. He was a candidate in the Holy Cross monastery."

"Did you get along together?"

"Yes, I think so."

"Would you consider him a friend?"

"Yes."

"During any of the times that you spoke with the defendant did he complain to you about anything that was going on at the monastery?"

"No. I don't remember specific examples."

"Did he ever tell you he was unhappy there?"

"No."

"Did he ever tell you that he wanted to go home?"

"No."

"Did he ever tell you that someone was bothering him, someone in particular, that he had a personal problem with anyone that lived at the monastery?"

"No."

Next, the line of questioning turned to Kofel's allegations of sexual abuse.

"Did he ever tell you that Father Abbot had touched him in private places?"

"No."

"Did he ever tell you that Father Damian had touched him in private places?"

"No."

"Has anyone done that to you?"

"No."

The prosecutor then asked several more questions about sexual misconduct, all of which Kopych answered in the negative, before turning the questions to religious life at Holy Cross.

"What's the purpose of becoming a monk?" she asked.

"To serve God, and you want to follow the commandments, you want to love your God with all your heart, with all your might, with all your strength, and you want to love your neighbor as yourself."

"Do you do that through prayer?" the prosecutor asked.

"Yes."

"Do you do that through obedience?"

"Yes."

"Do you live by a schedule?"

"Yes, we have schedule."

"Tell us about your schedule here in Miami."

"Basically, there is a time when to get up, when to go to bed. There is time for dinner, for morning prayers, for evening prayers. There is time when to study, when to go to school. There is time when we can go to play sports, when we can watch television."

"Is all of that designated times; for instance, what time you get up, is that decided by someone else and you follow that?"

"Yes, we have a schedule. Father Abbot makes the schedule and he asked us—he tells us he will make a schedule and tells us what the schedule is and then we follow the schedule."

"Do you have friends in Miami outside of the monastery?"

"Only friends that I went to school [with], that I took classes [with], that I know. Friends in a sense that I know their names and I took some classes with them."

"Do you seek to make friends outside the monastery?"

"No."

"Why not?"

"Because that would negate my purpose of wanting to become a monk."

Finally, Levine had Kopych answer questions about the events leading up to the death of Sister Michelle—the visit to the Youth Fair on Saturday, the haircuts, and a game of basketball the monk candidates, including Kofel, played in the afternoon. Kopych said he had not seen any cuts on Kofel's hands or scratches on his face until Sunday morning.

"Did you ask him how he cut his hands?" Levine asked.

"No, I didn't ask," Vasyl answered.

"Why not?"

"I thought it wasn't appropriate, or somehow I thought that I should not ask him."

Before she finished her questioning, Levine wanted to know about Sister Michelle. Had she ever been mean to him?

"No."

Had he ever heard her call the other Ukrainian boys names?

"No."

On cross-examination, Ray Taseff honed in on Wendt's absolute power over the monk candidates.

"Now, life in the candidates' house, the bedroom that we have described, you couldn't go to your bedroom to be alone unless you had the permission of Father Abbot, correct?" the assistant public defender asked.

"Yes, when it's not time to be in the bedroom."

"There were only certain things you can do in the bedroom, right?"

"Yes."

"The only thing you could do is sleep or change your clothes?"

"Yes, or pray."

"And to do anything else, to be by yourself in your own bedroom, you would have to go to Father Abbot, right?"

"Correct."

"And get permission, right?"

"Yes. If you want to do that during the time that you're supposed to do something else."

"If you wanted to do something other than what the

schedule required you to do, you had to speak to Father Abbot, correct?"

"Correct."

"Or Father Damian, correct?"

"Well, Father Damian would say talk to Father Abbot."

"So even Father Damian would defer to Father Abbot, correct?"

"Sometimes. Usually, I would say."

"My point is Father Abbot would make the final decisions about what you could do, correct?"

"Yes."

"And those included something like going to your bedroom, right?"

"Yes."

"You couldn't go to your bedroom during a time when it wasn't scheduled to go to your bedroom, correct?"

"Yes, you are not supposed to go to the bedroom."

Next, Taseff wanted to know about the books and magazines the monk candidates read. Who chose them?

"We don't read books that are not proper for the candidates—and the person who decides what's proper or not is the abbot," Vasyl answered.

"And as far as magazines, same thing, correct?"

"Yes, pretty much."

"It would be Father Abbot who determined which magazines were appropriate, correct?"

"Yes."

"To become a monk, it is Father Abbot who will make the decision when and if you are ready to go out into the world and be a monk, correct?"

"Correct."

"Now, Father Abbot stands in the shoes of Jesus on Earth, correct?"

"Symbolically, in a way. I and the candidates are apostles."

"It's as if he's Jesus and you are one of his disciples, correct?"

"Correct."

"And he gives directions and you follow, correct?"

"Yes, directions that deal with monastic life."

"And you are to obey Father Abbot as if you are obeying God, correct?"

"Yes."

"But you do have an allegiance of obedience to Father Abbot, correct?"

"Yes."

"And it's your responsibility to follow his directions, correct?"

"Yes."

"Now, it's not your place to judge Father Abbot, is it?"

"Well, to judge—in what way?"

"Well, it wouldn't be your place to judge his conduct as being either right or wrong?"

"No, Father Damian would point that out."

"That's my point. It's not your place to judge Father Abbot, correct?"

"Yes, correct."

"And it's not your place to judge whether his conduct is right or wrong, correct?"

"I'm not the one to judge Father."

"So it wouldn't be your place to judge his conduct, as his conduct relates to other people other than yourself, correct?"

"Correct."

In the afternoon, Sasha Korsak took the stand. He was twenty years old, one of six children, all boys. He worked as a cow herder in Ukraine before becoming a monk candidate. Korsak was also a talented artist whose specialty was iconography. He arrived in the United States on December 6, 1999.

During Levine's direct examination, Korsak said, in response to a question, "Monks should be obedient."

"Obedient to whom?" the prosecutor asked.

"To God and to Abbot."

He considered Kofel a friend. When asked if they ever talked about personal matters, Sasha said, "Don't remember."

"Did he ever talk to you about his feelings about becoming a monk?"

"Don't remember."

"Did he ever tell you he wanted to go home?"

"Don't remember."

He did, however, remember Kofel telling him, "Sister is dead."

"How was he acting when he told you that? Did he appear sad?" Levine asked.

"No," he replied.

"Did he appear like he had [had] a bad night's sleep or didn't sleep well?"

"No."

Levine pressed him. "What was his demeanor? How was he acting?"

"I would say he was surprised too—'Sister is dead and [I] don't know how it happened, why it happened.'"

Sasha corroborated Vasyl's testimony regarding the rules of the monastery and the fact that any deviation required the permission of Wendt.

During cross-examination, Edith Georgi honed in on the rules of the monastery and the degree of control Wendt exercised over the boys.

"You weren't allowed to speak in your own bedroom, were you?" Georgi asked.

"No."

"In fact, Father Abbot even decided what personal items you could keep or not keep?"

"Yes."

"Father Abbot even controls your future, doesn't he?"

"Father Abbot is in charge."

"Would you agree with me that he controls your life?"

"Yes, he does control my life."

Like Illya Hyrtsak, Korsak told investigators that he often heard footsteps going up and down the stairway at the candidates' house during the night. Georgi pressed him. He slept in the same bedroom as Vasyl and Yosyp. "So it had to be Mykhaylo or Petro, correct?" Georgi asked.

"Yes," Korsak replied.

"Petro's room had a separate entrance to another stairway, didn't it?"

"Yes."

"So, hearing these footsteps going up and down the stairs—and I'm talking about before March, before this horrible thing happened in March—you heard those footsteps many times?"

"Yes."

"But you never found out why?"

"No."

On redirect, Levine asked Korsak, "Would you lie for Father Abbot?"

"No."

"Even if he told you to do so?"

"Yes."

"Even if that would be breaking one of his rules?"

"Of course. If you are in the monastery, you can't lie. It's against God's commandments."

Georgi was on her feet. She had one question on recross.

"Sasha, in addition to Father Abbot being in charge of you, he is also the person to whom you give confession, isn't he?"

"Yes."

With that, Sasha Korsak was excused. If he lied on the stand, if he lied about not lying, he could confess and receive God's forgiveness through Father Abbot Gregory Wendt.

Yosyp Lembak didn't testify until the next day. He had only been at Holy Cross for seven months when Sister Michelle was murdered. His English wasn't good and, for the most part, his testimony corroborated what Vasyl and Sasha said on the witness stand, and buttressed the positions the prosecution and the defense would likely take at trial, where the prosecutors would argue that Kofel was a cold-blooded killer whose brutal and long-planned murder of Sister Michelle stemmed from his simmering hatred of her.

Kofel's attorneys could be expected to argue that their client was a victim, too; that years of sexual abuse by the priests caused Kofel to take out his anger and humiliation on Sister Michelle. It was time to depose the priests.

Petro Terenta's perpetuated testimony wasn't taken until December 2002. Terenta admitted to sharing a bedroom with Wendt, his adopted father, but he said he was never sexually molested by him or anyone else at Holy Cross. He also said that it was possible that on at least one occasion the two men shared the same bed.

During rapid-fire questioning by assistant public defender Ray Taseff, Terenta seemed unnerved by questions about sex.

"You took vacations to Naples on at least two occasions?" Taseff asked.

"Yes."

"To Orlando?"

"Yes."

"And to North Carolina?"

"Yes, we did."

"When you went to Naples, you and Father Wendt would stay in the same room together?"

"That's correct."

"And Mykhaylo and Father Damian would stay in the same room together?"

"Yes."

"And the other monastic candidates were in a separate room without adult supervision?"

"Yes."

"And when you went to North Carolina, you and Father Wendt stayed in the same bed together?"

"It's possible but I don't remember."

When asked why they shared a bed, Terenta replied, "To save money," and because, "I enjoyed his company and liked to stay with him. He's a great person to talk to."

Terenta said Wendt was "a great companion" and they were "a perfect match."

Petro also confirmed that Kofel, from the time he was fourteen, often stayed in the same room and "possibly" in the same bed with Father Damian Gibault when they traveled "because Mykhaylo could sleep when Father Damian watched television."

Gail Levine pressed Terenta about sexual abuse. "Are you celibate?" she asked.

"Yes," Terenta said.

"Have you had oral sex?"

"No."

"Anal sex?"

"No."

"Any sexual relations with Father Wendt?"

"No."

Terenta, who was adopted at age seventeen by Wendt, admitted that his biological father worked at the monastic center in Konsovo, and that he had privileges the other monk trainees didn't have.

For example while the others slept in the candidates' house, Petro was permitted to sleep in the monastery building where Father Wendt lived, but, he insisted, they slept in separate beds. He studied there and took his meals there and, unlike the other candidates, he traveled to Ukraine at least once a year. He also visited Holland and Belgium with Wendt, where they stayed in five-star hotels.

When asked why they stayed in Hiltons instead of seeking accommodations at local monasteries or rectories, Terenta replied, "It was for convenience reasons."

He also said that Wendt provided him with a car, a cell phone, credit cards, and a position as a director in one of the Holy Cross corporations.

"I am his assistant," Terenta explained. But to some of those who heard his testimony, he sounded more like a boy-toy, especially after he revealed more about his relationship with Father Abbot Gregory Wendt.

After characterizing it as "a father-son relationship," the young monk admitted that the priest did not introduce him to his relatives when they visited from South Carolina, nor could he ever recall Wendt introducing him to anyone as his son.

Before he left the witness stand after nine hours of testimony spread over two days, Levine had one last question on redirect—she wanted to know if Terenta and Wendt were together "for sexual reasons."

Petro's answer: "Not at all."

20

"When he entered his teenage years, Misha became more nervous, more reticent, more irritated when his father was drunk. He wanted to become independent and to leave his home as soon as possible. He dreamed of going to a monastery to become a monk."

—Marianna Tovt-Korhsynska, M.D., Ph.D.

September 3, 2002, was hot and steamy in South Florida. People were on edge, nervously watching the Caribbean where tropical storms Dolly and Edouard were wreaking havoc. Ten years and one week had passed since Hurricane Andrew cut a devastating swath across Miami-Dade County, and all the previous week the media recounted the catastrophe, which left forty-four dead and forty billion dollars in property damage.

A storm was brewing inside the Miami-Dade public defender's office that day, too. Wendt and Gibault and their attorneys were at the Miami-Dade public defender's office. They were under subpoena from Kofel's attorneys who were there, along with assistant State Attorneys Gail Levine and Priscilla Prado. If Kofel's defense team and the prosecutors expected to hear the priests answer questions, they were in for a big disappointment.

After identifying themselves for the record, Wendt and Gibault took the Fifth on every question put to them by the public defenders. Attorneys for the priests read a prepared statement into the record. It included an assertion of the priests' Fifth Amendment privilege against self-incrimination and a promise that they would answer questions if subpoenaed by the state. The prosecutors were not about to take that step, and the depositions, scheduled to last several hours, ended only fifteen minutes after they began.

"In my twenty years as a lawyer, I have never seen a witness invoke their Fifth Amendment privilege to each and every question posed, except when asked about their name and address," said a frustrated Edith Georgi. Kofel had come to America at age fourteen at the behest of Wendt, his spiritual advisor, and she wanted to question the priests about his life at Holy Cross.

"They had a woman murdered in their school and they have nothing to say? I guess they've forgotten all about her," said an exasperated Gail Levine.

Attorneys for the priests issued a joint statement: "If the state continues to believe that Father Abbot and Father Damian are under suspicion of wrongdoing, then it would be malpractice for an attorney to allow them to answer questions that might be used against them."

The defense attorneys filed a motion to compel the priests to answer their questions. Three weeks later, Ray Taseff was in front of Judge Crespo.

"This is a capital case where the witnesses who know the most about the character and background of the accused, [the people] who recruited him to come to the United States from his native Ukraine as a fourteen-year-old child, and who have relevant information about the death of Sister Michelle Lewis, have refused to answer a single question," Taseff told the judge.

He wasn't denying the priests' privilege to invoke their constitutional rights. Instead, he argued they had no right to "a blanket refusal to answer all questions."

The way the public defender framed his argument,

Kofel's right to a fair trial was at stake. Not surprisingly, the priests' attorneys saw it differently. Mel Black argued that the holy men should not be required to answer the defense's questions without a grant of immunity. After all, four agencies had investigated the holy men, none more aggressively than the MDPD and the Miami-Dade state attorney's office.

But Judge Crespo disagreed. The priests, the judge said, "cannot hide behind the veneer that since they are not subpoenaed by the state, they don't have to answer questions." Instead, he ordered them to appear again to be deposed. Afterward he would review the transcripts and decide whether or not to compel them to respond to questions they refused to answer, but they would have to invoke their constitutional rights question by question.

On November 26, two days before Thanksgiving, Wendt and the attorneys were back at the public defender's office. Round two began cordially enough.

"Good morning," Ray Taseff said to the cleric, who returned his greeting in kind.

"Can you tell me your name, please?"

"Frank Gerard Wendt, known in religion as Archimandrite Gregory, Father Abbot, with one *T*, Gregory or Father Gregory or Father Abbot."

"How would you like to be referred to by me?"

"The traditional, as Father Abbot."

"Okay. Father Abbot. My name is Ray Taseff. I am an attorney. I have been appointed to represent Mykhaylo Kofel."

He explained that "in the State of Florida in a criminal case, both sides have an opportunity to speak to the witnesses before the case goes to court, if in fact it ends up in court. This is a deposition."

Taseff then went on to ask the priest his date of birth, where he was born, and where he grew up. He asked him about his schooling—specifically, where he went to high school.

"St. John Vianny Minor Seminary," Wendt answered.

"Did you complete your high school education there?"

"Yes, I did."

"What year was that?"

"1962."

"Had you determined at that point in your life to pursue the priesthood?"

"Yes."

"At what point in your life did you make such a decision to come to such a realization?"

"When I was fifteen."

"What is it that precipitated that pursuit?"

"You can invoke privilege," Mel Black advised his client.

The cleric then read from a piece of paper: "Relying upon the advice of my counsel, due to the false allegations against me and my well-founded fear that these unjust investigations could lead to unfair charges and prosecution, I am reluctantly forced to invoke privilege and refuse to answer based on my constitutional rights guaranteed by the First, Fifth, and Fourteen Amendments."

"Was there any particular experience or event that led you to pursue the priesthood at age fifteen?" Taseff asked.

"Same advice," Black told Wendt who once again announced, "Relying upon the advice of my counsel, due to the false allegations against me and my well-founded fear that these unjust investigations could lead to unfair charges and prosecution, I am reluctantly forced to invoke privilege and refuse to answer based on my constitutional rights guaranteed by the First, Fifth, and Fourteen Amendments," the cleric said.

To save time the lawyers agreed to a shortened version. All Wendt had to say was, "I invoke the privilege on the grounds stated previously." And he did, again and again.

Of the nearly five hundred questions asked of him that day, the priest answered fewer than seventy. Among those that he refused to answer were, "When did you first meet Michelle Lewis?" "When did you first meet Mykhaylo Kofel?" "When did you first meet Mykhaylo Kofel's family?" and "Is Petro Terenta your adopted son?"

The session came to a close shortly before 5 P.M. It ended on a line of questioning about sexual abuse:

"When did you first learn that Mykhaylo Kofel had accused you of sexually molesting him?" Wendt was asked.

"I invoke privilege on the grounds stated previously," he responded.

"Have you ever had any sexual contact with Mykhaylo Kofel?"

"I invoke privilege on the grounds stated previously."

"Have you ever had any sexual contact with Petro Terenta?"

"I invoke privilege on the grounds stated previously."

"Have you ever had any sexual contact with Vasyl Kopych?"

"I invoke privilege on the grounds stated previously."

"Have you ever had any sexual contact with Sasha Korsak?"

"I invoke privilege on the grounds stated previously."

"Have you ever had any sexual contact with Yosyp Lembak?"

"I invoke privilege on the grounds stated previously."

"Have you ever had any sexual contact with any of those four candidates or any other candidates who were enrolled at Holy Cross Academy and Monastery?"

"I invoke privilege on the grounds stated previously."

But Georgi and Taseff weren't finished with Wendt. The deposition would be continued. There would be five more sessions before wrapping up on August 30, 2004.

In the interim, there would be hours of arguments, many of them heated, in front of Judge Crespo. From

Kofel's lawyers came motions to compel answers to their questions and motions to produce documents. From the priests' attorneys came motions for protective orders, motions for stays, and motions to deny the defense team's motions—"monk motions," the judge called them.

"Judge Crespo really struggled to be fair," Ray Taseff recalled. "We wanted to get as much information as possible, while the priests' attorneys wanted to give as little as possible."

While the lawyers argued, Mykhaylo Kofel cooled his heels in the county jail. He had been there since March 26, 2001. A voracious reader, he spent his time reading books and writing to his parents. His lawyers arranged for him to speak with them by telephone regularly, and they kept him abreast of developments in his case.

Kofel cooperated with his jailers, who became fond of him and called him Mike, and he got along well with his fellow inmates. Within weeks of his arrest, Edith Georgi said she observed a change in Mykhaylo. He had gained weight and "seemed more robust." Medications for anxiety and depression helped, Georgi said, but so did being away from Wendt and Gibault.

"When I got here in jail," Kofel said, "one of my classmates from Barry who works in the jail came to see me. She asked how I was doing, and she said that I spoke for the first time in jail." He explained, "It was because I had classes with Wendt. When I had classes with Wendt, I didn't say anything at all. I was scared of Wendt."

Kofel also spent time with doctors—the psychiatrists and psychologists his attorneys brought in to evaluate him. One of them was Professor Marianna Tovt-Korhsynska, M.D., Ph.D., a renowned and well-respected Ukrainian medical doctor and psychologist, and an assistant professor of medicine at Uzhgorod State University.

In 2003, Dr. Tovt-Korhsynska was awarded a Fulbright scholarship to the University of Pittsburgh Medical School. Before leaving for America, she met with the Kofels and others who knew Mykhalyo in Verkhovina Bystra.

"I met several times with Mykhaylo's parents, Yuri and Maria; with his aunt, Hanna Kahanec; his godmother, Olena Pavlyk; a former teacher, Hanna Saranych; and his best friend, Myhaylo Kulyk," Dr. Tovt-Korhsynska recalled in her written report to Edith Georgi. And she used the Russian version of the Minnesota Multiphasic Personality Inventory to obtain psychological profiles of Yuri and Maria Kofel. After she arrived in the United States, Dr. Tovt-Korhsynska also met with Mykhalyo in the county jail.

Her reports lent a unique perspective to the case. Unlike the other mental health professionals brought in to evaluate Kofel, Dr. Tovt-Korhsynska spoke to him, his family, and friend Myhaylo in their native language, and she had first-hand knowledge of the culture that shaped him.

Family and friends described Kofel as "very shy, modest, reticent, and introverted." He didn't express his feelings, and he didn't complain when someone offended him. Nor would he protest if others took advantage of him. "Both his mother and his teacher, Hanna Saranych, said he was obedient and could be influenced," Tovt-Korhsynska said.

Maria Kofel's MMPI, she said, reflected "much psychological distress, a tendency to resort to denial mechanisms, and moderate social introversion." She was a perfectionist who viewed the world "in terms of the extremes of good and bad." She instilled in her son the importance of studying "to be the best, especially as she was convinced of his very good memory."

From an early age, Mykhaylo "was able to read a page from a book and then recount it word by word. At the same time, she habituated Mykhaylo not to speak up for himself because 'it will be only worse.' These views are rather widespread in the post-Soviet society especially, among the lower socioeconomic classes," Dr. Tovt-Korhsynska said.

As for Yuri, his MMPI showed "psychological distress with marked depressive tendencies, social introversion, conformity, and conventionalism."

From her interviews with the Kofels, Tovt-Korhsynska learned that Yuri did not pay much attention to his son's upbringing. He loved his son, but did not really show it to him—it was "not customary," he told her. At least two to three times a week Yuri would be falling-down drunk. He became very angry when he drank, was physically abusive to his wife, and yelled at Mykhaylo but rarely hit him.

His father's alcoholism had a profound effect on Mykhaylo, according to Dr. Tovt-Korhsynska. It's what drove him to want to join a monastery. "When he entered his teenage years, Misha became more nervous, more reticent, more irritated when his father was drunk. He wanted to become independent and to leave his home as soon as possible. He dreamed of going to a monastery to become a monk."

His father's alcoholism was one of two pivotal factors in Mykhaylo's life. The other was the blow to the head Mykhaylo suffered in the 1994 explosion. Before it, Mykhaylo did well in school. After it, his grades fell.

Dr. Tovt-Korhsynska confirmed the sudden change with Mykhaylo's teachers and school records. "Possibly," she said, "the reason for the worse results in school could be the head injury he had at age twelve."

The circumstances of the explosion and the head injury were corroborated by Mykhaylo's aunt, Hanna, and his cousin Yevheniy. A bolt hit Mykhaylo above his right eye. It caused him to lose consciousness and bleed. After the accident, Misha complained of dizziness and sickness, and he lost his appetite. He slept a lot and seemed forgetful and nervous. His grades fell. Myhaylo Kulyk reported that "Misha often complained of feeling giddy."

As for Kofel's claims that he had been sexually molested by his father, Dr. Tovt-Korhsynska wrote, "Maria Kofel reported that Misha used to sleep in the middle between her and her husband in their double bed. It happened that her husband, when he was drunk, would look for his wife in the bed at night using his hand, but it was Misha he touched. When he got to his genitals, he touched them, and when he realized it, pulled his hand back."

Maria found it funny, and she thought Mykhaylo thought so, too. "But it is very likely that it irritated the boy, particularly as his father was drunk," Dr. Tovt-Korhsynska said.

"In the United States, he could interpret this behavior as molestation, especially as he was [allegedly] sexually abused by men whom he could perceive as very good people, better than his father."

Tovt-Korhsynska speculated that "maybe the idea that even his father could do something similar helped him somehow to survive the humiliation of the [alleged] sexual abuse in the United States."

When she met with Kofel in the county jail, Tovt-Korhsynska recalled, it was obviously painful for him to speak about the sexual abuse he allegedly was subjected to by the priests at Holy Cross.

"He became very tense, tried not to look at me, squeezed his legs and hands." She didn't press him on the details of the abuse, but he said the priests told him it would be a sin not to do as they told him, that God would be angry with him if he didn't, and that it would be a sin to tell anyone about it.

In her report, Tovt-Korhsynska wrote: "It is noteworthy that in our Transcarpathian region, especially in villages, the priests are very respected. People believe them and go to them for advice. Most of the Greek Catholic priests were in prison and some of them were even killed during the Soviet times because they didn't want to betray their faith, so the priests were considered to be honest, noble. So it could be very difficult for a boy like Mykhaylo from Ukraine . . . to fully understand that the two American priests cruelly abused him and lied to him."

When she asked him why he didn't report the abuse to the authorities, Mykhaylo said, "How could I go? It was easier for me to die, than to tell anybody about such a shame."

Besides, he was convinced that the police would not believe "a poor boy from such a country as Ukraine, but they would believe the American priests, who were . . . wealthy."

In Ukraine, Tovt-Korhsynska said, "it is a big shame to be raped, for men even bigger than for women," and it's not customary to report sexual abuse to the authorities. Their attitude, she said, is they have more important cases to investigate. Additionally, "all his relatives, teachers, and old friends described Mykhaylo as a shy, withdrawn, introverted boy, who would never speak up for himself. So for him it was especially difficult to report about being abused."

Regarding his mental state before the murder, Kofel told her, "I felt like I was turning crazy, and I didn't know what to do. It was like thousands of pieces of glass in my brain. But it was not exactly physical pain, because physical pain, it seemed to me, even relieved this pain. I tried to injure myself. I was thinking about suicide very often. I lost my faith, I think, the most important thing I had. Everything made me very nervous. I couldn't endure if somebody stood behind me or especially touched me, the slightest dirt irritated me, all the time I wanted to clean everything around myself and to wash myself.

"I began to drink alcohol. It helped me not to think all the time about what was happening with me. I had access to alcohol. There was a lot of alcohol of all kinds in their house, but I didn't drink too much. I didn't want them to realize I was drinking [because] they would be angry with me. I was really drunk only when it happened.

"And I took antidepressants. They encouraged me to take them at first, and I felt better for some time. But then the antidepressants helped less, so I took them more and more. That time I took five to six pills and more a day. That day it was really terrible, I was angry at the whole world, but I didn't want to kill anybody. I wanted to punish somebody. I drank a lot, never before I drank so much, and I took a lot of pills. I don't know exactly how much, but it was a lot. I was very drunk, never before I was like that, I didn't understand what I was doing. It was like not me, it was like somebody else was doing that. And I was very sick. I was vomiting.

"I was thinking about suicide, and also I wanted to punish somebody, because I felt that it was very unfair what happened with me. Why I went to her [Sister Michelle?] I didn't really understand, maybe because I was afraid of them, the two priests. They were very big and strong. She was available. And she was mean with us, she hated us. I came into her room and began to vomit because I was very sick. She woke up and jumped on me. I think I tried to protect myself. I didn't understand what I was doing."

While Kofel didn't reveal to Dr. Tovt-Korhsynska the details of the alleged sexual abuse he suffered, he had been more forthcoming with Dr. Philip Boswell, a clinical psychologist from Coral Gables, who met with him during several sessions in June 2001, which were arranged by the public defender's office. According to Dr. Boswell's notes, Kofel alleged that only hours before he murdered Sister Michelle, Father Damian had anally raped him.

He began by telling the psychologist, "I didn't tell you

everything about the sexual abuse before the murder. It was too painful to tell."

"Are you able now?" Dr. Boswell asked. "It can help to get it out."

In a slow and halting voice, Kofel said Gibault called him into his room. "He was only in his underwear. [He] made me also undress, like everything. I had to lie with him in bed."

Kofel said the priest then began touching him. "He started to touch my body, my private parts. He was also masturbating himself. I was lying faceup. He turned me facedown with his hand. He tried to have anal sex with me."

When Kofel tried to resist, the priest became angry— "Took me by my hair, pulling my head back," Kofel said. "In a nasty voice [he said], 'You better do what I say or I will throw you out! You'll go to hell if you don't do as I say!'"

Kofel told the psychologist that afterward he was in a lot of pain, that he bled from his anus, and that while he was being raped the priest called him a "bitch," and a "whore." Then he said, "The most terrible thing: 'You good fucking pussy.'"

Edith Georgi received Dr. Tovt-Korhsynska's report in May 2004. On June 8, she filed a "Notice of Intent to Rely on Insanity," informing the court that "The Defendant, Mykhalyo Kofel, through counsel, pursuant to Rule 3.216, F.R.Cr.P. [Florida Rules of Criminal Procedure], notifies this Court that he may rely upon the defense of insanity in this cause." She cited "Major Depressive Order" and "Posttraumatic Stress Disorder" as the basis for the plea and sent a copy to Gail Levine.

Among the witnesses she planned to call were Dr. Quintana, Dr. Koziol, and Detective Art Nanni.

21

> *"I was the Abbot of the Monastery of Exaltation of the Most Holy Cross. Today I am the Abbot of Protection of the Most Holy Theotokos Monastery."*
>
> —Father Abbot Gregory Wendt

Monday August 30, 2004, was another steamy summer day in South Florida. Exactly two weeks before, Miami-Dade's children went back to school following the long summer vacation, but for the first time since 1985 there would be no classes at Holy Cross Academy: The school had closed its doors.

The announcement came at the end of April when the *Miami Herald* broke the news. "Holy Cross Academy, which has struggled to keep its students since the 2001 on-campus stabbing death of Michelle Lewis, last week sold its ten-acre gated compound on Sunset Drive and Southwest 124th Avenue to a charter school."

What's more, Wendt was no longer Catholic. Neither were Gibault, Petro Terenta, Vasyl Kopych, or Yosyp Lembak. Their new affiliation was with the Orthodox Church of America, the OCA, which is not part of the Catholic Church.

Meanwhile, Catholic priests were making national and international headlines in August 2004, but it wasn't for saving souls. In St. Louis, the archdiocese announced it would pay two million dollars to settle eighteen claims of sexual abuse against clerics dating back to the 1970s, while in Austria a student priest—a seminarian—was convicted of downloading hundreds of pictures of child pornography. The story made headlines in both South Florida dailies, the *Miami Herald* and the *Sun-Sentinel*.

According to the news reports, authorities also found tens of thousands of pornographic photos and dozens of pornographic videos on computers at the seminary in the diocese of St. Poelten, fifty miles west of Vienna. Other photos of seminary students kissing and fondling each other and their older religious instructors were found, too. Pope John Paul II dispatched a papal delegate to exorcise the scandal.

Closer to home, hurricanes were once again very much on Floridians' minds. On August 13, Hurricane Charlie, a Category Four storm packing winds of 145 mph flattened Punta Gorda and Port Charlotte, two hundred miles north of Miami, while yet another hurricane was slowly churning across the Caribbean. Hurricane warnings and watches had been issued for the Virgin Islands and Puerto Rico, and forecasters were predicting that this one, Frances, a Category Three storm, would make landfall somewhere on Florida's east coast.

So it was understandable if the men and women who reported to Judge Crespo's courtroom at 11 A.M. for the final session in the seemingly never-ending deposition of Father Abbot Gregory Wendt were a bit edgy.

It was the sixth deposition session over a period of two years. The sessions, "continuations" in legalspeak, were often contentious and acrimonious. Prosecutors sat in on each one, but for this session no one from the state attorney's office appeared. The prosecutors would read the transcript instead. At this point the investigation into Kofel's allegations of sexual abuse had reached a dead end. Without corroboration or a confession, the state would not prosecute the priests even though virtually every lawman who spoke with the former monk came away convinced that he was telling the truth.

As for the defense attorneys, Holy Cross had been Mykhaylo Kofel's home for four years, and Father Abbot Gregory Wendt, the "highest authority" there, had been his spiritual shepherd and religious advisor for each of those years. Deposing him was an essential element of their investigation. Nevertheless, Wendt was argumentative and disingenuous. The priest, observers said, seemed contemptuous of the procedure and of the lawyers who asked him questions. Ray Taseff described the holy man's demeanor as "haughty" and "pompous."

And by his own admission, Wendt was verbose.

Following one long-winded response, Edith Georgi asked the priest, "Some people speak very verbosely and just maybe tend to answer a simple question with a paragraph . . . are you that kind of person?"

"I would tend to give complete answers, which might include explanations that are not necessary," Wendt replied.

That was apparent when Georgi asked if he had been hospitalized for any reason since the first monastic candidates, Petro Terenta and Mykhaylo Kofel, arrived in the United States in 1996.

"Yes, I had surgery on my left ankle," the priest replied. It would have been a sufficient answer, but Wendt didn't stop there. He continued: "I had a ruptured posterior tibial tendon, which required a tendon transfer with osteotome of the calcaneus involving the attachment with the cytanium bone screw. This was a mark or procedure on the left ankle, but it was also performed as an outpatient. I was able to return home by the evening."

It was also apparent when Georgi asked the priest if he considered Kofel as a "peaceful person."

"This question has to be carefully answered in order to give it its fair treatment," the priest began. "I want to say, first of all, that before the brutal murder of Sister Michelle, I have not known personally of Mykhaylo Kofel committing any violent acts in regard to someone else. So, that is the first statement in regard to this question.

"Then secondly, I think you have to distinguish between physical passivity such as a phlegmatic personality or reluctance to do physical work and in peacefulness, which to me [is] an interior disposition and governs more than one's actions at any particular moment.

"So I would say that exteriorly he stayed pretty much sitting at his desk as much as possible and even avoided doing the tasks that the other monastics were doing as part of their chores, keeping up with the candidates' house and so forth, even hiding at times when it was time to do these chores, but, you know, he would willingly at his own choice spend hours seated at his study carrel reading and studying.

"Now, in regard to my assessment of him as a peaceful person, interiorly when the monastic candidates came from the Ukraine they knew practically no English, almost literally no English, and so it was not surprising that they would be interested in action movies, movies that contained violence, because you don't have to understand the language to see what is going on.

"As time progressed and their knowledge of the language became more—they became more proficient in their knowledge of the English language, then I was somewhat disturbed that Mykhaylo Kofel still demonstrated an exaggerated interest in movies that were characterized by fighting and physical violence.

"I had talked with him in regard to this disregard and I also mentioned it to the other monastic candidates that vocation to the monastery is in essence of one who has as one of his titles the prince of peace. This is not to say that other vocations such as the military or so forth are not choices that Christians can make, but it is not a monastic vocation, and I questioned Mykhaylo Kofel in this regard, did he really feel he had a monastic vocation in pointing to the inappropriateness of this interest and there was also sort of an acting out of karate types of moves with other candidates.

"I also discouraged this and explained that this is not appropriate. In addition, there were things that were stolen such as the gold class ring of then Petro Terenta, a substantial amount of money from the petty cash of the monastery and my father's coin collection, which my mother had given to me to keep for her. I had put it on top of my filing cabinet, where it stayed for a very lengthy time, and there was never anything missing before, or since, Mr. Kofel's arrest. So I think that there are some things that I think would militate against a conclusion that he was a peaceful person interiorly or at least raise some grounds for question marks."

That was during the July 6, 2004, session. During the previous session in June, Georgi and Ray Taseff inquired about Wendt's educational background, basing their questions on a document, "Background on Father Abbot Gregory Wendt," that had been released on his behalf by Wragg and Casas, the Miami public relations firm. It indicated that the priest had "studied" at Oxford University in England, the University of Munich in Germany, and Fordham University in New York.

After clarifying that he had been "formally admitted to research," Georgi asked, "At which institutions listed here did you do research?"

"Oxford University, University of Munich, Germany," the priest replied.

"Do you recall the nature of the research?"

"My area of study is linguistics and included in that I took lectures."

"Well, that was the area of research that you did at Oxford?"

"My interests, academic interests are very broad, so when I was at any particular place I didn't limit myself, you know, to simply what I was writing on, but I would take advantage of what was available. As you know in response to your question as to universities or institutes or centers at which time I matriculated as opposed to those at which I did research, that question has been answered very clearly."

Georgi followed up. "Is there a record of the research you would have done at these various institutions?"

Apparently annoyed and exasperated, the cleric responded, "Now, if you are doing research, exactly where do you expect you would find a record?"

"Sir, I am asking you!" Georgi snapped back.

"I find the question a bit bizarre," the priest growled.

"Well, I could perhaps go into a library in Broward County and do some research. They would never know I was there."

"Exactly."

"I could say I did research at Nova [Southeastern University] and no one would know I was there. Is that the nature of your doing research at Oxford and Munich? Did you go there to use their libraries?"

"In case you are not aware, no one can walk off the street into the Bodleian Library in Oxford. You have to be admitted on the basis of academic credentials. I was so admitted," Wendt countered.

"Is there a record of your attendance and your research at the places you say you did research?"

When the priest didn't answer, his attorney answered for him. "You are asking if he knows whether there is—" but before Mel Black could complete the sentence, Wendt regained his voice. "Whether they keep records?" he asked.

"Do you know?" Georgi asked.

"Twenty years back?" Black asked incredulously.

After probing Wendt's undergraduate background—he had graduated from Alabama College—and his status as an archimandrite, Georgi asked, "Do you list Fordham University as being an institution, where you were formally enrolled in Fordham University, in terms of being registered with the registrar at Fordham?"

The question could have been answered with a simple yes or no. Instead, Wendt made a speech: "First of all, if you look at what I said, I said—I listed among the institutions John the XXIII, the Center for Eastern Christian Studies at Fordham University. John the XXIII Center was located in two buildings geographically, as I recall, on the west side of Fordham Road. The main campus being on the east side of Fordham Road. They were owned by the Fordham University Jesuits, the community lived, quite a bit, at least a very large community there of Jesuits, lived in that center. I lived there as a student. Classes were given in the classrooms of Fordham University. The other students lived in the dormitories of Fordham University. The students used the library of Fordham University. One registered for the center, at the center, therefore, you know, the question of the matriculation of the center's registration with the main registrar of the university is speculation, something of which I was not, I am not at all concerned.

"I find the question bizarre in the extreme."

"I would also like to present a couple of things which I got off of the Internet from the Google search by putting in John the XXIII and it says for example, Father George A. Maloney formed or founded John the XXIII Institute for Eastern Christian Studies, Fordham University. That is one.

"There is another one of the late Father Ciszek—in Siberia. He is up for canonization of saint of the Catholic Church. He was there at the time I was there. I lived there with him, conversed with him, ate with him and in his bio says worked at John the XXIII's Center at Fordham University. So this is a totally typical reference which seems to have been fallen upon scrutiny for reasons beyond my meager understanding."

Then finally, mercifully, he answered the question he found "bizarre in the extreme." "Yes," he said, "in terms of registering with the registrar."

As for Sister Michelle, Georgi wanted to know who had the authority to elevate the slain sister to the status of nun. "Are you the person who evaluated Sister Michelle Lewis to complete her religious training at Holy Cross Monastery?" she asked. "Were you the person who conducted the evaluation?"

"That would be the bishop," the cleric answered.

"Which bishop?" Georgi wanted to know.

"Whichever bishop had jurisdiction over the monastery at the time that she was supposed to be ready to be admitted fully into the status of a nun."

"Okay. The year 2001, who would that be?"

It was a simple, straightforward question, but instead of answering it, the priest turned to his attorney. "Do you want me to answer?" he asked.

"Nobody actually submitted her to any bishops, so it is not relevant," Mel Black declared.

Georgi disagreed. "I think it is relevant, the bishop over Holy Cross Monastery in 2001."

"I think that's all on this question, Ms. Georgi," the irate cleric barked.

Ray Taseff interjected, "You just answered it was the bishop who made the final determination and evaluation of her. Didn't you just say that?"

"There was no final evaluation, so she was—how would the bishop play in this question?" the priest replied. But Taseff persisted.

"You said there would be a final evaluation, one made by her bishop."

"That is the end of the answer. Thank you, Mr. Taseff."

Taseff wasn't about to give up. "Who would have made that evaluation?" he demanded.

"Are you badgering me?" the cleric snapped. "I already said I completed my answer."

"Do you feel badgered?"

"Yes."

"I am not badgering you. I am simply asking the questions," the defense attorney responded.

There was testiness between the attorneys, too. Tempers flared when Edith Georgi began probing Wendt's affiliation with the Orthodox Church of America.

"I was the Abbot of the Monastery of Exaltation of the Most Holy Cross," Wendt declared during the deposition of March 4, 2004. "Today I am the Abbot of Protection of the Most Holy Theotokos Monastery,"

"Has the name of the monastery at Holy Cross changed since November of 2002?" Georgi asked.

"The correct answer is that the Monastery of Exaltation of the Most Holy Cross no longer exists. That doesn't mean that the corporation has been dissolved. It is our intention to do so, but the community now exists in another monastery with a name that I gave you," the priest explained, adding, "The monastic community for spiritual reasons joined the Orthodox Church of America."

"What is that? I am sorry, sir, I really . . . sincerely don't know," Georgi said.

"Edith, you do know, you can't say you sincerely don't know, you have been communicating with them," Mel Black declared, a tinge of sarcasm in his voice.

"I don't know. I don't know, Mr. Black," the public defender fired back indignantly.

"You have been in communication with them, so how can you not know?" Black asked.

"I don't know what they are. What are they? What is it? You don't know what I know, Mr. Black, and I don't appreciate that. Now I am asking him, as the head of this entity what that Orthodox Church of America—What is it? I don't know if it is a religious entity, a structure? I don't know what the thing is. I certainly heard of it [but] I don't know what it is, okay?"

"You have heard of the Greek Orthodox Church and the Russian Orthodox Church?" Wendt asked.

"Absolutely," Georgi replied.

"The Russian Orthodox Church was the first Orthodox [church] to missionize the Americas, and as such its bishops served the pastoral needs of all other groups of Orthodox in America originally. In 1970 the original Russian Orthodox Church in North America was granted autocephaly—a-u-t-o-c-e-p-h-a-l-y, from self-head, a Greek word *self* and *head*, self-head together—by a legal proceeding of the Holy Synod of the Russian Orthodox Church in Moscow [which declared that] this Church of America was self-headed. It no longer depended on Moscow and became the Orthodox Church of America."

After thanking Wendt, Georgi stared at Black. "I am sure I already knew all that, right, Mel? Including autocephaly?"

But the public defender wasn't finished with the cleric. "Just to be very clear, my question is did this change from one name to the other . . ."

"Excuse me," Wendt interrupted indignantly. "To me it is more than a name."

After Wendt explained that the change in affiliation was purely for "spiritual reasons," Georgi asked, "Did the publicity from this case have anything to do with this transition?"

"Absolutely not," the priest answered, annoyed that the public defender would even ask such a question of him.

"Anyone who would make such a move as significant

as changing one's church affiliation for such a reason would not have any principles."

Holy Cross affiliated with the Orthodox Church in October 2003. The following month, Wendt wrote to the Orthodox congregations in the area announcing an open house at Holy Cross Academy. In the letter, he offered every Orthodox student who enrolled a five-hundred-dollar discount in the annual tuition, "and the Academy, in gratitude, would also contribute one hundred dollars per year to the local Orthodox church in which the student is a member."

Wendt closed the letter by assuring its recipients that "our monks made a faith-based decision to become part of the Orthodox Church for purely spiritual reasons, reasons for which we are now under attack by the Catholic Church."

Throughout the proceedings Judge Crespo was vigilant about preserving the priests' Fifth Amendment privilege against self-incrimination. When Georgi asked Gibault if he'd gone for counseling after he was asked to leave the seminary due to his alleged drinking problem, the judge sustained his right not to answer. Likewise when she asked Wendt if he filled out the tax forms for the monastery. But when Georgi asked the priest why he adopted Petro Terenta, the objection from his attorney was overruled.

"What is the relevance of that?" Mel Black wanted to know.

But Wendt answered, "Because of affiliation and paternity," he said. "And . . . to enable this young man the opportunity, in case I should die, to have whatever patrimony that would be available, enable him to pursue further studies."

"Could you please explain the word *patrimony*?" Georgi asked.

"Inheritance."

"Was there any other reason for the adoption?"

"At the time of the adoption, I had mentioned to the judge, just to be thorough, that it was pointed out to us that there is no direct benefit by this adoption in regard to INS, but there could be a psychological benefit, so I disclosed that to the judge."

"To what judge?" Crespo asked.

"The adoption judge, that was not the principle reason for the adoption, the principle reasons were the one I gave, but I did disclose that to the judge, which is what I had been told."

Georgi knew that Gibault had told the Kofels that he wanted to adopt Mykhaylo for immigration purposes. Wendt had given the same reason to the Terentas, so she asked him to clarify what he meant by psychological benefits.

"It was made known to me by the attorney handling the adoption, there would not be a direct INS benefit. In other words, he would not be, for example, granted a green card because of this adoption, but there could be a psychological benefit in regard to INS consideration of his status in remaining in this country. So I disclosed that to the judge, what I had been told, because you are not allowed to pursue an adoption for specifically these purposes, INS purposes."

"Were there any other reasons?"

"No."

> "*When you stabbed and beat her that day, five angels came and took her soul to heaven, that is where she is now with her father, grandparents, her aunts, and uncles.*"

> —Beverly Lewis

After several months of negotiations, Edith Georgi and Gail Levine struck a deal. Levine's boss, Miami-Dade state attorney Katherine Fernandez-Rundle approved it. She believed it was the right thing to do. Kofel believed it was the right thing to do, too. If the case went to trial, he risked life in prison without the possibility of parole.

The negotiations were under way in the fall of 2004. In a November 24 letter to Gail Levine, Edith Georgi wrote:

Dear Ms. Levine,

Prior to our communications of last Friday (November 19) we had entered into plea discussions. You summed up the situation quite well when you reported to Judge Crespo that we were "ten years apart" (your offer of thirty-five years vs. our offer of twenty-five years) and you hoped we would be able to reach an agreement in November. Last Friday, however, you stated that you are unwilling to go below thirty-five (possibly thirty-three). I was quite surprised at your unwillingness to negotiate, particularly in view of the reams of information we have discovered (and shared with you) concerning the entire underpinnings of the school and "monastic" environment formerly known as Holy Cross Academy. This information will obviously be very persuasive to a jury considering Mr. Kofel's culpability and should also affect your position on the case. Furthermore, based on your own experience, you must be aware of the logistical difficulties of completing our investigation in the Ukraine given the political situation and the infrastructure we have yet to penetrate. If you have read all of the records we have assembled as well as the sworn testimony of Fathers Wendt and Gibault, you must also be aware of the numerous fraudulent acts they have committed against others, not to mention the horrific treatment of Mr. Kofel.

I am writing to request that you rethink your position, or in the alternative, that we all meet with the State Attorney, Katherine Fernandez-Rundle, to further discuss this matter.

Sincerely,
Edith Georgi Houlihan
Assistant Public Defender

Less than three months later, there was an agreement. However, the final say would be Judge Crespo's. It would be up to him to approve what the State Attorney and the public defender had worked out, so at 9 A.M. on Thursday, February 10, 2005, two officers from the department of corrections led Kofel into Crespo's sixth-floor courtroom.

Instead of a prison jumpsuit, the former monk-trainee from Ukraine wore a solid blue shirt over a white T-shirt, black slacks, and a pair of handcuffs. He had been in the county jail for three years, ten months, and thirteen days. When he arrived there, he was a scrawny boy with a scraggly beard and an even scragglier mustache, but he would leave heavier, clean-shaven, and balding. And he would leave with a new name—while in jail Mykhaylo Kofel began calling himself Mike.

At about 9:15, the bailiff shouted, "All Rise," and the door leading to the judge's chambers opened. Judge Crespo bounded to the bench. There was a spring in his step that hadn't been there previously. For one thing, the judge was considerably thinner than he had been when he presided over Kofel's arraignment back in April 2001, the result of gastric bypass surgery the summer before. For another, he was on the verge of bringing the troublesome case to a close.

He had heard dozens of motions and issued scores of orders, wrestled with First and Fifth Amendment issues and endured depositions and the perpetuated testimony of monk candidates Yosyp Lembak, Vasyl Kopych, Sasha Korsak, and Petro Terenta. Many times the jurist's son, Manny Jr., called to ask his father to join him for lunch, only to hear his father say, "No. I'm up to my neck in monk motions."

As soon as he took the bench, Judge Crespo called the court to order in the matter of the *State of Florida v. Kofel, Case Number FO1-9820.*

"Counsel for the state and counsel for the defense, note your appearances for the record," he commanded.

Lead prosecutor Gail Levine rose to her feet. "Gail Levine, Priscilla Prado, and Penny Brill for the State of Florida," she announced.

Edith Georgi stood up next. "Edith Georgi and Ray Taseff, assistant public defenders on behalf of Mr. Kofel," she said.

After noting for the record that Mykhaylo Kofel was in the courtroom, too, sitting in the jury box between his lawyers, Crespo addressed Gail Levine. He asked the prosecutor if there had been a resolution of the case.

"Yes, Your Honor," Levine replied. "After continued discussions with the public defender, the State of Florida will offer the defendant a reduced plea from the charge of murder, first degree, and burglary with assault and battery. My understanding, the defendant is willing to . . . plead guilty to murder in the second degree of Michelle Lewis and burglary with assault and battery of Michelle Lewis, and receive a sentence of thirty years in the Florida State prison."

"Any other conditions to the plea?" the judge asked.

"No, Judge, thirty years for each count to run concurrent and coterminous." Afterward, Kofel would be deported to Ukraine.

"I would like the court to be aware that Michelle Lewis's mother, Beverly Lewis, is present and she would like to speak to you," the prosecutor added.

"I will be speaking to her," the judge promised. Turning to Kofel's lawyers, the judge asked if an interpreter was needed.

"His English is excellent," Georgi replied. "We would like the cuffs off."

As soon as the handcuffs were removed, Judge Crespo ordered Kofel to stand and raise his right hand to be sworn. The judge then began firing questions at the young defendant from Verkhovina Bystra, House #166, Zakarpattia Oblast, Ukraine. He wanted to be certain that Kofel was alert and coherent, and that he fully understood the consequences of the plea bargain.

"Now, the first question I want to ask you is exactly what I just asked your lawyer. Do you understand and comprehend the English language in such a manner and in such a way that you are not requesting, at this time, any assistance by any professional interpreter to assist you in understanding what it is you are doing here today and what is being stated here in court today?"

"Yes, Your Honor."

"You are fully understanding everything that's going on here today in the English language?"

"Yes, sir."

"How old are you, sir?"

"Twenty-two."

"What is your date of birth?"

"Seven-nine-eighty-two."

"Where were you born?"

"Ukraine."

"How long have you resided in the United States of America?"

"Eight years."

"Do you recall the date that you came to the United States?"

"Yes, Your Honor, it was '96, August 1, 1996."

"How far have you attended school?"

"I finished high school and I was in college for six months."

"So you have approximately less than one year of college."

"Yes, sir."

"Was your high school education completed in this country or Ukraine?"

"Here."

"What school did you graduate from?"

"Holy Cross Academy."

"Do you read and write the English language?"

"Yes, Your Honor."

"Do you read and write Ukrainian?"

"I do."

"So you are fully versed in both languages now?"

"Both languages."

Satisfied that Kofel had sufficient command of the

English language, Judge Crespo next sought to make certain that the defendant was not mentally impaired.

"Now have you ever, at anytime, in your life been treated for any type of mental illness or mental disturbance?"

"No."

"As you stand before this court here today, are you under the influence of any illegal drugs, alcohol, or any kind of prescription medication?"

"No, Your Honor."

"Anything that could possibly impair you or keep you from clearly and fully understanding what it is you are doing here today?"

"No, Your Honor."

"As you stand before me here today, are you clearly and fully understanding what it is that you are doing here today regarding your case?"

"Yes, Your Honor."

With that out of the way, Judge Crespo explained that before he could accept the plea, he had to be "convinced by a preponderance of the evidence that this action by you, this decision by you, has been done freely, voluntarily, without any duress or any pressure from anyone. And that you are taking this decision and making this decision because you believe, in considering the totality of the circumstances of this case, that this resolution is in your best interest."

He told Kofel that he would be giving up his right to a trial by a judge and a jury. "Do you understand that?"

"Yes, Your Honor."

And by pleading he would give up his rights to have his guilt proven beyond a reasonable doubt, to confront witnesses, and to appeal to a higher court. "This process, this plea," the judge explained, "has a finality to it. This closes your case. Do you understand that?"

"Yes," Kofel replied.

Judge Crespo then announced that he found Kofel to be

an "alert, intelligent young man, who fully understands the nature of the charges against him, and the consequences of his plea, and that the facts stated in the indictment and other documents, pretrial documents, "are sufficient to establish a *prima facie* case."

As he promised, Judge Crespo called on Beverly Lewis to speak. "I would like to address Mr. Kofel," the still-grieving mother said.

After being sworn, Mrs. Lewis began reading a letter she had written but never sent to her daughter's killer.

"I am Shelly's mother," she began, her hands shaking as she read. "You know her as Sister Michelle. I want you to know where she is now. She is in heaven," she said through tears. "When you stabbed and beat her that day, five angels came and took her soul to heaven, that is where she is now with her father, grandfather, her aunts, and uncles."

Mrs. Lewis recounted that she asked the funeral director if her daughter's casket could be open for the funeral. "I was told no," she said, her voice breaking. "I saw my daughter take her first breath. Your murdering her was so violent and brutal that I was not allowed to look at her and say good-bye. By the time she was nineteen years old, she could no longer see the big *E* and *T* on the eyeglass chart without glasses. How long did her glasses last when you attacked her? After they were gone, it shouldn't have been that difficult to kill her because she couldn't even see you. I am asking the court to make, as part of your sentence, every March 25 that you are put in lockup with crime scene photos."

Mrs. Lewis sat down. The courtroom remained hushed until Judge Crespo broke the silence. He thanked Mrs. Lewis, then explained why he would not be able to do as she asked.

"As to your request," the judge said, "after a period of time this court loses jurisdiction over his person and he becomes the jurisdiction of the department of corrections of the State of Florida, and I have no authority to order them to do that on a yearly basis. Even though I respect and understand your request, I must respectfully decline."

The judge then turned his attention to Kofel. "Before this court pronounces sentence on you, is there anything you would like to say to this court, more importantly to Sister Michelle's family?"

Kofel stood. "Yes, sir," he said. Then he began reading from a prepared statement. "I just want to say that I am really sorry. I want to take full responsibility for my actions. I wish I could turn back time and change the past. If I could, I will give my life for hers. Murder is wrong, no matter what."

He remained standing as Judge Crespo sternly meted out his sentence—thirty years in the state penitentiary on each count, with credit for time served in the county jail. "These thirty-year sentences will run concurrent and coterminous," the judge declared. "Do you understand what that means, Mr. Kofel?"

"Yes, sir," Kofel replied, but Crespo explained it anyway.

"As you serve one count, you will serve the other. When you finish one count, you will be finished with the other counts and, therefore, your entire sentence. Do you understand that?

"Yes, sir."

"Is that what you want to do?" the judge asked.

"Yes," Kofel replied.

Judge Crespo then ordered Kofel handcuffed. When that was done, he addressed everyone in the courtroom.

"This court, as many of you know, has been involved in the criminal justice system for well over thirty-five years now, and during that time, of course, I have been exposed to many, many cases, all tragic in their own way, but I have never really seen a case as tragic as this one because it has in essence put out the lights of a person who I did not personally know, but from what I have learned she was very special, a person whose life had not been easy at times. She would have to cross biblical paths but she felt and believed that she had found something that she really, really wanted to do. Once she found that, from what I know, she was at peace with that decision and she was looking forward to the rest of her life. After having made that decision, that [life] was snuffed out . . . terminated when Mr. Kofel took it upon himself to perpetrate this horrible act. What is most tragic about this case are the finalities of it.

"Nothing can bring Sister Michelle back. If he could, I am sure that what he stated, that he would trade himself for her, is true because I also believe that at this time, these years that, you have spent in that jail across the street, I sense in you a change. I sense in you a maturity that only time and a physically, emotional, mental burden can bring. And I am not talking just about maturity, that you look older because you are older, I am talking about more of an inner maturity.

"But the fact remains that this was an intolerable act and, even though the State has seen fit as part of the overall resolution of this case to offer what this court considers a very lenient sentence, a very lenient resolution, it doesn't take away the fact that the act remains intolerable and we as a society, as a community cannot tolerate such conduct. And because of that, you will be incarcerated for thirty years. You will be a middle-aged man by the time that you come out. You will not be able to reside anymore in this country. You are going back to your roots. What you do there is only up to you. I know that once you return there, you will find some kind of modicum of peace. This act will always be with you because, as I said, this act can't be taken back.

"So I know that you are going to return to the Ukraine. You may form a life. You will in all probability form a family, and hopefully you will live out your days as peaceably as you possibly can, but knowing that back in Miami on the twenty-fifth day of March, year two thousand one, you did an act that could never he condoned or forgiven, and for that may God have mercy on your soul. This court is adjourned."

With that, Judge Crespo left the courtroom. Kofel was taken back to the county jail where he remained until turned over to the custody of the state's department of corrections. With credit for the four years he already served in the county jail, the Ukraine native's sentence would be up in 2031. If he managed to stay out of trouble during his incarceration, he could get time off for good behavior, in which case he would be a free man by 2026. But whenever he's released, Kofel will be met at the penitentiary door by agents from United States Immigration and Customs Enforcement (ICE) and deported to his homeland.

Outside the courtroom, Gail Levine and Edith Georgi stopped to speak to reporters.

Flanked by Priscilla Prado and Penny Brill, Levine said, "We felt that the intolerable acts of Mykhaylo Kofel had to be considered in light of the intolerable conditions he lived [under] at Holy Cross Academy.

"We struggled in this case," she said, "and these so-called religious leaders blocked every one of our efforts."

The day before, Levine told the *Miami Herald*, "This wasn't a case of a bad man killing someone." Instead, "It was the case of a victim who turned around and victimized an innocent person." The state, the prosecutor said, believed Kofel had been abused, and that gave rise to "significant mitigation."

Mykhaylo Kofel, Edith Georgi said, "has accepted full responsibility for what he did. In my opinion, it's time the people who have wronged him took responsibility for what they've done."

Reached for comment, Gibault's attorney called the statements "outrageous," according to the *Herald*, and he blasted the allegations that had been leveled at the holy men of Holy Cross.

"They have found no evidence of sexual abuse and

haven't charged these men," Richard Hersch said, referring to both Gibault and Wendt. "The only evidence is out of the mouth of Kofel, a man who stabbed this lady ninety-two times, stomped her six times, and bludgeoned her with a blunt object and took extensive steps to cover up the crime."

Attorney Mel Black, who represented Wendt, said that prosecutors were frustrated because they couldn't get a tougher sentence and resorted to wrongfully accusing his client.

"They've been singing that duet for years, and it has gotten them nowhere," the defense attorney told the *Sun-Sentinel*. "There is sex appeal to the case. It's sensational, and it involves a religious institution. They wanted to win this one badly."

Despite the blistering criticism from the priests' lawyers, one week later, on February 17, sex crimes detectives Jose Cabado and Chavelin Moise, sat down with Mykhaylo Kofel in an interview room at the county jail. They were there to take a sworn statement from the former monk candidate. A stenographer was with them. At 1:22 P.M., the detectives began asking questions.

Kofel revealed details he had never before revealed to lawmen, prompting Cabado to ask, "Do you remember me talking to you a couple of years back about these incidents, and another detective, the second detective was Steve Signori . . . why didn't you tell us about these incidents in the past?"

Kofel drew a deep breath and explained: "In the beginning, the first time, I remember I didn't tell you about how Gibault raped me. And you know, I didn't even tell my lawyer, even my lawyer in the beginning. I told him within a year but not the first time. I just left it out because I was ashamed of myself, I didn't trust nobody. I was just embarrassed as hell."

Afterword

At first it seemed like a simple case of premeditated murder. A dead nun. A confession. A quick arrest.

"A slam dunk," observed criminal defense attorney Richard Hersch. But the murder of Sister Michelle Lewis turned out to be anything but a slam dunk.

It involved an army of lawyers, four law enforcement agencies, plus the U.S. Department of Justice and the Ukrainian Ministry of Justice, and it sent investigators halfway around the world to the Transcarpathian Mountains of southwestern Ukraine.

In the end, lawmen were unable to corroborate Mykhaylo Kofel's allegations of sexual abuse. Even if they had, it would not have relieved him of responsibility for the murder of Sister Michelle.

Ultimately, Kofel is responsible for what he did to Sister Michelle on March 25, 2001, but the seed for that crime was planted in Ukraine, where a young Mykhaylo witnessed his drunken father beating up his mother—"a classic case of the ongoing cycle of violence," says Ray Taseff. And while the seed was planted in a remote mountain village in Transcarpathia, it was nurtured in Miami at Holy Cross.

It was a bad idea to bring adolescent boys from eastern Europe halfway around the world to South Florida, to let them rub elbows with affluent American teenagers who themselves are just beginning to experience sexuality. Religious training is rigorous and it requires maturity, which is why the practice of admitting young boys to monasteries is virtually unheard of. For that, at least, the Holy Cross priests need to take responsibility. As for Kofel's allegations of sexual abuse, without corroboration there would be no prosecution, which means in the eyes of the law they are innocent.

At a meeting in the days after Sister Michelle's murder, Father Abbot Gregory Wendt reportedly assured about one hundred concerned parents that "the young men from the Ukraine underwent a lot of scrutiny" before they were brought to Holy Cross.

"They undergo clinical psychological tests. It sounded pretty official. It's a psychiatric test just to make sure they are balanced individuals," Frank Cordero said Wendt told the parents, according to the *Miami Herald*.

Which is not what the priest said under oath during his deposition.

"Was there any background check conducted by you or any other members of the Holy Cross Academy and Monastery of Mykhaylo?" Edith Georgi asked him.

"The recommendation of his parish priest," Wendt replied.

"Do you talk to them about his reputation?"

"I don't think the priest would recommend someone he didn't feel had promise."

"Well, how much information did you seek from the parish priest?"

"A normal amount."

"What's a 'normal amount,' sir? I don't do this business."

"I'm not asked this question either. This is the first time."

"Well, you are now so . . ."

"I've answered that."

"What sort of information did you seek?"

"What we considered to be the normal amount."

"What kinds of things would you be wanting to know?"

"Does this person seem to be interested in prayer, does he attend church regularly and so forth."

"What else?"

"If you're asking about behavioral questions, they are presumed. I mean, obviously, the priest is not going to recommend someone whom he considers to have a behavior problem."

"Did you want to know if there were any background issues, for example, with his family or anything like that?"

"I would have presumed that the priest would tell me, but no, we did not specifically ask for more than he told."

"Did you want to know anything about the type of person this is?"

"Yes, and in regard to the questions I've already described to you. We're interested in a religious vocation. So those would be the types of questions that we are asking and that would concern us."

Holy Cross Academy closed its doors in 2004. Wendt and Gibault along with Petro Terenta, Vasyl Kopych, and Yosyp Lembak now spend most of their time in Weaverville, North Carolina, at the Protection of the Most Holy Theotokos Monastery which is part of the Orthodox Church of America. Petro is now known as Hierodeacon Nicholas, Vasyl is Monk Seraphim, and Yosyp is Monk Mark.

I contacted Father Wendt by mail and by e-mail to request an interview. I received a letter dated October 23,

2006, from Joseph Blonsky advising me that "the abbot and the other members of the monastic community are out of the country at present. Upon their return, the members of the community will be in touch with you in response to your request." I have yet to hear from them.

I have heard from Mykhaylo Kofel several times. In a letter dated November 28, 2006, he wrote from his prison cell at the Okeechobee Correctional Institution, in Ockeechobee, Florida, about 140 miles north of Miami. Kofel wrote:

> I pass my time by reading, writing, watching TV, listening to a radio, exercising etc. Also, in here I work Inside Grounds, which means I either cut the grass or rake the dead grass; just keep the compound clean. Eventually, I will be able to work Outside Grounds, which means I will be able to go outside the gate and work there.
>
> I still pray for my parents, relatives, friends etc. but I don't pray for the priests (Wendt, Gibault) I still have a big hate for them. I know it is taught to forgive but after what they did to me and others it's impossible to forgive, I tried but it doesn't work. I still have nightmares of what happened to me in Holy Cross. It's psychologically devastating what happened to me in Holy Cross. I am going to have those nightmares, scars, and memories for many years.
>
> I am being treated nicely in here, much better than Holy Cross of course. They feed us three good meals a day, and on holidays the prison feeds special food to inmates. The institution provides everybody with good dental and medical care. Basically if you are not a troublemaker the officers will respect you. I constantly write to my parents, they write to me too, we talk on the phone once every three months thanks to the public defender's office.

I do get lonely from time to time. Sometimes I wish I had a brother or a sister or both. It is also hard for me because my parents are so far away from me and are not able to visit me. Likewise, it is hard for them, too. They miss me very much and can't do anything about it.

I would like my former classmates from Holy Cross and other people that knew me to know that I am not a bad person. I feel horrible for what happened and for what I did. My heart is full with remorse. I took the whole responsibility for what happened, the priests did not, they hid behind their lawyers.

Since I was locked up, I helped a lot of people. I taught some of them Russian and for some I helped to write letters to their families. I would share my food if anybody was hungry. If I had anything extra that anybody needed I would give it to that person.

I liked Miami because it was always warm and there are so many different people from different countries. I didn't like Miami because at night you couldn't see any stars like in a small town and unlike small towns everybody didn't know everybody.

I mostly miss my family and friends. I also miss skiing, hiking and playing hockey.

I haven't really thought what I will do when I am released from prison and return to Ukraine. It depends how Ukraine will be then. But I will definitely find some job, reunite with my friends and hopefully my parents will be still alive.

As for the others whose lives were touched by this tragedy, lead detective Art Nanni retired from the Miami-Dade Police Department in August 2006. He became a cold-case consultant for the department, working there three days a week. John King retired, too, and moved to another part of the state. Larry Belyeu and Joe Malott are still there, as is Doug McCoy who is now a sergeant.

Assistant public defender Edith Georgi is still fighting for the underdog, as is Ray Taseff, who left the public defender's office and is now in private practice in Miami, while prosecutors Penny Brill, Priscilla Prado, and Gail Levine are still prosecuting cases for the Miami-Dade state attorney's office.

Judge Manuel "Manny" Crespo, whose patience and evenhandedness in the troublesome case were remarkable, died on Sunday, January 8, 2006, at his home in South Miami. He was sixty years old.

He had been battling colon cancer but the disease did not keep him off the bench. He finished a trial the Friday before he died.

"Manny Crespo was an outstanding trial judge who was happiest trying cases and hearing motions in the morning, at night, or on weekends," said his boss, Joseph Farina, chief judge of the 11th Judicial Circuit. "His colleagues will miss his generous offers of assistance and his genuine affection. The public will miss a true champion of justice."

Beverly Lewis, Sister Michelle's mother, still lives in Ohio, not far from where her daughter is buried. While heartbroken, she's comforted somewhat by her belief that her deeply spiritual daughter is finally at peace, resting in the arms of God.

Appendix

FOR THE MIAMI-DADE
POLICE DEPARTMENT
SEXUAL CRIMES BUREAU,
MIAMI-DADE COUNTY, FLORIDA.

CASE NO. 168600-Z & 168765-2

INVESTIGATION INTO THE LEWD AND LASCIVIOUS FONDLING AND POS-
SIBLE SEXUAL BATTERY OF MYKHAYLO KOFEL, W/M/22, WHICH OC-
CURRED AT 12425 S.W. 72 ST. (HOLY CROSS ACADEMY) IN MIAMI-DADE
COUNTY, FLORIDA, BETWEEN APPROXIMATELY 1997 AND 1998.

SWORN STATEMENT OF MYKHAYLO KOFEL

Taken before Robin A. Benjamin, Steno-Reporter and Notary
Public in and for the State of Florida at Large, at the Miami Dade
County Jail, located at 1321 N.W. 13th Street, Miami Dade
County, Florida, on Thursday, February 17, 2005, commencing
at 12:22 p.m. and concluding at 1:16 p.m.

APPEARANCES   JOSE CABADO, DETECTIVE
                                     MIAMI-DADE POLICE
                                     DEPARTMENT
                                     SEXUAL CRIMES BUREAU

                                     CHAVELIN MOISE, DETECTIVE
                                     MIAMI-DADE POLICE
                                     DEPARTMENT
                                     SEXUAL CRIMES BUREAU

Thereupon,

MYKHAYLO KOFEL

after having been duly sworn, was examined and testified as follows:

EXAMINATION BY DETECTIVE CABADO:

Q: For the record state your full name?
A: Mykhaylo Kofel.
Q: How old are you?
A: I'm 22.
Q: What is your date of birth?
A: 7/9/82.
Q: What is your last address you lived at before coming here, do you re-
   member?
A: Yes, Holy Cross Academy, 12425 Southwest 72nd Street.
Q: Calling your attention back to when you lived at the Holy Cross
   Academy, did anything happen to you at that location?
A: Yes.
Q: Um (sic) let's start from the first incident and tell me what happened
   as far back as you can remember or, let me ask you do you remember
   when you first moved to the Holy Cross Academy approximately?
A: Yes, I came there in August 1, 1997.*
Q: When you came from Holy Cross where did you come from?
A: Ukraine.
Q: Is that your home country?
A: Yes.
Q: How did it come about you coming to Holy Cross?

———————————

*Due to a transcription error, the date of Mr. Kofel's arrival in the United
States was misstated in the sworn statement. Kofel arrived in the U.S. on
August 1, 1996.

A: Um (sic) well, I met, he was like a monk or priest he came to Ukraine. He was recruiting young candidates to become or to be a monk to come to the U.S.

Q: Did he introduce you to anybody in the United States in order to come to Holy Cross?

A: He was he came by himself and a translator and I was known to him by my local priest from the Parrish.

Q: So the person you spoke to that came to Ukraine, do you remember his name?

A: Wendt.

Q: How do you spell that?

A: W-e-n-d-t.

BY DETECTIVE CABADO: For the record I'm going to show you a photograph and can you tell me who is this person in the photo?

A: Well he has a beard.

Q: What is his name?

A: Last name is Wendt. His first name Is Gerard.

Q: Is this the same person that came to Ukraine to recruit you?

A: Yes.

BY DETECTIVE CABADO: For the record he identified the photograph of Frank Gerard, G-e-r-a-r-d, Wendt, W-e-n-d-t; date of birth of 06/07/1944.

Q: So what was his position?

A: Well actually he was like—

Q: What do you know him as to be?

A: We're supposed to call him Father Abbott (phonetic), the head of the monastery of the school.

Q: So you come to the United States and you came here straight to the Holy Cross, you tell me?

A: Yes. We spent like two weeks in the Ukraine in a rented house and he taught us some rules about Holy Cross. He told us a little bit, not everything, he didn't say everything.

Q: So once you arrived at Holy Cross, did anything happen to you when you were at the Holy Cross?

A: Well um (sic) the first at the beginning I came in August 1st so it was me and there were two candidates, me and Petro, P-e-t-r-e, (phonetic) and the last name is T-e-r-e-n-t-a (phonetic).

Q: So when you were at Holy Cross, do you remember the first incident called or anything happening to you that involved anyone at Holy Cross?

A: Well, um (sic) the first time we had to live it was called, it was just called Wendt's house where he lived. We were supposed to live in one room. There were two bunk beds in the same room and we lived like there until moved to another house like in three or four months. We moved to the official candidates' house. We were living in the second floor one room and the same bunk beds, and the downstairs room was where we had study chairs.

Q: And this house that you lived at where was it located?

A: The same area.

Q: Is it at the compound at Holy Cross?

A: Yes the same area, it's called Holy Cross Monastery and the school was called Holy Cross Academy. We come from Ukraine to be part of the first candidates who would actually become monks.

Q: So you lived with the other candidate, Petro on the second floor?

A: Yes and on the bottom floor was living the other priest.

Q: I'm going to show you a photograph and can you identify this person?

A: Yes, that's James Gibault. He had less beard.

Q: Is this the person you're saying lived in the first floor of the house you lived in?

A: Yes, by himself.

BY DETECTIVE CABADO: For the record, he identified James Albert Gibault, date of birth is 11/05/1954.

Q: Okay. Did anything happen to you when you were living in the house inside Holy Cross?

A: Yes.

Q: Tell me what happened tell me about the first incident you remember?

A: We were um (sic) I was upstairs in the candidates' house where we were supposed to study and I received this call from Wendt and he said to come over to his house. I don't know whose house it was in the beginning, but it was his own house.

Q: So the house that Wendt lived at, this is still inside the compound?

A: Holy Cross, yes.

Q: And who lived in that house beside himself?

A: Well in the beginning he lived by himself. When we moved to the candidate's house he stayed there by himself most of the time.

Q: So when he called you over to come to his house, did you go there?

A: Yes.

Q: Okay. Tell me what happened when you went there?

A: I went over there and he was there in the living room and there was TV by the couch, so he was sitting in the couch and he had like a book.

So he told me to sit down by him on the couch and um (sic) and so I did, I sat down and um (sic) he told me to teach him some you know to teach him how to pronounce some words in Ukraine—He was learning how to pronounce some words and I sat down next to him. I explained some words and that's when I first noticed that he put you know his hand on my chest his right hand on my chest.

Q: Was that over or under your clothing?

A: Over my clothes.

Q: And then what happened?

A: And he was going like circular.

Q: Like what some circles?

A: Circular motion and I noticed he was also like you know he was excited and he was breathing hard and so his hand was going down to my stomach.

Q: Did he say anything while he was touching you?

A: He could have said something but I know he said—you know I was uncomfortable when he did that, I was very stiff, I was motionless. He could have said, "It's okay."

Q: Did you tell him to stop his actions at anytime?

A: I was scared, I was surprised. It took me by surprise. I wasn't expecting him to do that. His hand moved to my thigh and then to my genitals and he did that and mostly he came back to my stomach and my chest.

Q: When he touched your genital area, was that over or under your clothes?

A: Over my clothes.

Q: Was he dressed or undressed?

A: He was dressed.

Q: What happened next?

A: So you know I didn't—I was scared, I was uncomfortable, I was shocked and he said "No, it's okay," you know, "it's God's will, you go to heaven if you do that." I was scared and he did that for five or ten minutes and he told me, "Let's go back in Gibault's house."

Q: Did you leave?

A: Yes.

Q: When you said you were scared, explain what you mean?

A: Because I never had this experience, this is a priest and I respect the priest. I know the priest in Ukraine is very respected and holy and I talk with my priest about God and nothing happened like that before. This American priest was touching me and I was horrified and then he kept on telling this is why, it's alright, it's God's will. I wasn't raised like that. I thought you know I'm going to sin. I was um (sic) he said if you disobey you're going to hell. I was confused you know.

Q: Do you remember when this occurred or do you remember the year or date?

A: I don't actually remember. I remember approximately the first year I came here, it was eight months. When I first got to Holy Cross it was like eight months. It was like in the spring of '97 or late winter of '97.

Q: Okay. Do you remember approximately what time of day this occurred?

A: I think I don't remember exactly but it was during the day.

Q: During the daytime?

A: Daytime.

Q: Did anything else happen after that?

A: I was at Holy Cross like a year and this thing continued. He would call me over and basically did the same thing each time. I was more willing each time I wanted to go back. I would move away and he said to me, "Do you know I'll punish you and send you back to Ukraine." He was brainwashing me, telling me things. I would be afraid of going to hell. I was very scared because I was very religious. I was very much into God.

Q: So, you said this continued, do you remember how many times?

A: Approximately six or seven times.

Q: And on these incidents you said it was the same thing basically touching you over the clothing, or did anything else happen?

A: No, it was just touching me over the clothes and just him saying him touching me and saying it's all right, it's God's will, brotherly love.

Q: He didn't do anything more than touching you basically?

A: Yes.

Q: Did he ever ask you to do anything to him?

A: No.

Q: During those six or seven incidents, where did it take place? I know the first incident took place at his house.

A: All of them took place in his house.

Q: Was anyone else inside his house during this time?

A: No.

Q: Was it always just you and him?

A: Yes, at the time.

Q: Was it always at the same time, could you tell me about that, or was there a specific time he did that to you?

A: It was always during the day. I don't remember the specific days, It was noon, sometimes like four o'clock, on weekends when I would be out of school, it would be around twelve or about one o'clock, or if it would be during the school times after school, after three o'clock or approximately four or five o'clock, you know I just remember it was during the days.

Q: So the first incident you told me it happened approximately eight months after you moved there, do you remember the last incident with Father Wendt occurred?

A: It was end towards the end of '97 and beginning of '98.

Q: That was the last incident?

A: Yes it just stopped you know actually I think it was before almost the end of '97 it stopped, so in the beginning of '98 in the winter of '98 we were there and there was you know workers Hispanic workers at Holy Cross compound so um (sic), they were fixing some rooms that still needed to be fixed, two rooms in his house on the top floor they needed to be fixed so they were fixing the two rooms. In the beginning of '98 there was also another candidate that came from the Ukraine. He came before then but he was there. We were still in the room top floor second loor bunks and in '98 the winter of '98 we were given different rooms on the second floor. I was given the middle room and Petro was in the other room towards the end and one candidate came from Ukraine he was called Ivan (phonetic).

Q: Do you know how to spell his name?

A: The first name I-v-a-n, and the last name is K-a-y-n-y-c-h. He stayed in the same room but, but we were separated in three different rooms and basically you know I noticed that Wendt stopped calling me over. It stayed like that for several months you know and um (sic) then the first incident that involve with Gibault the other priest was um (sic) just we weren't suppose to go out by ourselves outside. We couldn't go outside of the compound of the Holy Cross or even at evening times. We were on a schedule. The monks and priests they would never come but anyways the first time um (sic) Gibault asked me to go with him to help him with the groceries to a Winn Dixie or Publix. He took the car and we were going there. I was sitting in the passenger seat and he was sitting in the driver seat. He was driving and the first time I noticed that he put his hand all over my hand the first incident. I remember him touching me putting his hand over my hand and he put his hand over my thigh.

Q: When he put his hand over your thigh, was that over or under your clothing?

A: Over.

Q: Do you remember when that incident with Father Gibault occurred?

A: '98 winter, '98.

Q: Let me ask you—I know we have left that topic, do you know why Father Abbot or Father Wendt as you know him, stopped his assaults on you?

A: You know I don't really—probably I wasn't willing, he didn't like me or he wanted to try Petro, because at the same time we moved to separate rooms, Petro had to move his desk to Wendt's house so he had started there. He just said you know Petro is like an assistant and spent a lot of time over there even I think he had a bed there his own bed. It was to be separate beds and separate rooms. He had his own room in the candidates' house. During the time I would hear him go over, slam the door and go to Wendt's house. He said Wendt wanted himself to make love Gibault so probably Gibault was abusing Petro.

Q: Other than your suspicions, did you ever see anything between Wendt and Petro?

A: Yes, just one incident.

Q: When was that?

A: Approximately I don't remember but it could have been '99, I don't remember actually. It's you know I was um (sic) in the candidates' house and I was suppose to give Petre to return the keys or something. I went to Wendt's house and you know I caught them unexpectedly on the same couch. I had seen him touching Petro's chest.

Q: Any other incidents you observed between them two?

A: No.

Q: That was the only incident?

A: Yes.

Q: Did you ever question Petre about that?

A: No.

Q: Let's go back to Father Gibault, is that what you call him?

A: Yes.

Q: So the incident inside the car where he touched your leg over your clothing, did anything else happen on this particular day?

A: No.

Q: Did you say anything when he was touching you that day?

A: I think I say I could have said something in the car or outside—

come to his room later on that night when I was sleeping like after ten.

Q: Did he say that or you think he said that?

A: He said that, it could have been in the car or later on outside the car, I don't know.

Q: So did you come into the room that night?

A: I don't remember that night or the month. I know it happened. I was thinking it was later in the winter or early spring about the time he told me to come.

Q: And what happened?

A: The first time I went to his house and um (sic) he was, he had his bed his own bed and he told me to sit down and so he started in the beginning he started to do almost the same thing and he was touching my thigh, genitals and my stomach, chest, my arms and then so he told me to come almost like come every night. It was almost every night I was coming to his room and he would call me from his room or come outside and he told me to come to the house every time, so at night because all the candidates would be asleep after ten o'clock. So I was supposed to come and the same process to undress to my underwear and to lie in the bed you know and so he would also undress himself to his underwear and even to nothing. He told me to lie in his bed and get under the cover with me and he would touch me all over. I had no clothes on so he touched me all over my body.

Q: You said at first he was just touching you over your clothing and he called you to his room every night, do you remember how long of a time span this took place of the touching?

A: The same year '98 before summer like spring.

Q: Do you know how many times he would touch you over the—

A: I don't remember how many times. He did it a lot of times.

Q: Was it more than five?

A: Yes.

Q: More than ten?

A: Yes.

Q: More than fifteen?

A: Yes, this thing with Gibault in winter '98 had ended when I got here, it would be more like 2001.

Q: You said it progressed, now the first incident where you said you were both naked on the bed, continue to tell me what happened when you said he was touching you, where you both were laying on the bed, correct?

A: Yes.

Q: What happened?

A: He was touching himself and touching me you know my penis.

Q: What part of his body was he touching—you said he was touching himself, where was he touching himself?

A: On his penis and masturbating himself and he was also masturbating me. He would touch my penis.

Q: When he was masturbating himself, did he ejaculate?

A: He could have, I don't remember. The only bed but sometimes I remember I would lay on my side and he would turn me over touching me on my stomach with his penis on my stomach and I would feel wet.

Q: You said you felt wet, what do you mean by you felt wet?

A: He ejaculated on my stomach.

Q: And what happened to the semen on the stomach later on, do you remember what happened to the semen?

A: I think I don't remember actually, I think I just I was laying there paralyzed. I was really scared.

Q: So you don't remember if the semen was cleaned?

A: I don't remember, it could have gone on the sheet.

Q: Do you remember what happened to those bed sheets?

A: No.

Q: So, other than him putting his penis on your stomach and masturbating you and himself, did he tell you to do anything to him?

A: Yes, um (sic) he sometimes he would tell me to touch you know his stomach or sometimes bring my hand to his penis. I wasn't willing to do that. I was withdrawing, I wasn't willing to do that.

Q: Did he do anything else to you other than masturbation?

A: Yes in the summer of '98 is when I remember that clear. When Wendt took Petro and Ivan to Ukraine went back to Ukraine and me and Gibault was in the same house basically, there was nobody else, it was summer, no school and um (sic) so um (sic) the first incident I remember that happened before was like June in the same summer, it was well it was during the day and there was nobody around. He told me to come to his room and I did. I did that and umm (sic) so he told me to undress so I undressed and he told me to lay down on the bed and he completely undressed himself and he was masturbating himself and he told me to you know to lay down on my stomach and I did that and mostly what he did he pressed himself on me.

Q: He pressed himself?

A: Yes, on top of me and this was the first time he raped me.

Q: When you say he raped you, what do you mean by that explain that to me?

A: He put his penis in my anus.

Q: Do you remember the first time if he used a condom?

A: No.

Q: Do you remember if he ejaculated or not?

A: Yes, I felt warm inside of me and yes the first time the first incident I remember that.

Q: Did you clean yourself later with anything?

A: I remember taking a shower. I took a shower.

Q: And this occurred in his room on his bed?

A: Yes.

Q: On that incident day in the summer of '98, where you said he raped you, were there other similar incidents after that, where there was penetration?

A: From the summer till I came here.

Q: When you say you came here to the school, is that what you're referring to?

A: Yes, 2001 I remember he raped me. I clearly remember like eight times about, it was approximately ten times. During these incidents I would be maybe asleep and he would give me before that he would give me a pill. He used to have these pills that were anti-anxiety pills to sleep.

Q: He would give you pills?

A: Yes.

Q: Do you remember the name of the pills?

A: I remember how they look.

Q: What did they look like?

A: There were two pills basically. One pill was like a round pill generic and the other was bigger round but white.

Q: You don't remember what the pills were used for?

A: Anti-anxiety.

Q: For who?

A: Gibault.

Q: Was this a prescription?

A: Yes.

Q: And you would take them?

A: Yes.

Q: Voluntarily?

A: Yes, I would take them because he told me to but I had to obey.

Q: When you took them how did you feel?

A: I felt sleepy. I don't remember anything and I would wake up like 5:00 or 4:30 and he would wake me up to go to class. I had to wake up to shower and I would set the alarm and go back to the room and before I knew anything I would wake up and you know and on some occasions I would feel my head would hurt. I wouldn't remember anything. So the times I remember would be like seven or eight times I remember he raped me.

Q: When you said he gave you pills every time and every time you took the pills he gave them to you?

A: Yes.

Q: During these incidents was it always in his room?

A: Yes.

Q: Was it always on his bed?

A: Yes.

Q: Did there come a time when there was ejaculate on his bed sheets, how would the bed be?

A: Yes, stains.

Q: What would happen to the bed sheets, did anyone ever pick those up?

A: He would do his laundry on Saturdays. Um (sic) there were other times. In his room he had you know a TV in his room and he had a TV and so at night like around midnight or after that sometimes he made me watch some I would say like porno by satellite or HBO. Sometimes he would make me watch like sex scenes or sex movies and I remember the name of them. There was a series like one call *Queer as Folks*.

Q: And he would make you watch this?

A: Yes.

Q: And this was on cable you said?

A: Satellite.

Q: Satellite TV?

A: Yes.

Q: It was satellite TV, anything else?

A: Mostly there were also some movies that we were watching like sex movies.

Q: Right.

A: Like *Basic Instinct* with Michael Douglas. There were movies like had sex, always most of the movies had sex like one was called *Desert Passion*.

Q: Those were explicit kind of pornographic stuff?

A: Yes.

Q: Everybody was naked and having sex?

A: Yes.

Q: This was the type of material he exposed you to, anything else?

A: Yes.

Q: Basically cable, satellite, HBO, homosexual programs?

A: Yes, he made me watch those.

Q: Any other forms of pornography or just TV?

A: Just TV.

Q: Did he give you anything in exchange for the sexual activity—sexual intercourse he was having with you?

A: No. He just made me do it and said I would go to heaven, and I would be doing the right thing when I wanted to go. I was scared. I was not willing. I wanted to go back to my room and I was scared so he said I would be punished and I would go to hell. Sometimes he punished me and he would make me sit in the laundry room from seven to eight, and sometimes I would have to ask permission to have ice cream and during that time I would have to work during the summer time and this incident happened on many occasions and we would go on occasion like to the beach, Key West or Naples, rent a hotel by the beach and me and Gibault would stay in one room and Petre had to stay in another room. Me and Gibault had to stay in the same room. I remember on one occasion we went to Sanibel Island or Key West, it was always like that.

Q: So, on these different occasions was there also sex involved?

A: Yes, but I don't remember being raped over there. I remember him touching me. He told me to come to his bed. I remember the same room, two beds, so he told me I was supposed to sleep in his bed. So in the morning he would undress like he was sleeping in the one bed with me and he would sleep in the other bed if anybody came in. One time there was a house in North Carolina in a small town and he rented the house and there were three rooms and I had to stay with Gibault. So you know I slept with Gibault It was just one room.

Q: So, outside of Miami it was pretty much touching, there was no penetration?

A: No.

Q: During those incidents did you ever tell Gibault to stop or resist to what he was doing?

A: Yes.

Q: Explain that to me.

A: Sometimes I would cry, sometimes I would say I don't want to do this,

I want to go back. Sometimes he would push me down and tell me basically the same lecture.

Q: Did you ever tell anyone about these assaults?

A: No.

Q: The only one that you saw in the nude was Father Gibault, correct?

A: Yes.

Q: Do you remember any special markings or anything on his body that would be different that you could remember, anything that would help us out?

A: I remember he was circumcised. I remember he had a mole on his penis like small black dots.

Q: Small black dots on his penis?

A: Yes.

Q: What kind of dots?

A: I would say moles.

Q: Anything else that you remember about, anything on his body, under his clothing that stood out to you, any tattoos, scars, or markings, anything?

A: He had no tattoos, the scars besides his hands.

Q: Under his clothing only you could have seen?

A: He had no scars. I just remember that you know he had large thighs or fat thighs and he had stretch marks on his stomach, basically. I don't remember what kind of underwear, but I don't, I never seen no scars, tattoos.

Q: So just let me touch real quickly on the pornographic stuff. It was all cable TV and he showed you movies by satellite, is that correct?

A: Yes.

Q: Anything else?

A: No. Some scenes I remember.

Q: But I'm saying it was only TV. The pornographic stuff he made you watch?

A: Yes.

Q: Do you remember me talking to you a couple of years back about these incidents and another detective, the second detective was Steve Signori and I believe when he spoke to you about the incident with Father Wendt-Father Abbot, what you call him. Detective Signori covered the incident with Father Gibault, and I know certain things you told me today I didn't know from before. Is there any reason why you didn't tell us about these incidents in the past?

A: I say in the beginning the first time I remember I didn't tell you about how Gibault raped me.

Q: Right.

A: And you know I didn't even tell my lawyer even my lawyer in the beginning. I told him within a year but not the first time. I just left it out because first of all I was basically was just embarrassed as hell.

Q: Now the last incident with Gibault occurred you said—when was the last time anything happened with Gibault?

A: The last time was the night of the murder.

Q: Okay. It was the last incident between you and Gibault?

A: Yes.

Q: This incident was pretty much the same thing, penetration?

A: Yes.

Q: When there was anal penetration you said he never wore a condom?

A: Correct.

Q: Was there anything else he may have put on his penis, or was there anything else you remember he did to himself prior to the penetration?

A: No.

Q: You don't remember him doing anything else to himself or his penis prior to the penetration?

A: No.

Q: And he never offered you any gift or anything in exchange for him to do this to you?

A: No.

Q: Has everything you've stated been true and correct to the best of your knowledge here today?

A: Yes.

Q: Have you given this statement freely and voluntarily?

A: Yes.

DETECTIVE CABADO: Thank you.

(Whereupon the sworn statement was concluded at 1:16 p.m.)

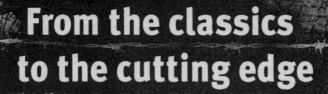